THE ENGLISH LANGUAGE

Stanley Hussey

THE ENGLISH LANGUAGE:
Structure and Development

LONGMAN
LONDON AND NEW YORK

Longman Group Limited,
Longman House, Burnt Mill,
Harlow, Essex CM20 2JE, England
and Associated Companies throughout the world.

Published in the United States of America
by Longman Publishing, New York

© Longman Group Limited 1995

First published 1995

ISBN 0 582 217628 CSD
ISBN 0 582 21761X PPR

British Library Cataloguing-in-Publication Data

A catalogue record for this book is
available from the British Library

Library of Congress Cataloging-in-Publication Data
Hussey, S. S., 1925–
    The English language : structure and development / Stanley Hussey.
        p.   cm.
    Includes bibliographical references and index.
    ISBN 0–582–21761–X (pbk.). — ISBN 0–582–21762–8 (CSD)
    1. English language—Grammar, Historical. I. Title.
    PE1101.H94   1995
    420'.9—dc20   95–5614
                                                                      CIP

Set by 5 in 10/12pt Bembo
Produced by Longman Singapore Publishers (Pte) Ltd.
Printed in Singapore

Contents

Preface   viii
Abbreviations and Symbols Used   xii
Some Useful Dates   xiii
Acknowledgements   xiv

Chapter 1   Introduction   1

Chapter 2   Choosing Words: The Vocabulary of English   13
Two examples   13
The expanding vocabulary: Old English and Middle English   17
The Renaissance: Copious language   27
Other borrowings   33
Alternatives to borrowing   34

Chapter 3   Arranging Words   48
The building blocs   48
The noun phrase   53
The verb phrase   58
The development of the verb   62
Adverbials   68
Conversion   70
Types of sentence   72
Grammatical acceptability   78

Chapter 4   How Words Mean   84
Semantics   85
Pragmatics   92
Cohesion   96

Chapter 5   Receiving Words   108
Sounds and spellings   108
O.E. and M.E.   111
Early Modern English   113
Present difficulties   115
Standards of pronunciation   117
Stress and intonation   119
Punctuation   122
Phonemes of Present-Day English   124

Chapter 6   Correct Words?   128
Standards and dialect   129
The growth of a standard   130
Dictionaries   137
Latin and a universal language   149
A standard for grammar   152

Linguistic Glossary   161
Appendix:
  Names   173
    Place names   173
    Personal names   177
Select Bibliography   181
Index   184

To our language may be with great justnes applied the observation of Quintilian, that speech was not formed by an analogy sent from heaven, It did not descend to us in a state of uniformity and perfection, but was produced by necessity and enlarged by accident, and is therefore composed of dissimilar parts, thrown together by negligence, by affectation, by learning, or by ignorance.

(Samuel Johnson, *Plan of A Dictionary* (1747))

For William

Preface

English is very much in the news these days, principally in the debate over the kind of English children should be taught and what kinds of literary texts should be examined. Almost every year seems to produce a government-inspired Report – or, at the very least, a Revised Curriculum. From its very first page, the Kingman Report of 1988 takes a strong line against what it sees as fashionable but misguided views on the teaching of English:

> The distraction today is in part the belief that this [learning]
> capacity can and should be fostered only by exposure to varieties
> of English language; that conscious knowledge of the structure and
> working of the language is unnecessary for effective use of it; that
> attempting to teach such knowledge induces boredom, damages
> creativity and may yet be unsuccessful; and that the enterprise
> entails imposing an authoritarian view of a standard language
> which will be unacceptable to many communities in our society.[1]

It argues that much of what an earlier Report (that of the Bullock Committee of 1975) recommended has not been implemented. Kingman was followed in 1989 by the Cox Committee's recommendations for the basis of a National Curriculum, but these have been seen in some (especially governmental) quarters as too imprecise, and too liberal in the choice of literary texts, so the proposed revised curriculum of 1993 advocates more attention to traditional grammar, spelling, standard English, and the choice of classical texts for English literature examinations. All these committees have been assailed by 'evidence' – much of it anecdotal in character – that school-leavers cannot spell, cannot punctuate, do not know what many ordinary words mean: in short, they cannot use their native language. This is assertion, not argument, and its tone is often moralizing, for language 'corruption' must surely indicate social or national corruption. It is easy, on the other hand, to travesty proposals for a stricter curriculum, to talk of good old-fashioned parsing and the short, sharp spelling and grammar tests which, on those Friday mornings long ago, sorted out the sheep from the goats and showed how the latter could be turned into the former. The more liberal educationalists argue that nothing is more calculated to bore the young, to destroy all their natural creativity, to make them feel that if this is the sort of English language needed to appreciate English literature they want little part of either.

One trouble is that both sides speak of 'English' as if it was one clearly-defined thing. In fact, there are many 'Englishes', if only because English is used as a first or second (or even common) language in many different countries of the world. Each of us, too, has his or her own **idiolect,** our own personal English, influenced by where we were brought up, the kind of professional and social circles we move in, our age and sex, and a host of other matters. Paradoxically, the greater knowledge of language in the last generation or two has made it so much more difficult to say just what 'English' is. **Linguistics,** the formal, scientific study of language as a phenomenon (strictly not of languages, although it is natural to use one's native language as an illustration) has made it clear that speech is as important as writing (the older English grammars concentrated on written English). **Sociolinguistics** emphasizes language as a vehicle for communication and considers the daily interactions of different kinds of people as manifested in the language they use. Social categories are clearly important in the study of English, and it soon becomes evident too that, over the centuries, changes in English have often been socially motivated. **Stylistics,** another branch of Linguistics, recognizes that variation is conditioned, not simply by who we are but to whom we are speaking or writing and even by the kind of material we are dealing with, for this may bring its own expectation of an appropriate language – legal language, for example, or religious language. Our letter to the tax inspector will hardly use the same style as our letter to a close friend. To some extent sociolinguistics and stylistics overlap: sociolinguistics is a kind of socially conditioned stylistics.

Yet among all this variety there must be some common ground, some received practice, otherwise communication would break down. The difficulty lies in defining the limits of this received practice and in identifying its difficult or disputed features. Not long ago *The Sunday Times* produced a number of booklets with the general title *Wordpower*. One of the interesting contents was a Glossary affording 'Easy Reference to English usage'. In so far as this stressed present-day usage it was valuable, but it was a hotchpotch, simply arranged alphabetically, of questions of acceptable usage (*hopefully*, split infinitives); grammar and syntax (*can* v. *may*, dangling participles, coordination – but not, incidentally, subordination); spelling (often differentiating between English English and American English, e.g. *programme* v. *program*, *-ise* v. *-ize* in verbs); punctuation (comma, quotation marks); changes of meaning (*decimate*) and discrimination (*lady* v *woman*); and definitions of technical terms used in language study (*dialect*, *etymology*, *intensifier*). All this can be useful for ready-reference, but heaven forbid that anyone should attempt to learn it by rote.

A more valuable approach is through understanding something of the history of English. To quote Kingman once more:

> [To] understand that English, like all languages, is subject to change, and have some knowledge of the history of the English language as well as of current changes, with an appreciation of language change in relation to past as well as contemporary literature.

I believe that many readers and listeners possess a well-developed critical faculty and a quickness in recognizing the effects aimed at in a particular passage. They are perhaps less good at first in perceiving how these effects are achieved, at seeing how a great writer or speaker exploits (or occasionally deliberately contradicts) the linguistic conventions of his age. The further back we go, this operation naturally becomes more difficult. Understanding the simple meaning of the words on the page is reasonably easy with most nineteenth- or twentieth-century English. But seventeenth-century Milton is read far less often than he was and Shakespeare himself seems yearly to be growing more difficult. And how about Chaucer? People are intrigued by the past, but not so many of them for its own sake. It needs to be contrasted with, or else used to explain, the present. Why does that word or that construction now seem unusual or especially significant? When did English acquire it? What are, or were, the alternatives? How, in fact, has English got the way it has? Roger Lass's book *The Shape of*

English is a longer and a much denser book than mine, but I cannot improve on his formulation: 'A language is at least three things at once: a self-contained system, a reflection of its past history, and a prelude to its own future.'[2] My book more often adopts a stylistic approach, but in taking a historical viewpoint in its explanations, it aims to provide a firm sense of both the structure of the language and much of its history.

I should like to acknowledge several debts, some particular and some general. It has been both a pleasure and a stimulus to have shared the teaching of the History of the English Language with David Burnley, Tony Gilbert, Richard Hogg, Helen Phillips and Meg Twycross. To Meg Twycross I owe the passages from Lodge and Bunyan in the first chapter and the idea of the expanding cats in the second and to Avril Bruten the Jane Austen passage in the third: they are not of course responsible for what I have made of them. I often consulted Katie Wales's *Dictionary of Stylistics* and *The Oxford Dictionary of English Grammar* (Eds. S. Chalker and E. Weiner) to check a particular point and came away much better informed in general. The anonymous reader for Longman suggested one beneficial reorganization of material and pointed out several infelicities together with a few downright errors. Longman has been helpful to a degree beyond that which an author has a right to expect of his publisher. I cannot now remember the sources of some other ideas and examples, and if anyone remains unacknowledged, I apologize. To generations of students in London and Lancaster go my thanks for their attention and for their questions which sometimes made me realize I did not understand the point perfectly either.

NOTES

1. *Report of the Committee of Inquiry into the Teaching of English Language* (London: HMSO, March 1988). The quotations are on pp. 1 and 53.

2. Lass, 1987, p. xi.

Abbreviations and Symbols Used

O.E.	Old English
M.E.	Middle English
E. Mod. E.	Early Modern English
P.D.E.	Present-Day English
S	Subject
O	Object
d O	Direct object
i O	Indirect object
C	Complement
NP	Noun Phrase
VP	Verb Phrase
IPA	International Phonetic Alphabet
RP	Received Pronunication
OED 1	*Oxford English Dictionary*, 1933
OED 2	*Oxford English Dictionary*, 2nd. edition, 1989
[ ]	sounds are written between square brackets.
/ /	phonemes are written between oblique strokes.
< >	graphemes (i.e. spellings) are written between angle brackets.
*	a hypothetical form dependent upon reconstruction

Some Useful Dates

c. 410	Departure of Roman forces from Britain.
mid 5th century	Invasion by Angles, Saxons and Jutes (and probably Frisians).
597	Beginning of conversion of the English to (Roman) christianity.
793	First recorded hit-and-run raid by Scandinavians. Followed by invasions in ninth and tenth centuries.
878	Alfred halts Scandinavian advance. Danelaw established.
1066	Norman Conquest.
c. 1342–1400	Geoffrey Chaucer
1476	William Caxton sets up his printing press at Westminster.
1564–1616	William Shakespeare.
1603	Death of Elizabeth. Accession of James I.
1611	Authorized Version of the Bible.
1623	First Folio edition of Shakespeare's plays.
1660	Restoration of the established monarchy (Charles II).
1755	Johnson's Dictionary.
1884–1928	Gradual publication of the *New English Dictionary*.

Acknowledgements

We are grateful to the following for permission to reproduce copyright material:

Faber & Faber Ltd for poem 'Thrushes' by Ted Hughes from *Lupercal*; Faber & Faber Ltd/Harcourt Brace Inc for extracts from poems 'East Coker' & 'The Waste Land' from *Collected Poems 1909–1962* (World excluding USA)/*Four Quartets* (US) by T.S. Eliot. Copyright 1943 by T.S. Eliot, renewed 1971 by Esme Valerie Eliot; the author's agents for poem 'Thou' by J. Heath-Stubbs from *Collected Poems 1943–1987*, pubd. Carcanet Press Ltd 1988; Manchester University Press for poem 'Mi Gronfeyther' by Samual Laycock in *Songs of the People* ed. B. Hollingsworth (MUP 1977); Director of Savings for extracts from National Savings *Children's Bonus Bonds* leaflet which is 'Crown Copyright'; Times Newspapers Ltd for an extract from the article 'Put the class before the forms' by Colin Ward in *The Times* 10.10.90. & an extract from A.A. Gill writing as a TV critic in *The Sunday Times* 19.6.94. Copyright Times Newspapers Ltd 1990, 1994.

Chapter 1

Introduction

English is big business. In 1776 (the date of the American War of Independence) there were around 15 million speakers of English, under 2 million of whom were in the United States of America. Now there are some 350 million whose first language is English and the majority of native English speakers live outside England, in North America, Australia, New Zealand, South Africa, the West Indies, and so on. To these we must add those who use English as a second language, for business or technological purposes, and even those who use English as a link language in a country where the national languages are either mutually incomprehensible or else competitive in nationalist terms. The only competitors to English are Hindi (which has perhaps twice the number of native speakers) and Mandarin Chinese (with possibly three times as many).[1] And of course English has been used in Britain for over 1,500 years. The exact number depends upon whether you count from the landings of the Germanic invaders in the mid fifth century AD or from the first written records in English, around 700. Faced with figures of that magnitude, how can we approach the complexity of English or seek to explain the present state of the language in terms of the past?

Yet it is not that difficult. We might begin with four versions of the Lord's Prayer:

> Dū ūre fæder, þe eart on heofonum, sȳ þin nama ġehālgod.
> Cume þīn rīċe. Sȳ þīn willa on eorþan swāswā on heofonum.
> Syle ūs tōdæġ ūrne dæġhwāmlīċan hlāf. And forġyf ūs ūre gyltas
> swāswā wē forġyfaþ þæm þe wiþ ūs āgyltaþ. And ne lǣd þū
> nā ūs on costnunge, ac ālȳs us fram yfele.
>
> (Old English (Ælfriċ, c. 990))

> Oure fadir, þat art in heuenys, halewid be þi name. þi kyngdom
> come to. Be þi wille don as in heuene and in erþe. ʒive to us

þis day oure breed ouer oþer substaunse. And for3iue to us oure
dettes, as we for3iuen to oure dettouris. And leede us not into
temptacioun, but delyuere us from yuel.

(Middle English (Wycliffite Bible, c. 1385))

Our Father which art in heaven, hallowed be thy name. Thy
kingdom come. Thy will be done in earth, as it is in heaven. Give
us this day our daily bread. And forgive us our debts, as we forgive
our debtors. And lead us not into temptation, but deliver
us from evil.

(Early Modern English (Authorised Version, 1611))

Our Father in heaven,
Thy name be hallowed;
Thy kingdom come.
Thy will be done,
On earth as in heaven.
Give us today our daily bread.
Forgive us the wrong we have done,
As we have forgiven those who have wronged us.
And do not bring us to the test
But save us from the evil one.
For thine is the kingdom and the power and the glory, for
ever.

(Later twentieth century (New English Bible, 1961))

Ælfric was a Benedictine monk who translated part of the
Bible from the Latin version (the Vulgate). As novice-master
of his monastery, with responsibility for the trainee monks,
he was naturally interested in the spread of education. The
translation of the Bible into Middle English (hereafter M.E.)
during Chaucer's lifetime used to be attributed to John Wyclif.
Nowadays we believe that he masterminded the work but that
much of the actual translation was carried out by his assistants:
hence 'Wycliffite'. Wyclif's early career was in Oxford as a
lecturer in logic and philosophy, but he gradually became more
and more dissatisfied with Roman control of the Church and
with some of its teaching. By 1382 popularized versions of
his ideas were being preached around the country by Lollard
sympathizers and initial contact through preaching was followed
up by bible study and reading circles. The thrust of the Lollard
message was that the clergy should be better than they were
and that religion should be less formal and more personal.

Also a lack of Latin should not be a bar to understanding God's word – hence the demand for the Bible in English. The New Testament translation was begun in 1382 and the Old Testament followed later. The Wycliffite Bible exists in two versions, an 'Early', often very literal, version and a more idiomatic 'Later' one. All of this was naturally anathema to the church authorities, the 'proud prelates', as the Wycliffites called them. If men could read the Bible in their own tongue, they could think for themselves about their own salvation. In 1407 there was a clear prohibition on the making or using of English translations and for some time it became dangerous to own or read a Wycliffite bible. The debate about the desirability of having the Bible in English was really only resolved by the publication of the Authorised Version in 1611. In 1604 King James I convened a conference at Hampton Court of forty-seven eminent scholars and clergy. The task of revision and re-translation occupied three and a half years: the result is surely one of the few elegant works to emerge from a committee. In 1947 a new translation was undertaken by a joint committee of all British churches (except the Roman Catholic). Once more there were panels of translators but this time they were assisted by literary advisors. The declared aim of this New English Bible (New Testament 1961, Old Testament and Apocrypha 1970) was to produce not only a more accurate version but also one more intelligible to twentieth-century readers. It has not been universally welcomed, but it has effectively superseded other translations made between the seventeenth and twentieth centuries. The language of these four versions of the Bible is inevitably a blend between the general possibilities of the language at the time of translation and the choices made, within these possibilities, by the authors in order to reach a particular audience or to achieve certain literary effects.

The first thing that strikes us about the Old English (hereafter O.E.) version is probably the strange letters. þ and ð (Ð is the capital and ð its lower-case counterpart) are called *thorn* and *eth* respectively. Ideally they represent two different *th* sounds. ð is the voiced *th* in *bathe* where we can hear the vibration as we place our fingers over our vocal cords, the two 'lips' inside our adam's apple. þ is the *th* we hear in *bath* and is voiceless (or unvoiced), where the breath passes through the vocal cords unimpeded. Unfortunately the O.E. manuscripts do not show this distinction in writing, although in later O.E. there is a tendency to use þ initially and ð in the middle and at the end of words. æ is pronounced rather like the *a* in *sat*. I have – although O.E. did not – also distinguished two types of g and two types of c. Those letters without a dot above (gyltas, Cume) are pronounced 'hard', as they still are in *guilt* and *come*. Those with a dot above are pronounced like *y* (*todæġ* and *forġyf*) and *ch* (*riċe*) respectively. Here Present-Day English (hereafter P.D.E.) improves on O.E. by using distinct letters for different sounds. 'Hard' g is spelled g (*good, game*) and 'soft' g usually y (*today, young*). So (outside this passage) O.E. *ġeorn*, 'eager', is the same root as P.D.E. *yearn* and O.E. *benċ* is today spelled *bench*. The O.E. word for 'cat' was *catt* ('hard' c) but for 'church' it was *ċyriċe* which we now spell with ch at both beginning and end. I have also marked the long vowels: ā, ū, and so on. Try reading the first passage aloud with these remarks in mind and much of it becomes surprisingly intelligible. The second passage continues to use þ but has the letter ȝ (called *yogh*) for the y sound (ȝive and forȝiuen were pronounced in this way in this dialect of M.E.). It does, however, spell *kyngdom* (O.E. *cynedom*) with a k, in recognition of the 'hard' sound.

Some words from the earlier passages are recognizable immediately, such as *fæder, heofunum, nama, Cume, þīn wille, eorþan*, all from the first two lines of the O.E. *hlāf* ('loaf') and *ālȳs* ('loosen') can be added after a moment's further reflection. But others are more puzzling: *riċe* is later replaced by *kingdom, Syle* by *Give, gyltas* by *debts* and *costnunge* by *temptation*. If we know German, *riċe* may suggest *Reich*: the two words are cognates, formed from the same root. Or we may think of the suffix in *bishopric*, the bishop's domain. *Costnunge* has simply dropped out of the language – its last recorded use is about 1200 – and has been replaced by *temptation*, a word originally Latin but borrowed into English via French in the Middle Ages. We still have *guilt*, although it is now an abstract noun and not found in the plural. *Dettes*, lacking its *b* in the Wycliffite version, is also borrowed from French, but the *b* was restored in the sixteenth century when the classicizing Renaissance was determined to recognize the word's Latin origin in *debitum* (a similar thing happened with the *d* in *adventure*, the *l* in *fault* and the *p* in *receipt*). O.E. *ālȳs* has given way to borrowed French *deliver*. The difficult word is perhaps *Syle*. It looks like *sell* and is derived from O.E. *sellan*. But surely we cannot be inviting God to *sell* us our daily loaf? In fact, *sellan* meant 'give', whether or not in return for money. It is interesting that in the related (cognate) Scandinavian language *selja* meant either 'give up' or 'sell'. So a word may retain its original form but its meaning may subsequently change. Some words drop out of the language altogether (*riċe, costnunge*) but many more are borrowed from other languages and appear in English – sometimes in an anglicized form – as the demand grows, both for new words for new ideas and for a vocabulary to express finer shades of meaning. The vocabulary of the New English Bible is of less use for direct comparison, since its translators were concerned both to produce more exact translations and to avoid anachronisms. Hence, *the wrong we have done* for *debts* (or the equivalent *trespasses* in the 1662 Prayer Book) and *test* instead of *temptation*. In some modern versions *your* even replaces *thy* which is apparently thought unacceptable, even when confined to a religious context.

We could recognize *heofonum* and *eorþan* easily enough, but what are the *-um* and *-an* doing on the ends of those words? If we contrast the first passage with the second and the second with the third, we notice a diminishing number of strange endings: *in heofonum* becomes *in heuenys*; *on eorþan* is later *in erþe; we forgyfaþ* turns into *we forȝiuen* and, eventually, *we forgive*. But P.D.E. does have endings: Thy name *be* hallowed and Thy will *be* done use subjunctive *be*, expressing a wish, instead of the indicative *is*; similarly Thy kingdom *come* has subjunctive *come*, not indicative *comes*. In a sentence we need to know who is doing what to whom and, in the case of the verb, whether this is happening now or happened some time in the past. One way of managing this is by changes within the word itself: one form for the subject, say, and another for the object, and still others to show whether we are speaking of singular or plural. The most common way of achieving this is to use different endings (or inflections): *boy/boys; walk/walking/walked*. But it need not be a matter of the ending; the change can be in the middle of the word: *man/men, drive/drove*. Several languages (Latin or German, for instance) make extensive use of endings and O.E. also indicated the relationship of one word to the others in the

sentence by using a particular ending. In the O.E. version, the
-*aþ* ending of *forgyfaþ* and *agyltaþ* indicates that the verb
is in the present tense plural. Most O.E. prepositions were
followed by the dative case: hence on heofon*um*, on eor*þan*,
on costnung*e* and fram yfel*e*. P.D.E. has far fewer endings
but has to compensate by such devices as a greater use of
grammatical words (sometimes called *function* words) and a more
fixed word order. **Grammatical words** are the small change of
language. They do have a meaning which can be looked up in
the dictionary, but their function, their place in the grammar of
the language, is far more important. Words such as pronouns
(*you, they*), prepositions (*to, from, of*), determiners (*the, that, some,
any*), conjunctions (*and, or, but, since*), and auxiliary verbs (e.g.
the various forms of *have* and *be*) are grammatical words. They
belong to what linguists call a *closed class* into which new words
are hardly ever admitted: almost all of them have been in the
language since O.E. times. Most words, however, are **lexical** (or
content) **words**, where the content is the most important feature
(*boy, girl, paper, language, beautiful, describe, say, invariably*). Some
of these too, have been in English from its beginnings, but
thousands more have been borrowed over the centuries and
others are still being added. Nor surprisingly, these are termed
open class words.

A comparatively fixed word order is another feature of P.D.E.
Consider the two sentences, 'The man loved the woman' and 'The
woman loved the man'. In changing from the first of these to the
second we have not changed the form of any of the words but we
have reversed the meaning. Since we have come to expect that,
on the whole, subjects precede verbs and that objects follow
them, we have no difficulty over changing the meaning in
this way. In a language where endings reveal relationships of
words to each other, word order is far less important; it may
assume certain patterns (putting the verb at the end of a Latin
sentence) but these are a matter of style, not of necessity. So
the O.E. version of the Lord's Prayer has *Sȳ þīn willa* and
the M.E. *Be þi wille don*, whereas the two later versions have
Thy (your) will be done. The drift of English has therefore been
away from a language which uses many endings (a *synthetic*
language) towards one which uses fewer endings but employs
other strategies to indicate relationships (an *analytic* language);

however, P.D.E. has not yet arrived at the state of being a purely analytic language.

In considering these four versions of the Lord's Prayer, we have stumbled upon a method of describing the different ways we can approach a language. We can examine its **Vocabulary** (or *lexicon*, the stock of words in that particular language), its **Grammar and Syntax** (the latter is the study of how words are combined into longer units, such as sentences; the word derives from two Greek elements, *syn*, 'together' and *taxis*, 'arranging'), or its **Transmission** (pronunciation in speech and spelling and punctuation in writing). We also need two other kinds of terminology if we are to look at P.D.E. in the light of its origins. The first kind I have used already in referring to O.E., M.E. and Early Modern English. O.E. used to be called Anglo-Saxon; it covers the period 700 to 1100. M.E. runs from 1100 to 1500, and Early Modern English (hereafter E. Mod. E.) extends from 1500 to 1700. After 1700 we have markedly less difficulty in understanding the forms of the language; we do not need to translate Pope or Wordsworth. (Some linguists simply label the whole period following 1500 'Modern English'. 'Modern English', however defined, therefore includes P.D.E., but it is not synonymous with P.D.E. and must be distinguished from it.) It would be possible to use more exact dates, to say that O.E. ended with the Norman Conquest in 1066 and E. Mod. E. began with the first printing press in England, set up by William Caxton in 1476. But that might be misleading, for language changes gradually and often imperceptibly. No one went to bed on the last night of 1066 speaking O.E. and miraculously woke up on 1 January 1067 speaking M.E. The periods themselves, like their dates, are conventional and, up to a point, useful. They serve to contrast major changes in the language, for instance the predominantly 'Germanic' vocabulary of O.E., supplemented by numerous 'Romance' borrowings into M.E. That terminology is the second kind we shall need.

Individual languages are almost always members of larger groups. Most European and Indian languages can be traced back to a very large group called (Proto-) **Indo-European** (see figure 1).[2] It should be emphasized that this is a linguistic construct, based on a careful comparison of many apparently similar forms in the individual languages. We have no record

8

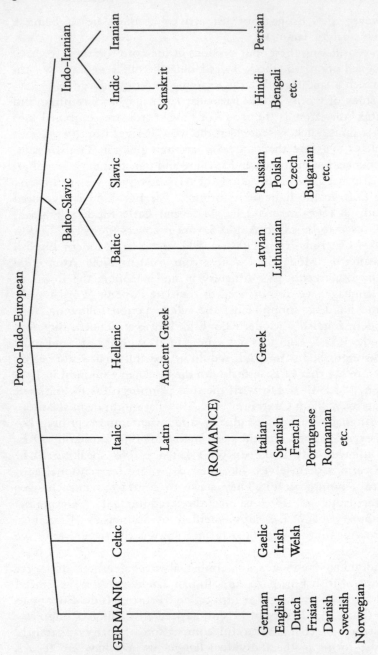

Figure 1

of this parent language. We do not know who spoke it, or when, or where they lived. Perhaps it was really not one language at all, but a group of closely-related dialects. It is probable that, during a period of migrations, certain groups split off from Indo-European; for a considerable time there was little contact with the parent group but there was contact with other peoples, and that would introduce some new linguistic features and modify others. Eventually (again, we do not know when) further separation resulted in the Germanic group of languages of which English is a member. Germanic may have been spoken in north-west Europe shortly before the beginning of the Christian era. To take another considerable jump, the 'English', speaking *englisc* and living in *Engla-land*, arrived in this country in the middle of the fifth century AD as invaders from the part of Germany nowadays called Schleswig-Holstein. Some of them probably came from Frisia, part of Holland – Frisian is the Germanic language closest to English – and perhaps from Jutland. Early (but not contemporary) accounts speak of Angles, Saxons and Jutes, but the presence of the Jutes (from Jutland) is sometimes disputed. The newcomers drove the native Celts (the 'ancient Britons') northwards and westwards to areas such as Cornwall, Cumbria and Wales, but the settlement of England was a gradual and partial process. In fact, for the O.E. period, we should not think of one England, with one language, English, but of different tribes speaking different dialects: Northumbrian, Mercian, West Saxon and Kentish. Northumbria was, logically enough, England north of the Humber; Mercian was spoken in Mercia, the present Midlands, the area between the Humber and the Thames; West Saxon was the language of Wessex, central southern and south-west England, the kingdom of Alfred the Great; Kentish covered an area somewhat larger than present-day Kent. Eventually, in the later ninth and tenth centuries, Wessex won political and cultural supremacy, and West Saxon almost (but not quite) achieved the status of a written standard, understood over all areas of the country.

It is the **Germanic** and **Romance** language groups with which we shall be most concerned. English is basically a Germanic language. The Romance languages, represented by French, Italian, Spanish, etc., descend from Latin. Characteristics of English (occasionally only of earlier English[3]) which are Germanic and are not shared by non-Germanic languages (including Latin and the Romance languages) are:

1. A complex pattern of sound-shifts, taking place very early in Germanic and affecting certain consonants. This change did not take place in non-Germanic languages and enables us to see the original relationships between two words whose form now seems wholly different, e.g. (native English words first): *f*oot v. *p*edestrian; *h*earty v. *c*ordial, *h*undred v. *c*entury; *t*ooth v. *d*ental, *t*en v. *d*ecimal; *g*arden v. *h*orticulture; *b*rother v. *f*raternal, *b*reakable v. *f*ragile. (Of course the Latin words have subsequently been borrowed into English.) This is called *Grimm's Law* after the nineteenth-century philologist Jacob Grimm (who was, incidentally, one of the two brothers responsible for the fairy-tales).

2. In Germanic languages, including English, the main stress of a word comes as near to the beginning as possible. In Romance languages word-stress is more variable. For this reason we can often pick out words borrowed into English which have not yet accommodated themselves to our pattern of stress, like *promenáde, bizárre, cartóon, connoisséur* (all from French) or *bravádo* (from Spanish).

3. In O.E. there was simply a two-tense system in the verb, present and past (*see* and *saw, like* and *liked*) which was marked by different forms. Later on we developed a much more complex system of tenses based on Latin but using auxiliary verbs rather than the Latin endings (*I am seeing, I shall see, I was seeing, I have seen*, and so on).

4. A two-fold classification of adjectives, that is a complete set of endings for each of two different uses of the adjective, depending upon whether or not the adjective was immediately preceded by a determiner, e.g. *those expensive clothes* v. *expensive clothes* or *those clothes are expensive*. This was present in O.E., but disappears during the M.E. period when it was evidently thought no longer necessary, and remains in modern German. Two other features of English are not peculiar to Germanic languages but are strongly represented in them:

5. Numerous compound words.

6.   A category of 'weak' verbs, those which in P.D.E. form their past tenses and past participles in *-ed*, such as *loved, helped, walked*, or in *-t*, such as *swept, built*.

We shall often have occasion to contrast Germanic features of English with those borrowed from Romance languages or from Latin which was understood throughout western Europe in the Middle Ages and the Renaissance. At different times in our history we shall see that this contrast has been used for cultural and political purposes. A greater use of French and Latin might indicate social superiority or, contrariwise, Germanic features could seem more 'pure', reminding us of our ancestry. Nowadays the two are more often distinguished as constituents of different styles of English, although it is worth remembering that a choice of style can itself be a powerful factor in trying to establish dominance.

All this may seem a great deal of information presented in a bald and fairly unappetizing manner and often hedged around with qualifications. Future chapters of this book will treat the different perspectives on language separately. How do we choose words? How do we put them together in sentences? How do we transmit them in both speech and writing? Another point which is very important: to what extent are our choices and our methods conditioned by what happened to English in earlier periods? To answer these questions we need the terminology outlined in this introduction, if only sometimes as shorthand forms to avoid the tedious repetition of definitions. We shall also need several illustrative examples, for generalizations about a language will take us only so far: different authors (even from the same period) and different kinds of writing may only partly conform to the general remarks made. Language, or *a* language like English, is a complex phenomenon, but also a marvellously sensitive one for saying what we want to say and saying it in a way we trust will be understood and appreciated.

NOTES

1.   Bailey (1992: p. vii) suggests that the proportion of the world's population making regular use of English may actually be declining

as a result of population increases in Third World countries where local languages are spoken.

2.   For further information see Robinson 1992. Some languages spoken and written in Europe are not part of the Indo-European family, for example Finnish, Hungarian, Turkish and Basque.

3.   R. Lass, *Old English: A Historical Linguistic Companion* (Cambridge: Cambridge University Press, 1994) is a full treatment of its subject, especially in phonology and morphology.

Chapter 2

Choosing Words: The Vocabulary of English

Vocabulary is a good place to begin our study. It is the aspect of a language which is easiest to appreciate. It is often the result of historical events. The Norman Conquest of 1066 began the introduction of hundreds of French words into the Middle English vocabulary; Elizabethan explorations brought back new words from the Americas. Some linguists talk of *external* pressures like these, as opposed to *internal* pressures on a language which result in a search for economy of expression and the gradual removal of ambiguities. Perhaps because it has been exposed to so many outside influences – some of them invasions, like the Norman Conquest or the Scandinavian settlements of the ninth and tenth centuries, but others operating in more peaceable ways, like the borrowings from Latin which was a prestige language for so many centuries – the vocabulary of English is especially rich, and this often allows us to choose between several ways of expressing the same idea.

We might begin with two descriptions of Hell, one contemporary, the other from three centuries ago. In the first extract taken from *Nice Work* by David Lodge, Robyn Penrose, a feminist university lecturer in English Literature, is directed to 'shadow' Vic Wilcox, the manager of a Midlands factory – and he her – in furtherance of a government-inspired scheme to make universities and industry more aware of each other. The idea is to visit each other's place of work, to observe, and wherever possible to join in, what is happening, to see, as it were, how the other half lives. Robyn regards the whole business as a great waste of time (of *her* time, especially) but she cannot really refuse since her university post has still not been confirmed. Passage 1 describes her first visit to the factory. John Bunyan became famous as a Puritan preacher and Part I of *Pilgrim's Progress* may have been written in Bedford jail where he had been imprisoned for preaching without a licence. His hero, Christian, is on a pilgrimage from the City of Destruction to the Celestial City and at this point of the story is passing through the Valley of the Shadow of Death. The book is full of biblical and allegorical figures, and folklore creatures too, such as the monster Apollyon whom Christian had overcome with great difficulty not long before. Its language is usually simple and direct; Bunyan mistrusted stylistic display.

In looking at these passages we should ask ourselves several questions. What kinds of words are chosen? What effect on us do they have? When did these words come into English and where did they come from? Do they suggest a particular kind of English, defined according to the situation in which it is used: the sort of English we might expect to hear in, say, a sermon, a football commentary or a war correspondent's report, or read in an epic poem, a letter from a close friend or the telephone directory? Clearly this concept of **register**, as it is called, overlaps with style, and in the 1960s and 1970s *register* was so overused that it lost much of its original more precise meaning. Nevertheless it remains a reasonably useful term. Does the particular word the writer chooses make us think of other words with which it is commonly associated (with which it *collocates*) or are we pulled up short because we were *not* expecting that particular word in such a context? To discover the origin of a particular word and when it entered English, we need a large dictionary. The fullest is the large *Oxford English Dictionary*, but *The Oxford Dictionary of English Etymology*, in a single volume, will serve for quicker reference and many other dictionaries also give the word's **etymology**.

Passage 1

> What *had* she expected? Nothing, certainly, so like the satanic
> mills of the early Industrial Revolution. Robyn's mental image of
> a modern factory had derived mainly from TV commercials and
> documentaries: deftly edited footage of brightly coloured machines
> and smoothly moving assembly lines, manned by brisk operators
> in clean overalls, turning out motor cars or transistor radios to the
> accompaniment of Mozart on the sound track. At Pringle's there

was scarcely any colour, not a clean overall in sight, and instead
of Mozart there was a deafening demonic cacophony that never
relented. Nor had she been able to comprehend what was going
on. There seemed to be no logic or direction to the factory's
activities. Individuals or small groups of men worked on separate
tasks with no perceptible relation to each other. Components were
stacked in piles all over the factory floor like the contents of an
attic. The whole place seemed designed to produce, not goods for
the outside world, but misery for the inmates. What Wilcox called
the machine shop had seemed like a prison, and the foundry had
seemed like hell.

(David Lodge, *Nice Work* (1988))

The noise in the factory seems to Robyn a *deafening demonic
cacophony* that never *relented*. Why does this phrase stand out?
Partly, of course, because of the alliteration, but more through
the choice of *cacophony*. The word probably entered English via
French, but it is originally Greek. There are several Greek-derived
words in modern English, especially in medical and scientific
writing (words with prefixes like *arch-* or *poly-* or suffixes like
-ology or *-ism*) but their appearance in the common language
does not begin to compare with the number of words from
French or Latin. Furthermore, this is a *demonic cacophony* and
demonic, too, comes from Greek. It is not a *ghastly din* where both
words would be native English. Robyn's vocabulary, as befits her
profession, is a literary one. The cacophony never *relented* (not
stopped) and she cannot *comprehend* (rather than *understand*) what
is going on. The various jobs in the factory have no *perceptible*
(instead of *clear* or *obvious*) relation to each other. These three
words are all borrowings from French. The *satanic mills* of the
opening line is meant to recall Blake's poem *Jerusalem*. Her mental
image of a factory is also conditioned by TV commercials and
documentaries. Here there is little room for unusual words. The
illustration of smooth efficiency is achieved by choosing terms such
as *components* or *manned*, but still more by the adjective compounds
deftly edited, brightly coloured, smoothly moving. Lodge does not use
hyphens here, but compounds do not absolutely require them; the
idea of a single unit, which can often be replaced by one word,
is of greater importance. Here the compounds, together with the
balanced adjectives – *brisk* operators in *clean* overalls – supply the
imagined air of efficiency about to be so abruptly shattered. In

the last four lines of the passage the vocabulary becomes much simpler in its attempt to describe the real factory: components are *stacked in piles* like *the contents of an attic*. The place reminds her of a *prison* with *inmates* (the latter word makes us think of an asylum). The satirizing of Robyn's view of life, with its imagined, sanitized order ('there seemed to be no logic or direction') is largely achieved by the replacement of a literary-sounding vocabulary by a more colloquial one.

Passage 2

> About the midst of this Valley, I perceived the mouth of Hell
> to be, and it stood also hard by the way side. Now, thought
> Christian, what shall I do? And ever and anon the flame and
> smoke would come out in such abundance, with sparks and
> hideous noises (things that cared not for *Christian*s Sword, as
> did *Apollyon* before) that he was forced to put up his Sword and
> betake himself to another weapon called *All-prayer*; so he cried in
> my hearing, *O Lord I beseech thee deliver my Soul*. Thus he went
> on a great while, yet still the flames would be reaching towards
> him: also he heard doleful voices, and rushings to and fro, so that
> sometimes he thought he should be torn in pieces, or trodden
> down like mire in the Streets. This frightful sight was seen, and
> these dreadful noises were heard by him for several miles together:
> and coming to a place where he thought he heard a company of
> *Fiends* coming forward to meet him, he stopt, and began to muse
> what he had best to do. Sometimes he had half a thought to
> go back. Then again he thought he might be half way through
> the Valley; he remembred also how he had already vanquished
> many a danger; and that the danger of going back might be
> much more then for to go forward; so he resolved to go on.
> (John Bunyan, *The Pilgrim's Progress* (1678))

Hell is appropriately the very last word in the first extract; it occurs in the first line of the second. For Bunyan it is no metaphor but a clearly-visualized region. What Robyn termed a *demonic cacophony*, Christian thinks of as *hideous noises*. The number of unusual words in the second passage is obviously much smaller. But we should not write off Bunyan's work as casual and unconsidered. It includes words more characteristic of the seventeenth century than of the late twentieth – *midst, hard by, way side, ever and anon, betake himself, beseech, doleful, to and fro, mire, fiends, muse.* Some may remind us of biblical passages: in the New Testament parable some of the sower's seed fell *by the way side* and the Old Testament prophet Jeremiah sank *in the mire. Frightful* and *dreadful* (linked by their shared suffix – *ful*) were stronger words then than now – these are truly terrifying sights. The restricted register which Bunyan for the most part employs is paralleled by other usages (which are both lexically and grammatically unusual to us) such as *would come out* and *would be reaching out* (where *would* means 'continued to'), *cared not* ('did not care'), *should be torn* ('was bound to be torn'), *he had best to do* ('would be best for him to do'). These would not have seemed strange to a seventeenth-century reader, although some of them might have seemed rather old-fashioned. I would not want to claim that Bunyan is representative of seventeenth-century English which has a wide range of registers and styles. He is selecting, for his own purposes, from what was possible in his vocabulary, just as Lodge, more self-consciously and for very different ends, is selecting from the lexicon of late twentieth-century English. And in the last two lines Bunyan's register changes, just as Lodge's had done, but in the opposite direction: *vanquished* (French, with a memory, perhaps, of knightly combats) and *resolved* (from Latin) are more literary. Christian is emerging from Hell, Robyn is entering more deeply in.

THE EXPANDING VOCABULARY: OLD ENGLISH AND MIDDLE ENGLISH

In looking at these two passages we have become aware of words borrowed into English from other languages and the fact that some of them may, in practice, be limited to certain registers. We have also noticed, although less often, the effect of some compounds. Many of the compounds, as we shall see, achieve the kind of concentration aimed at in very different kinds of writing: advertising or poetry for instance. It is sometimes suggested that most compounds are native English in origin; many are, but once a word has become accepted in English it is able to become part of a compound. *Gentle* was borrowed from French and soon joined with O.E. words to form *gentleman* and *gentlewoman*, and, with an O.E. suffix, *gentleness*.

We should not ignore the native English basis of our vocabulary, although it is not often going to strike us as especially notable. If we ask how much of our vocabulary is **Old English** in origin, the answer will depend upon how often we count each word. Almost all of the grammatical (or function) words mentioned earlier are native English, except for *they, them, their* and *both* which are Scandinavian. So if we counted every grammatical word each time it occurred, the proportion of O.E. words in a passage would be correspondingly high. Naturally, too, the percentage of native and borrowed words will vary with the content of the passage being analysed: more complex or deliberately impressive styles will contain a much higher proportion of borrowed words (**loan words**). In addition to the grammatical words, several short, simple lexical (content) words are native English. These include parts of the body, like *arm, bone, eye, foot, hand, heart*; words for natural phenomena, for example *day, earth, field, land, night, water* (but not *sky* which is Scandinavian); farm animals such as *cow, horse, lamb*; in the house, *house* itself, *home, door, floor*; close family relationships: *father, mother, child, son, brother* (but *uncle* and *cousin*, less close, are borrowed); representative common verbs, e.g. *choose, eat, look, love, see, sit, sleep, speak*, and adjectives *busy, deep, good, high, many, wide*. Only a small number of abstract nouns, such as *care, love* and those with the suffix *-th* (*health, strength, wealth, worth*), can be traced back to O.E. We should not assume, however, that all short, basic words are native English; *street, law, face, very, pray, seem, dinner* are all borrowed, although admittedly they have been in the language for some centuries. Some O.E. words which have subsequently disappeared from the general language can still be found in dialects or place-names (see p. 177–80).

Like all living languages, however, O.E. (c. 700 to c. 1100) changed, and in particular supplemented its vocabulary in order to provide new words for new ideas. In all probability the borrowings began on the Continent, before the Angles, Saxons and Jutes invaded England in the mid fifth century and became the English. O.E. *wīn, butere, strǣt* (Latin *via strata*, 'paved road'), *weall, disċ* ('dish'; O.E. *sċ* is pronounced *sh*), *ċīese* ('cheese') are easily recognizable words which in fact are Latin borrowings. Some religious words – the invaders were not yet christian but were in contact with christian settlements – include *biscop, munuc, angel, dēofol* and *ċyriċe* ('church'). *Ċyriċe* was from Greek *kyriakon doma*, 'the lord's house'; contrast Latin *ecclesia* and French *église* from a different root, although we borrowed *ecclesiastical* much later on. *Saturday*, too, was borrowed from Latin (Saturn's day). It is the only day of the week whose name is not Germanic in origin: *Sunday* (O.E. *sunne*, 'sun'), *Monday* (*mōna*, 'moon'), *Tuesday* (Tiw, god of war and of the sky), *Wednesday* (Woden), *Thursday* (Thor, son of Woden), *Friday* (Friga, consort of Woden and goddess of marriage and childbirth). In French the names of some of the days reflect their Latin origins: *mardi* (Mars), *mercredi* (Mercury), *jeudi* (Jove), *vendredi* (Venus) and *samedi* (Saturn). With the conversion to Christianity in 597, Latin was once again being spoken in England by people in a position to influence the vocabulary, for education and the copying of texts was almost entirely in the hands of the Church, especially the monasteries. *Pope, priest, abbot, clerk* ('cleric'), *mass, altar, hymn, psalm, creed, school* were all borrowed into English. Later, after the reform of the monasteries in the tenth century, *cloister, verse, grammar* (O.E. *grammatic cræft*, 'grammatical skill') and *history* were among several others added. From the beginning, then, Latin has contributed to the growth of the English vocabulary; it was the only sizeable source of loan words in Old English, but even so it represented only a small proportion of the whole vocabulary.

The English, who had themselves invaded this country and eventually established themselves as a nation, were in turn invaded in the ninth and tenth centuries by the **Scandinavians**. I use 'Scandinavians' as a cover term for Danes and Norwegians; these invaders are sometimes called Vikings and the *Anglo-Saxon Chronicle* (from which much of our information comes) refers to them indiscriminately as Danes, *Dene*. The attacks on England were part of a large pattern of raids on western Europe beginning at the end of the eighth century. Indeed, their voyages took them further still, eastwards to Russia (mostly Swedes) and perhaps to America. The first Scandinavian hit-and-run raids on this country were in the 790s, often on monasteries like Lindisfarne, Jarrow and Iona which, being near the coast, were readily accessible and, being undefended but full of valuable objects, were easy targets for the heathen attackers. It was the Norwegians who plundered in the extreme north and who sailed round northern Scotland to attack (and subsequently colonize) parts of Ireland, including Dublin; the Orkneys and Iceland also came under their domination. The Danes came due west across the North Sea to ravage targets in northern and eastern England. Plundering gradually gave way to settlement and the influence of Scandinavian upon English could begin. Alfred eventually halted their drive southwards and westwards, and in 878 made a truce establishing what we would call 'spheres of influence': to the north and east of Watling Street and the River Lea was to be Danish territory while the south and west remained English. In the tenth century much of the *Danelaw*, as it was called, was recaptured, although York remained under Scandinavian rule until 954. From 900 onwards there was fresh penetration into the north-west (the Wirral, Lancashire, Westmorland, Cumberland and north-west Yorkshire), chiefly by Norwegians coming from Ireland, and, at the end of the tenth century, a new wave of Danish invasions along the south and south-east coasts culminated in Danish rule during the early eleventh century: for a short time Canute was king of England, Denmark and Norway. The English dynasty was restored in 1042 and lasted until the Norman Conquest of 1066. One further point is that, although the Scandinavian influence on the English vocabulary took place in the Old English period, many of the words are not *recorded* until early Middle English. This is because the areas in which most O.E. documents were written were in the south and west, far away from northern and eastern England where the invaders predominated.

The influence of the Scandinavian languages on the English vocabulary precedes that of French and is altogether different and far less immediately noticeable. This is almost entirely due to the fact that Scandinavian is, like English, a Germanic language and French is a member of the Romance group. A typical list of Scandinavian loans indicates their unremarkable and unsophisticated nature:

nouns: *anger, birth, cake, dirt, egg, fellow, knife, law, leg, loan, skill, skin, skirt, sky* (initial *sk-* is typical), *window, wrong*.

verbs: *call, cast, die* (apparently not in O.E. which did have *dead* and *death*), *get, give, hit, scold, score, scowl, scream* (four other *sk*-sounds), *thrust*.

adjectives: *awkward, happy, ill, low, rotten, scant, ugly, weak*.

These are all straightforward, simple terms. There was no cultural superiority to the native Anglo-Saxons and consequently no real areas of supremacy from which words might be borrowed. While a few Scandinavian loans replaced their O.E. counterparts (*rodor* and *wolcen* gave way to Scandinavian *sky, niman* to *take, hātan* to *call* and *weorpan* to *cast*), in other cases the two related (cognate) words continued side by side and in some cases eventually diverged in meaning. *Shirt* (O.E.) and *skirt* (Scandinavian) were originally synonymous. Other pairs are (O.E. first): *sick* and *ill, wrath* and *anger, shin* and *skin, blithe* and *happy, foul* and *ugly, craft* and *skill*. Since the invaders eventually settled in the north and east, their influence can be seen in many place-names from those areas, especially those with *-thorp* ('farmstead'), *-by* ('settlement'), *-toft* ('plot of ground'), *-beck* ('stream') and *-thwaite* ('clearing'), and also in some dialect forms: *kirk* ('church'), *dike* ('ditch'), *flit* ('move house'), *mun* ('must'). The Scandinavian influence on English, then, is not so much in the number of words supplied as in the fact that many of them are frequently-used words. But, unlike French and Latin, Scandinavian gave us a few grammatical words, most important the third-person plural pronouns in *th-* (*they, them, their*) and also *both* and *though*. The period of major influence is also surprisingly short, beginning in the ninth century and lasting into the very early M.E. period. Thereafter there has not been much strong or continuous contact between England and the Scandinavian countries, so post-medieval borrowings have been few: *batten, doze, oaf, rug, skittle, squall, cosy, muggy,* and the more recent *ombudsman*. A few other loans are of more specifically Scandinavian objects: *fjord, saga, ski, smorgasbord* and *troll*.

The one date every schoolboy in England knows is the Norman Conquest of 1066. Before the Conquest English was the language in which an extensive and remarkable literature had been composed and it was also the language of legal and administrative documents. Things did not change overnight after William the Conqueror defeated Harold at Hastings: language does not work in that way. Latin replaced English as the language of official records, a position it held for the next 350 years. Gradually, however, **French** became established in England as a prestige literary language and also, by the mid thirteenth century, as the language of the law. The Normans of 1066 and their immediate successors represented only a minority of the population of England, perhaps one Norman to every nine or ten Englishmen, but they were in a position to commission books and to influence education. The

Jerseyman, Robert Wace, wrote in the mid twelfth century of 'rich folks who possess revenues and silver, since for them books are made and good words are composed and well set forth'.[1] New writing, now in a language we can properly call Middle English (c. 1100 to c. 1500), and already beginning to be influenced by Norman French, begins to emerge alongside the French of the invaders. The last entries in the Peterborough version of the *Anglo-Saxon Chronicle*, written in 1154, while clearly in a language derived from O.E., contain enough new features (originating in the spoken language) to justify our placing it on the far side of the dividing line between O.E. and M.E.

It is possible to distinguish in M.E. two periods of borrowing into English from French. For some 200 years after the Conquest a form of French (Norman French, or better, *Anglo-Norman*, the French spoken and written in England) was the language of the upper classes and the higher clergy and English of the subject lower classes. The Norman invaders thought of home as across the Channel and that was where they wanted to be buried (as William is at Caen). William's eldest son, Robert, succeeded him as Duke of Normandy and the younger son, William Rufus, as King of England. Richard I, the 'Lionheart' (1157 to 1199), the second son of Henry II and Eleanor of Aquitaine, spoke no English and spent only a few months of his reign in England. The feudal aristocracy had possessions in both France and England and regular contact between the two countries was thus maintained. Englishmen found it to their advantage to learn French because, as historians remind us, the distinction was not really racial so much as social: the change to modern ideas of nationalism comes only slowly during the later Middle Ages. There must, however, surely have been more bilingualism than we know of, especially if we extend the concept of bilingualism to include Englishmen who could understand French and also speak it after a fashion. On estates people learnt to use French-derived words like *tax, duty, pay*, and from French-speaking clerics they picked up terms like *religion, saviour, pray* and *trinity*.[2] These are quite simple words, and other early borrowings (*age, change, city, fresh, large, letter, people, please, second, try, use, very*, for instance) plus *bacon, castle, market* and *prison*, all four of which may have entered English even before the Conquest, seem now always to have been part and parcel of English.

The situation changes during the thirteenth century with the gradual loss of English possessions in France (Normandy itself was lost in 1204) following the 1244 decree of Henry III of England and King Louis of France that nobles could not hold lands in both countries. They thus began to think of themselves as either English or French. The French words borrowed into English in the later Middle Ages do not come from Norman French but from the now prestigious Central French dialect (*francien*) which was to become the basis of standard French. Some of these words (those needed to describe the often abstract concepts of chivalry or courtly love for example) seem more learned than their earlier counterparts and they were often borrowed through literature rather than through speech. As with the Renaissance Latin borrowings to be described later, turning over the pages of a standard history of the language (such as that by Baugh and Cable, 1993) will indicate the very large numbers of words involved. This is how Chaucer concludes the description of his knight, the first pilgrim in the *General Prologue* to the *Canterbury Tales* (the words from French are italicized):

He nevere yet no *vileynye* ne sayde
In al his lyf unto no *maner* wight.
He was a *verray*, *parfit*, *gentil* knyght.
But for to tellen yow of his *array*,
His hors weren goode, but he was nat *gay*.
Of *fustian* he wered a *gypoun*
Al bismotered with his *habergeoun*,
For he was late ycome from his *viage*,
And wente for to doon his *pilgrymage*.[3]

Some of the words are abstract: *vileynye* ('offensive words'), *verray* ('true'), *parfit*, *gentil*, *gay* ('dressed up'); others are technical: *fustian*, *gypoun*, *habergeoun*. *Viage* (perhaps 'military expedition') and *pilgrymage* are more general. Yet O.E.-derived *wight*, *knyght*, *tellen*, *hors*, *ycome* occur too. By this time French had been added to earlier borrowings from Latin and Scandinavian, so that a *knight* (English) is called *Sir* (French), his wife is *Lady* (English, but compare *madam*, from French), and the wife of an *earl* (English-Scandinavian) is a *countess* (French). *King* and *queen* are English, but *sovereign*, *royalty*, *rule*, *reign*, *court*, *govern* and *parliament* are all French. It has recently been argued that the Anglo-French of the second half of the M.E. period is sometimes creative, using words in senses not found in Continental French, or at least not found until later.[4] *Carpenter*, for instance, is found in both French and English, but *joiner* ('worker in wood'), although in English from 1322, is not found in French until later. So in this case it would be inaccurate to say the word was 'borrowed' from French; it looks as though English itself formed *joiner* as an agent noun from French *joindre* (on the model of *porter/porteur*). *Bribe* occurs in French as a noun ('small piece', 'scrap'), but the modern sense of the verb ('to corrupt by offering money') is evidently in use in Anglo-French from the mid fourteenth century. This is less surprising if we remember that many upper-class people in England still normally spoke a form of French.

In the later part of the fourteenth century, and increasingly in the fifteenth, English started to make a comeback, and became the natural language for all classes of Englishmen to use. After all, Chaucer (c. 1343 to 1400) wrote in English and not in French. But, as J. H. Fisher says, his background was cosmopolitan:

> Born into a family with a French name, married to the daughter
> of a Flemish knight, living in an Anglo-French court, serving in
> capacities that required him to write daily in French and Latin,
> Chaucer was bicultural and bilingual to a degree that it is hard for
> us to comprehend.[5]

In 1362 the Chancellor opened Parliament in English for the first time, and in the same year it was decreed that English and not French was to be used in the law courts (this was probably often disregarded). In the later fourteenth century and in the fifteenth century, French in England became a cultivated second language rather than a necessity. There were even books claiming to teach French. We shall have occasion later in this book to look at the rise of a new standard English in rather more detail, but a growing English nationalism certainly played its part. There are even complaints about how the French have appropriated into their own literature the great English hero Arthur and have generally exploited the English.[6] Even today, there is sometimes not much linguistic love lost between the two languages. If you leave the battle early, you 'take French leave' in English, but if you are French you 'filer a l'Anglaise'.[7]

Where does this leave French in popular regard at the close of the Middle Ages in England? The peak of borrowing had certainly passed by 1400, but French words still sometimes stuck out in

English because French is a Romance language whereas English is a Germanic one. In Chaucer a French loan word will usually require another French loan word to rhyme with it: *maistrie* and *jalousie*, *resoun* and *consolacioun*, *purveiaunce* and *governaunce*, *conclusioun* and *disputisioun*. These examples happen to come from the *Franklin's Tale*. Incidentally, the last word in the description of the Franklin in the *General Prologue* is *vavasour*, an outmoded word even then, from chivalric romance. The impression of a rather old-fashioned country gentleman, who will later tell a Breton *lai*, a possibly old-fashioned type of story, is crystallized by finally calling him a *vavasour*. It is worth noting that some of these abstract words are among the most difficult to translate properly into Modern English. French had provided English with an abstract vocabulary – God's *governaunce* over man and the lady's *ordinaunce* over her lover. In less aristocratic vein, fun could be had with what was obviously not the French true Frenchmen really used (or Englishmen at court, for that matter). Chaucer says that his Prioress's French, although spoken *ful faire and fetisly* ('most beautifully and elegantly') was

> After the scole of Stratford atte Bowe
> For Frennsh of Parys was to hire unknowe.[8]

Langland is not usually regarded as a comic writer, but his Avarice, when commanded by Repentance to make restitution for his ill-gotten gains, states (or pretends) that

> 'I wende riflynge were *restitucion*', quod he, 'for I lerned nevere rede on boke,
> And I kan no Frenssh in feith, but of the ferthest ende of Northfolk'.[9]

Chaucer's Miller can pronounce a polysyllabic French word, even though it may be a struggle:

> But first I make a *protestacioun*
> That I am dronke; I knowe it by my soun.[10]

– that over-careful articulation we have all heard from a man the worse for drink. Miller and Reeve, in the ensuing conversation, are adamant that nobody is calling anybody else a cuckold, although the Miller adds that there may be some things it is better not to know, especially, perhaps, if you were to know them in French:

An housbonde shal nat been inquisityf
Of Goddes *pryvetee*, nor of his wyf.

God's hidden secrets, perhaps something terrible – but *nor of his wyf*, his wife's 'private parts'? He continues:

So he may fynde Goddes *foyson* there,
Of the remenant nedeth nat enquere.

'God's plenty', perhaps a phrase used at harvest time, is here turned into a dirty joke.

From the point of view of this book, we need to consider the effect on Present-Day English of all these French borrowings. They were not always new words for new ideas. Some of them replaced the O.E. word, as *wyrd* was replaced by *fortune; here, fyrd* and *werod* by *army; wīg* by *war; lof* by *praise; wlite* by *beauty*. In other cases the O.E. and French-derived words continued side by side and eventually acquired different shades of meaning. Consider the different contexts in which we would use (O.E. word first) *heart* and *courage, forgive* and *pardon, lust* and *pleasure, sing* and *chant. Love, blithe* and *mood* seem quite ordinary; *passion, romance, jealousy* and *desire* are truly romantic. But several of these distinctions are ours. If we confine ourselves to the Middle Ages, the proportion of French borrowings, although large (in comparison with, say, the three per cent or so of Latin loans into O.E.), is still not as high as we might have thought, as David Burnley points out:

> It is worth noting that despite the great numbers of lexical items borrowed from French, the most frequently used words continued to be those of English and sometimes Scandinavian origin. In Early Middle English the lexicon still consisted of 91.5 per cent words of English origin; in later Middle English this figure had fallen to 78.8 per cent. But counted in terms of the number of occurrences of English-derived words in continuous text, the figures are 94.4 per cent for the earlier period, and falls only to 87.5 per cent for the later (Dekeyser, 1986), reflecting both the more exotic nature of French borrowings, and the fact that the function words of the language remain English.[11]

After the Middle Ages, we continued to borrow words from French, often in rather specialized fields in which French was thought to be superior to English. Military language was enriched by *attack, campaign, communication, manoeuvre,* and ranks such as *captain, colonel* and *commandant*. In dress, *blouse, beret, lingerie, suede, boutique* have been borrowed, and in food and drink *café, champagne, chef, chocolate, restaurant* and *soup*, not to mention several individual dishes on the *menu*. More general words are *apartment, burlesque, memoirs, routine* (all seventeenth century), *bureau, canteen, communism, etiquette, police, route* and *souvenir* (eighteenth and nineteenth centuries), and *baroque, chauffeur, cliché, garage, questionnaire, renaissance* and *repertoire* (twentieth century). Then there are phrases like *au pair, avant garde, carte blanche, déja vu, enfant terrible, faute de mieux, faux pas, haute couture, joie de vivre, nouveau riche, raison d'être, savoir faire*, and still others in which the French word-order of noun plus adjective – English has adjective plus noun – gives the game away: *attorney general, court martial, heir apparent, life immortal, malice aforethought, proof positive* and *sum total*. Several of the post-medieval borrowings look and sound French because the French pronunciation is retained in English. Compare the 'sh' sound in *chef, chauffeur, chic, chiffon, champagne, machine* with the anglicized 'tch' of *chief, chase, change, check, choice* which were all borrowed into M.E., and contrast the French and English pronunciations of *age* and *garage*. Or else the spelling still looks more French than English: *quay, fruit, physique, critique*. We even retain the French accent in a few words: *café, cliché, fiancée*. Or again, the stress, which in a Germanic language like English is normally as near the beginning of the word as possible, is on a later syllable in more recent French loans like *capríce, connoisséur, prestíge, silhouétte*.

THE RENAISSANCE: COPIOUS LANGUAGE

In the Middle Ages it is sometimes difficult to be sure whether a word was borrowed into English direct from Latin or, as more frequently happened, via French, for French was itself descended from Latin. Sometimes the M.E. spelling of the word will help; for instance, spellings with *-aunce, -ee, -ioun, -esse* (*substaunce, charitee, confessioun, gentilesse*) will normally signify a French borrowing. Sometimes the same word has been borrowed into English twice: the simpler *blame, count, feat, sure, sever* from French into M.E. and the corresponding Latin loans *blaspheme, compute, fact, secure* and *separate* later on. On the whole, the longer and more technical-sounding the word, the more likely it is to have come direct from Latin, e.g. *comprehend, contempt, contradiction,* *conviction, divide, equivalent, include* and *exclude, frustrate, immortal, implication, individual, inferior, interrupt, legal, legitimate, moderate, necessary, nervous, rational, subordinate, summary, ulcer.*[12] But this is a somewhat grey area; by the later Middle Ages all educated men in England could read French and Latin and, of course, English as well.

It was during the Renaissance, however, that Latin borrowings entered English thick and fast. Education was easier to obtain: there were more grammar schools, the Inns of Court were beginning to challenge the dominance of the two universities of Oxford and Cambridge, and the spread of printing (from the late fifteenth century on) meant that books became cheaper and more widely available. Men's horizons, and their minds too, were expanding, and English seemed inadequate to express all that needed to be said. Here is Skelton (c. 1460 to 1529), poet laureate, satirist and stylist, whose poetry often juxtaposes learned (i.e. Latin-derived) and popular registers

Our naturall tong is rude,	
And hard to be enneude	*made fresh*
With pullysshed termes lusty;	*pleasant*
Our language is so rusty,	
So cankered and so full	
Of frowardes, and so dull,	*awkward words*
That if I wolde apply	
To write ornatly,	
I wot not where to find	*know*
Terms to serve my mynde.[13]	

rude (together with *ineloquent* and *unpolished*) become pejorative terms for English in the sixteenth century. If he is to write *ornately* the poet will have to turn to Latin. But not everyone who could read knew Latin. So almost all the great Latin authors and some of the major Greek authors too were translated into the vernacular, and this was no doubt one method by which several Latin words found their way into English. Even so, there was a danger that some readers would find the Latinate English too elaborate and too difficult. Richard Mulcaster, headmaster of Merchant Taylors School in London (where the poet Spenser had been a pupil) considered the position in his *Elementarie* (1582). He pays tribute to English as *verie forcible and stout*, especially in its preponderance of monosyllables. But where the matter was more elaborate or the style needed to be more eloquent, English alone would not do: 'Commonesse for euerie man, beawtie for the learned, brauerie [i.e. boldness] to rauish'. So his own vocabulary is based on English but the demands of the subject-matter may require borrowing. The loan word, however, must not be borrowed merely for its own sake; it must be fit for the context and may itself need to be changed in form a little to make it appear more English:

> For mine own words and the terms, that I vse, they be generallie English. And if anie be either an incorporate stranger, or otherwise translated, or quite coined a new, I have shaped it as fit for the place, where I vse it as my cunning will giue me.[14]

Mulcaster's is a sensible solution to the problem. Whether or not English should borrow words, and if so how many, exercised some of the best minds in the Renaissance. Some objected to the wholesale importation of what they sarcastically called 'inkhorn' or 'inkpot' terms, bookish language. Undoubtedly Latin words were sometimes borrowed simply to sound impressive, but more pragmatic writers like Mulcaster realized both that English had always borrowed words from other languages and that, in this case, a compromise was necessary.

Thousands of words were borrowed into English from Latin (and Greek) during the sixteenth and the early seventeenth centuries. Some soon dropped out as being superfluous, but many others remained and helped to provide English with some of the different shades of meaning I mentioned earlier. Renaissance and eighteenth-century dictionaries helped to spread and to authenticate some of these. To get some idea of the number of words involved and what sort of words they were, turn over the pages of the relevant chapter in one of the standard histories of the language, such as Baugh and Cable, Pyles or Millward, where the borrowings are classified under different subject-headings. An absurdly short and selective list may nevertheless give some idea of the range:

> allurement, allusion, amnesty, anachronism, antipathy, antithesis, axis, atmosphere, autograph, appropriate, agile, *anonymous*, antique, caustic, capsule, chaos, chronology, climax, *catastrophe*, comma, crisis, critic, criterion, conspicuous, consolidate, dedicate, denunciation, dexterity, disability, disrespect, disregard, *drama*, education, emphasis, energy, enterprise, enthusiasm, excursion, expectation, exert, expensive, external, extinguish, eradicate, exist,

halo, *heterodox*, habitual, hereditary, harass, *idiosyncrasy*, impersonal, index, insane, ingenious, jurisprudence, jocular, larynx, *lexicon*, malignant, meditate, *misanthrope*, mundane, parenthesis, pathos, pastoral, parasite, pneumonia, protest, scheme, skeleton, system, susceptible, *tantalize, thermometer, tonic*, tactics, verbosity.

The italicized words probably came directly from Greek; they are fewer in number than the Latin borrowings and the degree of anglicization is less. Other words on the list, common to both Greek and Latin (*antithesis, chronology, crisis, enthusiasm, scheme, system*, for example) are likely to have been borrowed through Latin which was more familiar.

English may have contained some 44,000 words by 1623, the year of the First Folio (Fl), the collected edition of Shakespeare's plays produced by his associates Heminges and Condell (Shakespeare died in 1616), and almost one-quarter of these are recorded as having made their first appearance between 1580 and 1623. Shakespeare therefore shared in this considerable expansion of the vocabulary.[15] He may have introduced some 600 words into English, excluding compounds. Not surprisingly he has always been the best-recorded English author and some words previously attributed to him may well have been used earlier by another writer (some 50 words credited to Shakespeare by the large *Oxford English Dictionary* were actually first used by his contemporary Nashe). Among the many words which Shakespeare was, so far as we know, the first to use are *abstemious, accommodation, admirable, comply, counterpart, educate, fixture, generous, pedant, pious, quarrelsome, supervise* and *tranquil*. These are direct borrowings; other words first found in Shakespeare are hybrids where the affix (prefix or suffix) may be from one language and the root from another, such as *dislike, employer, intermingle, resound, surname, undervalue*. Renaissance borrowings from Latin are apt to seem rather learned words, not surprisingly since they were almost always borrowed through writing, in contrast to many of the earlier speech-based loans into English, such as Scandinavian words in the ninth and tenth centuries and the earlier French borrowings in the years following the Norman Conquest.

How can we know, though, which words struck the audience in the Globe theatre in 1600 as new or unusual? We cannot always be certain, but we do have some evidence. The large *Oxford English*

Dictionary gives the etymology of words in English since 1100 and dated contexts for their use. The single-volume *Oxford Dictionary of English Etymology* gives the etymology of the word and the century – not the actual date or an illustrative context – in which it was borrowed. There are also concordances to Shakespeare (the best is the Harvard Concordance by Marvin Spevack) which show how often Shakespeare used a particular word. Dictionary and concordance can be used together, plus the Shakespearean context which may be even more useful. Does the word seem to need definition? Is it linked to a simpler synonym or even paraphrased? The enormous influx of Latin words allowed a writer to 'place' a word strategically so that it coincides with major stress and carries increased emphasis, or else it could be used in conjunction with other words, near synonyms, to create what the Elizabethans called *copious* language:

> How weary, stale, flat, and unprofitable
> Seem to me all the uses of this world!
>
> (I. ii. 133–4)

cries Hamlet in one of his soliloquies, and the copious vocabulary conveys the impression of unbearable tedium.

> Brutus is noble, wise, valiant, and honest;
> Caesar was mighty, bold, royal, and loving.
>
> (*Julius Caesar* III. i. 126–7)

which is Mark Antony's view, immediately after Caesar's death. There are examples in almost every play. Not all the words in the list need be Latinate, although it is unusual to find a group without one or two examples.

We perhaps think first of Donne as a great love poet. Yet he was, in later life, Dean of St Paul's. This is part of a sermon he preached there in January 1626. The magisterial effect is achieved both by the grouping of the words and also by the balance of the syntax (which we shall return to later). Donne is an expansive writer and it is often easier to follow the progress of his thought at paragraph rather than sentence level:

> I would always raise your hearts, and dilate your hearts, to a holy
> Joy, to a joy in the Holy Ghost. There may be a just feare, that
> men do not grieve enough for their sinnes; but there may bee a

just jealousie, and suspition too, that they may fall into inordinate
griefe, and diffidence of Gods mercy; and God hath reserved us
to such times, as being the later times, give us even the dregs and
lees of misery to drinke. For God hath not onely let loose into
the world a new spirituall disease; which is, an equality, and an
indifferency, which religion our children, or our servants, or our
companions professe; (I would not keepe company with a man
that thought me a knave, or a traitor; with him that thought I
loved not my Prince, or were a faithlesse man, not to be beleeved,
I would not associate myself; And yet I will make him my bosome
companion, that thinks I doe not love God, that thinks I cannot
be saved) but God hath accompanied, and complicated almost all
our bodily diseases of these times, with an extraordinary sadnesse,
a predominant melancholy, a faintnesse of heart, a chearlessnesse, a
joylessnesse of spirit, and therefore I returne often to this endeavor
of raising your hearts, dilating your hearts with a holy Joy, Joy in
the holy Ghost, for *Vnder the shadow of his wings*, you may, you
should *rejoyce*.[16]

   This is by no means an untypical paragraph in a Donne sermon,
but remember it *is* a sermon and therefore a certain amount of
redundancy of expression will be necessary to get the message
across, for the listeners cannot turn back, as they can with the
pages of a book. Such pairs as *dregs and lees* or *an equality, and an
indifferency* are simply synonyms. So are *keepe company* and *associate
myself*, but these two are separated by several other words; the
fact that each is preceded by *I would not* . . . leads us to place
them together. Not all examples of copious diction are, however,
synonyms: *a just fear . . . a just jealousie, and suspition too* proceed
in an ascending scale of horror. Similarly *griefe and diffidence,
accompanied and complicated*, and *a knave, or a traitor* advance in each
case from the less to the more specific. As Donne reaches his climax
he produces a longer list, *an extraordinary sadnesse, a predominant
melancholy, a faintnesse of heart, a chearlessnesse, a joylessnesse of
spirit*, linked by the articles and the repetition of the *-ness* suffix
and made more weighty still by the addition of the two Latinate
adjectives *extraordinary* and *predominant*. Almost at the end of the
paragraph he speaks of *raising your hearts, dilating your hearts*. But
this is exactly how he had begun: *I would always raise your hearts,
and dilate your hearts*. The copious vocabulary both adds weight
to the expression and, because it is a matter of often associated,
but not necessarily synonymous, words (members of the same

lexical set, to use a more technical expression), it enables Donne to make distinctions and thus advance his argument. Copious language is not, of course, peculiar to the Renaissance; it would be relatively easy to find comparable passages from later English. But the expansion of the English vocabulary during the Middle English and Renaissance periods allowed the development of quite sophisticated styles.

OTHER BORROWINGS

While Latin and French, with Scandinavian as a rather poor third, have been the chief sources of words borrowed into English, many other languages have each contributed a few. Italian has been prominent in the fields of music (*piano, opera, tempo*) and architecture (*balcony, portico, studio*) and has also supplied *fiasco, mafia, manifesto, pizza, regatta* (originally a boat race held on the Grand Canal, Venice), *replica, spaghetti, umbrella* and *vendetta*. Among the borrowings from Spanish are *alligator* (*el lagarto*, 'the lizard'), *bonanzo, bravado, canoe, embargo, hurricane, potato* and *patio*. *Al* is also the definite article in Arabic, hence *alcohol, algebra* and *alkali*. *Sugar, syrup* and *coffee* are also probably Arabic in origin, the latter amusingly defined by Francis Bacon in 1624 as '*caffa*, a drink black as soot and of a strong scent, that comforteth the brain and heart and helpeth digestion'. Dutch has contributed *brandy, cruise, dock, easel, gin, landscape, pack, skipper* and *yacht*. *Tea*, originally Chinese, entered English from Dutch. The colonization of India in the seventeenth and eighteenth centuries gave us *bungalow, curry, guru, jungle* and *shampoo*. Several of these words no longer seem foreign since we use them so often; a few (*algebra, alkali, portico, tempo*) still seem restricted to special subjects. Indeed English is indebted to so many languages: *angst, kindergarten* and *protein* from German, *yoghurt* from Turkish, *lilac* from Persian, *kamikaze, karate* and *tycoon* from Japanese, and recently *glasnost* from Russian. Some of these latter words have not yet been especially anglicized and so still look 'un-English'. It has even been suggested that English has occasionally borrowed words for things it views with suspicion and leaves them in a foreign-looking form, words like *liaison, gigolo* and *madame* (all French), *innuendo* (Latin) and *bordello* (Italian).

Christopher Ball very properly reminds us that the borrowing of a word into another language is a gradual process.[17] At first only bilingual speakers will understand it. Then monolingual speakers become conscious of the new word as either filling a gap or as simply fashionable, and so they themselves use it. The loan word may be assimilated into English in pronunciation and perhaps spelling; it may produce its own derivatives (gentle*man* or beauti*ful*) and it may subsequently change its meaning. It originally has no collocational relationships in the new language and has been deprived of those it had in its original language. It may develop a wider or a more restricted range of use. To see the effect of loan words in English, other than those quickly assimilated into the core vocabulary, we need above all – as I have tried to show – a range of contexts.

ALTERNATIVES TO BORROWING

Open your morning paper and you will not have to look far before coming across a **compound**, often several together. In the extract from *Nice Work* we saw that compounds could suggest efficiency and smoothness ('deftly edited footage of brightly coloured machines and smoothly moving assembly lines'). They also achieve a concentration which is a boon to the writers of newspaper headlines where space is at a premium. This is especially so in the adjectival compound whose second element is a participle, as in the three examples above. Some of the energy of the verb seems to have become encapsulated in the participle; the alternative might well have been a longer and less striking phrase where the energy would have been dissipated. Advertisers, too, love compounds, especially novel ones. They hit us in the eye and sometimes convey an air of scientific skill, or, at least, a considerable amount of thought expended which must (surely?) imply efficiency and professionalism. Who could fail to be impressed by a VW Scirocco GTi car with 'internally-ventilated front disc brakes, allied to rear drums by a fail-safe diagonally-linked dual circuit'? We might be more sceptical about a mail-shot which offered us an investment with all the advantages and none of the drawbacks, but the effect aimed at is the same (I reproduce the format: italics, single-sentence paragraphs, and all):

> It's one that benefits from the *tax-free advantages* of investment through a Personal Equity Plan (or PEP, for short).

One that offers a *specially-constructed portfolio* of established
unit trusts, investing for income in three distinct sectors.

And one that has the sort of *long-term potential* that we believe
only a stock market-based investment can provide.

English, being a Germanic language, is full of compounds. O.E.,
as I suggested, borrowed comparatively few words and those
principally from Latin in the spheres of religion and learning.
Instead it preferred to use the resources it had to form longer
words. It borrowed *grammar* but also coined *stæf-cræft*, literally
'letter-skill'. 'Literature' is *bōc-cræft*, a school is *lār-hūs* ('teaching
house'),[18] 'charitable' is *ælmesġeorn*, 'eager of alms', 'passionate'
is *hāt-heort*. The alternative would almost always have been a
Latin loan word, often polysyllabic, and English did indeed
subsequently borrow many of these Latin terms. Sometimes
O.E. – almost deliberately, it seems – refused to borrow the
Latin word but instead 'translated' the idea into its O.E. equivalent.
So, in these 'loan translations', Latin *prae-posito*, 'preposition',
becomes *fore-set-nes* ('placing before'); *discipulus* (literally 'little
learner') *leornung-cniht* ('learning boy'); and *hospitalitas, giest-liþ-nes*
('stranger + gracious + the abstract suffix -*nes*). Compounds are
especially prevalent in O.E. poetry. This is a short passage from
Beowulf, the greatest of the O.E. heroic poems, in which Hrothgar,
the Danish king, tells the hero about the home of the monsters,
Grendel and his mother:

Ic þæt *londbūend*, lēode mīne,
selerǣdende, secgan hȳrde,
þæt hīe gesāwon swylce twēgen
micle *mearcstapan* mōras healdan,
ellorgǣstas. Ðǣra ōðer wæs,
þæs þe hīe gewislīcost gewitan meahton,
idese onlīcnes; ōðer *earmsceapen*
on weres wæstmum *wrǣclāstas* træd,
næfne hē wæs māra þonne ǣnig man ōðer;
þone on *geārdagum* Grendel nemdon
foldbūende.

(1345–55)

(I have heard that those who live in that land, my people,
counsellors in the hall, say that they have seen two such huge
prowlers in the border regions, alien intruders, occupying the

wastelands. One of them, so far as they could tell, was like a woman; the other wretched creature trod the paths of exile in the form of a man, except that he was bigger than any other man; from days of old those who dwell on the earth have called him Grendel.)

I have italicized the compounds; notice how many there are in these few lines. Some of them are transparent enough: *selerædende* ('hall advisers'), *londbūend* ('land dwellers'), *foldbūende* ('earth-dwellers'), *ġeārdagum* ('year-days'). Others are more imaginative, appropriate for poetry: *mearcstapan* ('march-steppers' – the Marches, as in the Welsh Marches, are the borderlands between two clearly-defined regions, a fitting habitation for monsters); *ellorgǣstas* ('elsewhere spirits'; *gǣst* eventually gives us 'ghost'); *earmsċeapen* ('wretched-shaped thing'); *wrǣċlāstas* ('exile paths'): exile from your homeland and your countrymen was the worst of fates in Anglo-Saxon poetry). It has been estimated that about one-third of the vocabulary of *Beowulf* consists of compounds. The most imaginative of all the O.E. poetic compounds, where the meaning has to be teased out, are known as *kennings*: a mortal feud is *ecghete*, 'sword hate', ice is *wæl-rāpas*, 'water ropes', the shore is *ȳðlāf*, 'wave remainder', what is left when the tide has gone out. Where the compounds are clustered together the effect is like a mosaic, a deliberate patterning.

The desire to borrow words into M.E., especially from French, may have effected a permanent change in our language habits. French, a Romance language, is not particularly fond of compounds, although the number seems to be increasing in recent years. Think of the French equivalents to some Modern English compounds: *warship* is *vaisseau de guerre*, *bathroom* is *sal de bain*, *hairbrush* is *brosse à cheveux*, *wineglass* is *verre à vin*, and the *high-speed train* is *train à grande vitesse* (TGV). The English is a compound word but the French is a phrase. I recently noticed, in a hotel bedroom, a plastic bag for dirty laundry. It was labelled *Laundry bag, sac à linge, Wäschebeutel* – two 'Germanic' compounds plus a French phrase. The number of new compounds in M.E. is therefore much fewer than in O.E. But of course, as the Elizabethans recognized, borrowing words and compounding words are not necessarily alternatives, and consequently they did both. Side by side with their extensive Latin loans, they also coined many compounds. Mulcaster (p. 28) had mentioned the number of monosyllables in English; Nashe resolved to join them together and exploit them 'like the Apothecaries use more compounds than simples, and graft words as men do their trees to make them more fruitful'. And so he did. 'Old excellent he was at a bone-ache' (describing a torturer); 'the shop-dust of the sights I saw in Rome'; 'this supereminent principal metropolis of the red fish' (Yarmouth); 'an ale-crammed nose' are some of his better efforts. Nashe arrived in London, fresh from Cambridge, in 1588; by the end of 1601 he was dead. He was a journalist before his time, seeking out gossip from the fringes of the nobility. If he were alive today, he would probably be writing for *Private Eye*.[19] For those patriots who objected to the wholesale borrowing of Latin 'inkhorn' terms, compounds could be presented as a much more intelligible alternative. In his translation of St Matthew's gospel, Sir John Cheke coined *foresayer* for prophet, *hunderder* for centurion, and *gainrising* for resurrection., Elsewhere he uses *skullplace* for cemetery. But this minority approach was doomed to failure. A curious parallel, equally ineffectual, was a nineteenth-century attempt to replace foreign scientific terminology with native English: *fireghost* for electricity and *deemstery* for criticism.

I have been speaking of compounds, but in histories of the language it is usual to distinguish between compounding and affixation. In compounds two independent words are joined but no part of either word is lost and the two can still exist separately, as in *paperback, lipstick, highrise, joy-riding* and *traffic-warden*. As it happens, all these are reasonably 'transparent' compounds where the meaning can readily be ascertained. But not all compounds are transparent: *airmail* is, but *blackmail* is opaque. The presence or absence of a hyphen does not seem significant. The frequency of use is sometimes said to be the reason we dispense with the hyphen, but why then should *week-end* have a hyphen, *pullover* not, and *bus stop* usually be written as two separate words? The hyphen may rather be used to avoid an ugly-sounding (or ugly-looking) group of letters: *fire-escape, still-life, sell-by date*. Compounds which are similes tend to be hyphenated (*knee-deep, blood-red*), so do those where the second element is an adverb or preposition (*passer-by* and *looker-on*) and also compounds with more than two elements *hit-and-run* driver, *ready-to-eat* meal, *round-the-clock* talks). What seems to be important in recognition of a compound is the feeling that the compound is a unit (and can frequently be replaced by a single-word synonym). Examples like *point of view* and *way of putting it* qualify for another reason: they can be preceded by adjectives (*interesting* point of view, *unusual* way of putting it), just like ordinary nouns.

Affix is a comprehensive term covering both prefix and suffix. Prefixes precede the stem of the word and suffixes follow it. The process of **affixation** is the same as that of compounding, except that affixes are not separate words: hence dark*ness*, *hyper*market, *pre*fabricate, social*ist*, *sub*-title. Occasionally the borderline between compounding and affixation is a narrow one. *Self-service, self-drive, self-sealing, self-satisfied* are probably compounds, since we do have a word *self*. *-hood* in *motherhood, widowhood*, etc., is now clearly a suffix, but O.E. *hād*, from which it derives, was a full noun meaning 'status', 'position'. The same is true of *-dom*, as in *boredom, freedom, kingdom, officialdom, wisdom*; the O.E. noun *dōm* meant 'judgement'. We have retained several of the affixes present in O.E.: *un-*, *mis-*, *-ful*, *-y* (adjectival, as in *speedy* or *silly* – it was spelled *-iġ* in O.E.), *-ness*. But we have borrowed others, such as *ante-*, *dis-*, *re-*, *-ate*, all from Latin; *anti-*, *arch-*, *poly-*, *-graph*, *-ism*, *-ize*, *-scope* from Greek; *en-*, *-able*, *-age*, *-ess*, *-ment*, from French. Furthermore, once a borrowed word is popularly accepted as being part of English, it can itself engage in compounding or affixation, for instance *unreliable* (O.E. + French + French), *affectionate* (French + Latin), *fire-escape* (O.E. + French). Compounds can spawn further compounds, as when *wastepaper* produces *wastepaper basket*. Affixes seem to go in and out of fashion. '*Television?*' sneered the great *Guardian* editor C. P. Scott, earlier in the century, 'the word is half Greek and half Latin. No good will come of it!' *-ish* (O.E. *-isċ*) seems originally to have meant simply 'belonging to', as in *ċildisċ* ('child-like') or *ūtlandisċ* ('foreign'); compare the different connotations today of *childish* and *outlandish*. Then, later on, *-ish* suggested 'rather like', especially of colours: *blueish, yellowish*; we seem to have extended this use, as in *earlyish, ten-o'clock-ish*. *-ish* can sometimes, but by no means always, have a derogatory force, as in *childish* and *outlandish* above, or *babyish, womanish* (contrast *womanly*), *uppish*, and so can *-ist* (*plagiarist, theorist, purist* – but scarcely in *scientist* or *tobacconist*, nor, nowadays, in *feminist*). Dr R. W. Burchfield has recently speculated about the declining popularity of *-ess*.[20] Following the Norman Conquest it was seen as a useful feminine suffix: *countess,* *duchess, mistress*, and later on *patroness, poetess, actress, waitress* and several others were added. But the later twentieth century's dislike of gender-related terms has signalled a decline, although *actress, waitress* and some others are still with us.[21]

Another way of looking at affixation is to include affixes within the category of bound morphemes. A **morpheme** is the smallest distinctive unit of grammatical analysis and it can reach below the level of the word. *-s* (for forming noun plurals), *-ing* (as in present participles of verbs) and *-ed* (past tense and past participle of weak verbs) are bound morphemes since they have no independent existence. Free morphemes are words in their own right, so *call-ed* and *tree-s* each consists of one free and one bound morpheme but *encyclopaedia* of only one free morpheme. Since affixes are not words they too can be termed bound morphemes, although some linguists distinguish them as *derivational* (or *lexical*) morphemes because they possess word-forming capacity, unlike grammatical morphemes which are simply endings. Affixes can turn one part of speech into another and show up the relationship between them, e.g. *sure* and *ensure*; *active* and *activate; sudden* and *suddenly; thought, thoughtful, thoughtless* and *thoughtlessness; civil* and *civilization.*

Compounds, however, seem more interesting than affixes. Journalists and government ministers thrive on them, and, like affixes, compounds sometimes sparkle for a time and then disappear from public view. *Bench-mark* was fashionable until fairly recently; *level playing-field* may well go the same way. The 1992 General Election gave us *bratpack*, adopted from earlier American English. The recession can at least prove inflationary in this respect: *exchange-rate* mechanism, *buy-out, kick-start* the economy, *supply-side.* Sometimes a compound makes it out of slang or technical language into Standard English: *double-whammy* (a combination of two bad things coming together) owes its present prominence to its use in one particular political speech. If the new compound fills a need in English – a shorthand form for an idea which would otherwise take much longer to express – it will probably remain: *look-alike* and *sound-bite* seem to be established, but *wannabe* not yet. Several 'new' words in English are compounds, although upon investigation they often turn out to be older than we imagined. *Hotline* dates from the early 1960s (to be followed later by *helpline* and *chatline*); *soap-opera* from as early as 1939; *user-friendly* was used of computers in the late 1970s. *Wheel-clamp* (now usually

abbreviated to *clamp*) and *phone-card* (previously *card-phone*) come
from the 1980s. The recent jokey *snail-mail* ('surface mail') contrasts
with *airmail, E-mail* and *fax*. But of course the recognition of the
compound as an English word comes through frequency of use; it
may well have been recorded some time before.[22]

Poets and poetic dramatists are more individual and creative.
Some poets are especially notable for the number and variety
of their compounds: Keats, Hopkins and Dylan Thomas come
to mind immediately. Shakespeare's plays are full of compounds
(and examples of affixation too). He particularly responded to the
concentration of energy in the adjectival compound of which the
second element is a participle. In *Romeo and Juliet*, an early play,
there are some 70 compounds, nearly two-thirds of which are of
this kind, beginning in the opening Chorus:

> From forth the fatal loins of these two foes
> A pair of *star-crossed* lovers take their life;
> Whose misadventured piteous overthrows
> Doth with their death bury their parents' strife.
> The fearful passage of their *death-marked* love . . .
>
> (1 Chorus 5–9)

proceeding through the play:

> *Earth-treading* stars that make dark heaven light.   (I. ii. 25)

> The *grey-eyed* morn smiles on the frowning night.   (II. ii. 188)

> Come, civil night,
> Thou *sober-suited* matron, all in black.   (III. ii. 10–11)

> *Dove-feathered* raven! *Wolvish-ravening* lamb!   (III. ii. 76)

until the tragic end of Romeo's suicide:

> O here
> Will I set up my everlasting rest
> And shake the yoke of inauspicious stars
> From this *world-wearied* flesh.   (V. iii. 109–12)

In *King Lear*, to choose a later play, the old monarch tries to *outface,
outscorn, outjest* and *outfrown* almost everybody and everything,
including the storm on the heath.[23] The play also contains several
of the 93 coinages of words beginning with *un-* attributed to
Shakespeare; once more, Lear is seen most characteristically in

opposition. Nevertheless, the play has its share of compounds too:

Unfriended, *new-adopted* to our hate.   (I. i. 203)

Thus out of season, threading *dark-eyed* night.   (II. i. 119)

Wine loved I deeply, dice dearly, and in woman
Out-paramoured the Turk.   (III. iv. 87)

       . . . gave her dear rights
To his *dog-hearted* daughters.   (IV. iii. 44–5)

             . . . to be *tender-minded*
Does not become a sword.   (V. iii. 32–33)

Blends are a sort of compound except that part of one or both words is lost when they are run together: *smog* is *smoke* plus *fog; electrocute, electric* plus *execute; motel, motor* plus *hotel; dictaphone, dictation* plus *telephone.* Some recent examples are *guesstimate, guess* plus *estimate; breathalyzer, breath* plus *analyzer; fanzine, fan* plus *magazine; chunnel, channel* plus *tunnel. Cam-corder, camera* plus *recorder,* is evidently first recorded in 1982, although it has grown in frequency of use since then. In colloquial English we sometimes shorten words which, in their new form, find their way into the general language: *(tele)phone, tele(vision), exam(ination), pub(lic house), bra(ssiere), disco(theque), (re)fridge(rator).* New nouns are formed from initials: MP, BBC, HP, AIDS, TV, YUPPIES, QUANGO, VAT, and immediately behave as nouns (talk to *your* MP, get it on *the* HP, setting up yet *another* quango, *including* VAT). This practice has become so common that new organizations often choose their titles with such abbreviated sets of initials (acronyms) in mind. Technically acronyms (AIDS, QUANGO) are pronounced as if they were words and the others (MP, BBC) are abbreviations only. But it scarcely seems worth making the distinction. From proper nouns we have coined *sandwich* (from the eleventh Earl of Sandwich who apparently did not wish to leave the gaming table, even for meals, and *guy* (Fawkes); from literary characters *malapropism, quixotic;* from places *bikini* (the island of the first atomic explosion which blew practically everything away) and *brussels* (sprouts). Trade names, originally given to a particular product, are later used more generally: *hoover* is any kind of vacuum cleaner, while *aspirin, nylon* and *xerox* have similarly widened their range.

Since I have often referred to the inventiveness of poets in their use of vocabulary, we might consider how some of these processes work in a particular poem, *Thrushes*, by Ted Hughes.

Terrifying are the attent sleek thrushes on the lawn,
More coiled steel than living – a poised
Dark deadly eye, those delicate legs
Triggered to stirrings beyond sense – with a start, a
          bounce, a stab
Overtake the instant and drag out some writhing thing.
No indolent procrastinations and no yawning stares,
No sighs or head-scratchings. Nothing but bounce and
          stab
And a ravening second.

Is it their single-minded-sized skulls, or a trained
Body, or genius, or a nestful of brats
Gives their days this bullet and automatic
Purpose? Mozart's brain had it, and the shark's mouth
That hungers down the blood-smell even to a leak of its
          own
Side and devouring of itself: efficiency which
Strikes too streamlined for any doubt to pluck at it
Or obstruction deflect.

With a man it is otherwise. Heroisms on horseback,
Outstripping his desk-diary at a broad desk,
Carving at a tiny ivory ornament
For years: his act worships itself – while for him,
Though he bends to be blent in the prayer, how loud and
          above what
Furious spaces of fire do the distracting devils
Orgy and hosannah, under what wilderness
Of black silent water weep.

Some of the compounds seem quite usual. *Overtake, nestful, horseback, desk-diary* are, initially at least, prosaic enough. Yet *streamlined* is used about a shark and the man *outstrips* his desk-diary; these are unusual collocations. *Head-scratchings, single-minded-sized* and *blood-smell* strike us as deliberate coinages. *Head-scratchings* follows two examples of adjective plus noun, *indolent procrastinations* (where both words are borrowed from Latin) and *yawning stares*. In all three cases their length is important: thrushes don't waste time like that, instead they *bounce* and *stab*, monosyllables.

Three lines earlier these words are conversions, *a start, a bounce, a stab*. *Triggered* and *hungers* are further conversions, as are *Orgy* and *hosannah*, used as verbs in the penultimate line. These two words, in uniting body (*orgy*) and soul (*hosannah*), contribute to the comprehensive nature of many of the actions described. Two unusual words contrast the very different approach to life of bird and man. *Attent* in the first line looks like a blend of *attentive* and *intent*. *Blent*, near the end, may mean one of several things, or more likely all of them: 'blended', 'absorbed', 'blinded' (O.E. *blendan*) and, by a metaphorical extension of this, 'confused' or 'deceived'.

NOTES

1. Quoted in *Layamon's Arthur*, edited and translated by W. R. J. Barron and S. C. Weinberg (Harlow: Longman, 1989), p. xxv.

2. Millward, 1988: p. 122. Also R. Berndt, 'The Linguistic Situation in England from the Norman Conquest to the Loss of Normandy (1066–1204)', in *Approaches to English Historical Linguistics*, Ed. R. Lass (New York: Holt, Reinhart and Winston, 1969), pp. 369–91 and M. Laing, 'Anchor Texts and Literary Manuscripts in Early Middle English', in *Regionalism in Late Medieval Manuscripts and Texts*, Ed. F. Riddy (Cambridge: Brewer, 1991), pp. 27–52.

3. References to Chaucer are to *The Riverside Chaucer*, Ed. L. D. Benson (Oxford: Oxford University Press, 1988).

4. W. Rothwell, 'The Missing Link in English Etymology: Anglo-French', *Medium Ævum* 60 (1991), pp. 174–96.

5. J. H. Fisher, 'Chaucer and the French Influence', in *New Perspectives in Chaucer Criticism*, Ed. D. M. Rose (Norman, Oklahoma: Pilgrim Books Inc., 1981), p. 191.

6. T. Turville-Petre, 'Politics and Poetry in the Early Fourteenth Century: The Case of Robert Manning's Chronicle', *Review of English Studies* 39 (1988), pp. 1–28 and 'The "Nation" in English Writings of the Early Fourteenth Century' in *England in the Fourteenth Century*, Ed. N. Rogers (Stamford: P. Watkins, 1993), pp. 128–39; S. S. Hussey, 'Nationalism and Language in England, c. 1300–1500', *Nations, Nationalism and Patriotism in the European Past*, Ed. C. Bjørn, A. Grant and K. J. Stringer (Copenhagen: Academic Press, 1994), pp. 96–108.

7. Third leader, *The Times*, 4 May 1991.

8. General Prologue, pp. 125–6.

9. *The Vision of Piers Plowman* (B–text), Ed. A. V. C. Schmidt (London: Dent, 1978), passus V, lines 235–6.

10. *Canterbury Tales*, I (A), 3137–8.

11. J. D. Burnley in Blake 1992: 432.

12. There is a longer list in Baugh and Cable 1993: pp. 180–1.

13. *Phyllyp Sparwe*, 774–83, in *John Skelton, The Complete English Poems*, Ed. J. Scattergood (Harmondsworth: Penguin, 1983).

14. R. Mulcaster, *The First Part of the Elementarie* (1582), Scolar Press Facsimile (Menston, 1970), p. 269. Another writer who sees the new possibilities of stylistic variation is Richard Carew (1555–1620): '. . . the long words that we borrow being intermingled with the short of our owne store, make up a perfect harmonie, by culling from out which mixture (with judgement) you may frame your speech according to the matter you must worke on, majesticall, pleasant, delicate, or manly more or less, in what sort you please.', *The Excellencie of the English Tongue*, quoted Bailey 1992: p. 44.

15. For a more detailed discussion see S. S. Hussey, *The Literary Language of Shakespeare* (Harlow: Longman, 2nd Edn., 1992) from which several of the examples are taken. Shakespeare is quoted from the New Penguin edition.

16. *The Sermons of John Donne*, Eds. E. M. Simpson and G. R. Potter (Berkeley and Los Angeles: University of California Press, 1954) VII, pp. 68–9.

17. In his chapter on Lexis in *The Sphere History of Literature in the English Language*, Ed. W. F. Bolton (London: Sphere, 1975) X, pp. 214–45.

18. *scōl* and *discipul* (below) were indeed borrowed into O.E. from Latin, but they were not used very often.

19. C. Nicholl, *A Cup of News* (London: Routledge, 1984), p. 3.

20. R. W. Burchfield, *The Sunday Times*, 2 September 1990.

21. Crystal (1988) gives useful lists of common noun suffixes (p. 93) and of adjectival suffixes (p. 143). We can all create our own examples: I found the indignant writer of a recent essay speaking of attempts to *zombify* the language.

22. I am indebted to Tulloch (1991) and to J. Green, *Neologisms: New Words Since 1960* (London: Bloomsbury, 1992).

23. M. Mack, *King Lear in Our Time* (Berkeley: University of California Press, 1965), p. 88.

EXERCISES

1. This article, entitled 'Put the class before the forms', appeared in *The Times* of 10 October 1990. Its author, Colin Ward, obviously deplores what he sees as undue and disastrous government 'management' of education. The article is too long to quote in full, but I have tried to preserve its argument intact and to include enough for us to examine the careful choice of words.

> There always was a golden age of schooling, and it never was the present. For some people it was (but only in retrospect) the time when they were at school. For grandparents it was often their children's schooldays in the years of expansion and optimism. For many teachers just retired, it was the middle years of their working life, when they had mastered the multifold skills involved, had developed their own philosophy and were intimidated neither by any classroom situation nor by instructions from above.
>
> Many people in other professions express similar sentiments about the most creative period of their careers. But the busy governments of the 1980s, with four major Education Acts in ten years, have achieved an unprecedented demoralisation of teachers. A just-retired primary head in East Anglia, where I live, said: "I joined a profession and left a trade.". . .
>
> But the erosion of the teacher's professional autonomy and judgment has done far more damage. Alan Chedzoy, a member of Dorset education committee, was right to inveigh in a letter to *The Guardian* last week against Education Department "initiatives" that have "distracted and exhausted teachers with tasks which have required them to give their energies to meetings, paperwork, writing yet more courses and indeed, anything rather than teaching children".
>
> The vogue for market terminology has sought to reduce teachers to production-line operatives "delivering" an added value to a raw material. Hence the ministerial mania for quality control at every stage of the process . . .
>
> Hardly had teachers and pupils adapted to it [the GCSE] when new analogies from the Victorian age occurred to the paymasters, such as payment by results. So we were to have not only a national curriculum but the testing of attainment targets for every child at every level of schooling. No one in

authority gave any thought to the incredible amount of time, labour and paper this involved, a deduction from the time available for actual education.

Needless to say, the private sector of education, including the ill-fated city technology colleges (for which the government's financial input is usually several times larger than the capital allocation for *all* other schools in a particular local education authority area), are exempt from the requirement to adhere to the national curriculum . . . . Last month Mr MacGregor [the then Minister of Education] instructed the examining boards that the standard reminder to examiners of their task to assess pupils' understanding of a particular subject, not their mastery of English, was "simply not good enough", since consumers increasingly expect higher standards. Yet his own inspectorate has reminded him that pupils in London schools have a total of about 180 home languages.

This kind of high-level detailed intervention is the mark not of political maturity but of demagogy. . . . As a person of no political affiliation, I am grieved that none of the parties has recognised that a national curriculum is a dangerous innovation, that no politician recognises that most of our conscript children live in a profoundly anti-educational culture, or that the measure of any successful lesson is not examination results but the establishment of a dialogue between teacher and pupil. It is an encounter that has nothing to do with market relationship.

The first thing to strike us may well be the extensive Latin- and French-derived vocabulary. Which of these words could be replaced by simpler terms? Are all of them unusual (e.g. not *expansion, political, culture*)? Are some merely part of the technical vocabulary of education (e.g. *curriculum, assess*) but is *inspectorate* deliberately chosen rather than *inspectors*? Of the remainder, which words are emotionally loaded? Find examples of a Latinate or Romance polysyllabic adjective immediately followed by a noun of the same kind. Most important is the choice of a register not usually associated with teaching – which? Do you find the use of *Victorian* and *conscript* more sinister? Is *encounter* in the last line, at first sight deceptively neutral, in fact more hostile than the *dialogue* of the preceding line?

2.   Is it true that O.E.-derived words are always more 'basic' than their synonyms which happen to be loan words? Compare *bloody* and *sanguine, broad* and *large, carve* and *cut, choose* and *select, holy* and *sacred, loving* and *affectionate, sing* and *chant, truth* and *loyalty*.

3. What kinds of words and affixes has Greek contributed to English? Start looking in the fields of a) literary criticism, b) medicine.

4. Make a guess at the approximate date these compounds entered English: *agony aunt, beefburger, bar-code, bottle bank, drop-out, fail-safe, minibus, multistorey, nitty-gritty, phone-in, piecework, second-class, speed-limit, spin-doctor, telecast.* Then check with a good dictionary (*OED* 2 if possible) and see how often you were right.

5. From one day's (or one week's) newspapers pick out 20 compounds which strike you as significant. What parts of speech are they? In what kinds of writing (e.g. news, features) were they found?

Chapter 3

Arranging Words

THE BUILDING BLOCS

A lot of nonsense is talked about grammar. It is not a nasty medicine we have to be given, when young, for our own good, but a number of ways we can put words together into longer units which we recognize have meaning beyond a mere jumble of separate words. We know much of our grammar instinctively from an early age and we get it right far more often than we get it wrong. Such intuitive knowledge of grammatical structures – what is or is not acceptable in English – is sometimes called our linguistic *competence*. Yet there are many advantages in discovering the flexibility and variety of English and how these qualities can be achieved by a mastery of grammatical use. Equally we need to recognize and sort out ambiguity and imprecision of expression.

For too long the English language was considered a poor relation to Latin. We saw this in sixteenth-century views of English vocabulary as 'unpolished' and 'ineloquent'. The same was thought to be true of English grammar. Elizabethan schoolmasters taught English constructions simply as better or worse ways of translating Latin – and then sometimes took away the original and made their unfortunate pupils put the whole back into Latin! In the eighteenth and nineteenth centuries, and even well into the twentieth, English grammar often continued to be taught as if it were Latin grammar. This is manifestly absurd. Latin is a **synthetic** language, made up (by synthesis) by adding to the stems of words a variety of endings which express the relationships between different parts of the sentence. Old English, too, is a synthetic language, although of course with different endings from Latin. But although Present-Day English (P.D.E.) retains some endings, it has become much more of an **analytic** language, making more use of grammatical words and word order to express these relationships. In *the man killed the lion* we know it is the man who did the killing because these two words come before the verb. Equally the unfortunate lion gets killed because it follows the verb in this particular sentence. Yet turn the order round (don't change a single word) and you have reversed the killer and the killed: *the lion killed the man*. Admittedly we know that the action took place in the past because of the *-ed* suffix in *killed*, but in Latin the subject of the sentence (the person or thing which acts out the verb) would also have had a distinctive ending to show that it was indeed the subject (or nominative case) and the object (who or what is acted upon) would have a different ending (and take the accusative case). Since English does not now work like this, there seems little point in learning many of the terms of Latin grammar. Much better to take English sentences to pieces to see how they work in practice and whether we could put them together again differently. Not surprisingly, Latin-based teaching of English grammar concentrated on formal, written language. It had practically nothing to say about informal, spoken language. And it was very ready to say what was wrong or sub-standard. Saying what is wrong with English sentences is still something of a national pastime. Do you accept:

1. Hopefully the economic situation will get better.
2. Everybody is entitled to their opinion.
3. There's an article in the paper about how men leave their wives when they get fat.
4. I only want some peace.
5. He only saw Bill yesterday.
6. I intend to really get down to my revision next week.
7. There was a large amount of people at the match, but less than at last week's.
8. Driving away from the town, the street is the third on the left.
9. If he was to come tomorrow, I shouldn't be here.

All of these? Only some of these? None of these? If not, why not? Might you *say* some of them but not write them? I will return to these sentences once we discover more about how the parts of the sentence fit together.

One possible area of confusion which it is best to resolve before going any further is that between form and function. **Form** is what a constituent of a sentence is, for example a noun, a verb or an adjective. **Function** is what that constituent does in the particular sentence. It is all very well to say that a noun is 'the name of a person, place or thing', to quote a very old definition. That depends on the meaning of the noun, but what does a noun *do*? Most commonly it can be subject or object – either direct object or indirect object – but it can also be the complement (see below for definition of these terms) or even act as if it were an adjective:

> My *electricity* bill for this quarter seems much too high.
> *Mary's* car had to go back to the garage.

Conversely the adjective can take up the function of a noun (it can act as a noun):

> The *poor* are always with us.
> From the *sublime* to the *ridiculous*.

or, in some sentences, a 'noun' can become a verb:

> He began to *bargain* his way out of the difficulty.

or even a 'verb' a noun:

> If you find out any more, give me a *ring*.

We shall see that the same plasticity of language is true of the Noun Phrase or the Prepositional Phrase. So function will usually yield better grammatical returns than form, and the emphasis in the study of English grammar has been increasingly on function.

We might begin our more detailed examination of English grammar by taking a very simple sentence and seeing how it can be expanded.[1] (This is represented in Figure 3.1) *Cats purr*. That is a complete sentence, with a subject (*cats*) and a verb (*purr*); I shall abbreviate subject to S, and verb to V. But it is obviously a very simple sentence and each of its two parts is capable of expansion. When this happens, we use the terms **subject** and **predicate**. In most (but not all) English sentences, S precedes V; it either 'acts out' V or, less often, is 'acted upon'. The predicate is what is said about S; it indicates an action, a process, or a state of affairs. Its main component is the verb. V may be followed by a **direct object** (dO): *I opened the tin*. In this case dO is what is 'affected' by the action of the verb. There can, however, be another kind of object, the **indirect object** (iO) as well as the direct object (dO); this iO is the 'recipient' of the action of the verb:

> I (S) gave (V) the cats (iO) their dinner (dO).

Not all verbs can take objects, however. Those which can are called *transitive* verbs:

> The boy kicked the ball.
> The girl wore her best dress.
> The man killed the lion.

Those which cannot are *intransitive* verbs:

> Cats purr.
> He worked late.
> She smiled knowingly.

Still other verbs do not take objects but **complements**. These are 'linking' verbs like *be, appear, seem, feel, become, get, look, sound.* In several such sentences the complement (C) refers back to the subject:

> My sister is *a nurse.* (S V C)
> We became *friends.*
> She sounded *silly.*

whereas in *The boy kicked the ball,* S *boy* and dO *ball* are clearly two distinct things. But C need not do this, since not all complements are subject complements. An object complement can be seen in:

> They elected Stanley *chairman.*
> Everyone thought them *mad.*

and an adverbial one in

> My shoes are *in the wardrobe.*

The complement, by definition, *completes.* Thus, armed with some ideas about how the sentence may be put together and some basic terminology to describe what we are doing, we can proceed to look more closely at the individual building blocs and the expanding cats. In order to keep hold of the basic SV sentence, I shall put both CATS and PURR in capitals.

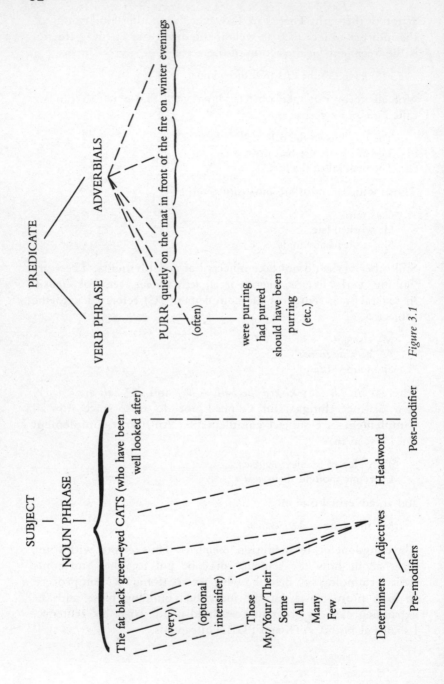

Figure 3.1

THE NOUN PHRASE

CATS is the subject. But we can place a **determiner**[2] in front of the noun, limiting or specifying its reference:

The/Those/My/Your/Their/Some/All/Many/Few CATS

and one or more adjectives following the determiner. Between determiner and adjective may come an optional intensifying adverb:

The [*very/quite/too/rather/unusually/incredibly*] fat, black, green-eyed CATS.

(There are other such adverbs which would not fit this particular sentence, like *largely* or *properly*.) The resulting **Noun Phrase** (NP) is felt to be one grammatical unit. Like the single word CATS, the complete NP acts here as the subject of the verb PURR. Nevertheless CATS is the most important word in the NP (it is sometimes called the *head*) because it controls the agreement of subject and verb: *cats* (plural) *purr* but *the cat* (singular) *purrs*. However, the NP does not have to be the subject of the sentence. It can equally well be the direct object:

I fed *the fat, black, green-eyed CATS.*

or the indirect object:

I gave *the fat black, green-eyed CATS* their dinner.

(where *their dinner* is the direct object, what was given). Determiners and adjectives in the NP are sometimes called *pre-modifiers*, since they both precede the noun and modify (or limit) its meaning, in this case to describe one particular type of cat. We have not finished with the NP yet, however. We can follow the head CATS by a *post-modifier*. Post-modifiers tend to be phrases or clauses rather than single words; my example includes a relative clause:

The fat, black, green-eyed CATS *who have been well looked after* PURR.

The post-modifier could take other forms, for instance an adverbial phrase:

The fat, black, green-eyed CATS *from around the corner.*

or even both adverbial and relative clause together:

. . .CATS *from around the corner who have been well looked after.*

The usefulness of the description of the sentence as comprising NP plus Verb Phrase (VP) will be seen to be even greater when we take a brief look at the historical development of English grammar. O.E. relied on endings to show the relationship of words within the sentence. The number of endings is not so great as in Latin (they are of course *different* endings) and in O.E. prose we can see clear signs of a SVO/C word order. But in O.E. it was perfectly possible for a subject to follow the verb or for an object to precede it: þone *cyning lufaþ þæt wīf* means not 'the king loves the woman' but 'the woman loves the king' because of the accusative form of the definite article þone. And the definite article varies (for us it is an invariable *the*) because the system of gender in O.E. nouns is not our system. We think of *king, policeman*, and so on, as masculine nouns and *queen, girl*, and so on, as feminine, and we tip all other nouns which suggest neither masculinity nor femininity into a huge rag-bag called neuter. O.E., on the other hand, had what is called grammatical gender, where *cyning* or *munuc* may indeed be masculine, but so are *stān* ('stone') and *fisċ* ('fish'). We have to remember the gender of the O.E. noun, just as we do now with nouns in French, German, Italian or Latin. In O.E., for no apparent reason, 'wheat' was masculine, 'oats' feminine and 'corn' neuter. Feminists will derive little comfort from the fact that *wīf* ('woman' or 'wife') was neuter. Worse yet, the definite article and the adjective declined fully to reflect the gender of the noun as well as its case in that particular sentence:

Se gōda cyning seah þone munuc	(The good king saw the monk)
Se munuc seah þone *gōdan* cyning	(The monk saw the good king)
Se cyning seah þā *gōdan* munucas	(The king saw the good monks)
Seo hlǣfdiġe seah þā *gōdan* cwēn	(The lady saw the good queen)
Seo gōde cwēn seah þā hlǣfdiġan	(The good queen saw the lady)

In the M.E. period many of these endings disappeared, especially in the definite article (which was almost invariably þe by Chaucer's time) and the adjective. As a result the NP carried few or no indications of case and gender. So two things happened: word-order became more important, with the subject normally preceding the verb and the object following it, and O.E. 'grammatical' gender gave way to 'natural' gender.

In the noun itself, the ending *-as* represented the subject and object plural of only one of the large declensions of O.E. nouns (there were other declensions with other endings). By Chaucer's time this *-as* had become *-es* and by Shakespeare's *-s*. Furthermore, in M.E. *-es* became the usual form for the whole of the plural, not just the two plural cases, nominative and accusative, and more and more nouns effectively moved into this one declension, however they may have been declined in O.E. The O.E. plurals *suna, bēc*, for example, became M.E. *sones* and *bokes*. Our regular noun plural ending in *-s* therefore derives from O.E. and so does the genitive singular in *'s* (O.E. *-es*). The apostrophe in the genitive (*'s* in the singular – the *boy's* cap – and *s'* in the plural – the *boys'* caps) is of course only a written sign and we do not hear it. Very little else of the complex system of O.E. noun declensions now survives. There is an *-en* plural in three nouns, *oxen, children* and *brethren* (of which only *children* is a word in common use) but there were several more such plurals in M.E., sometimes simply as alternatives to the usual *-es*. P.D.E. has what we would term irregular plural endings in *men, women, feet, teeth, geese, mice, lice*, although these are in fact the survivors of a fairly small group of O.E. nouns. We also have a few plurals with a form the same as that of the singular: *sheep, deer*. We shoot *grouse*, catch *salmon*, or order two grilled *plaice*. These five words are the normal plurals in English although *fish* with zero ending signifies a class ('We'll have fish for dinner tonight.') whereas *fishes* simply suggests 'more than one', as in the biblical miracle of the loaves and the [two] fishes. A few plurals have the voiced form of the consonant whereas the singular has the corresponding voiceless sound. *Loaf/loaves, wife/wives, house/houses* are examples. Not all singulars ending in *-f* conform, however: *proof/proofs* and *chief/chiefs* do not, while one or two nouns of this kind have alternative plurals: *hoof* and *hoofs/hooves* or *dwarf* and *dwarfs/dwarves*. Some nouns later borrowed into English from other languages have retained their foreign plurals, although it is noticeable that they are not really in general use: *crises, phenomena, fungi, data, gateaux*, for instance, but even here some are beginning to become acclimatized. *Agenda* is 'properly' a plural (singular *agendum*), but we ask for an item to be put on *the* agenda, just as we sometimes blame the *media* (there, however, we may be using a collective noun and thinking of press, radio and television). So while CATS (regularly) PURR, *children* chatter, *men* fight, *sheep* baa and *crises* occur.

Why did so many of these endings disappear between the end of the O.E. period and the fourteenth century? Three explanations are commonly given:

1. Since English, as a Germanic language, has its main stress at the beginning of the word, there was a loss of distinctiveness in the endings which consequently carried little stress. Many endings came to be pronounced with the 'neutral' vowel [ə] (the sound heard in *a*bout) and several were certainly spelled with an indistinctive -*e* in M.E.
2. Social upheavals, following the Scandinavian invasions in the ninth and tenth centuries and the Norman Conquest in the eleventh, might lead non-native speakers to concentrate on the root of the word, as a means of being understood, and not to bother overmuch about the grammatical endings.
3. From the thirteenth century, French nouns had only one singular and one plural form, and in a period like M.E., when so many influential people spoke both French and English, this pattern became more common in English.

Some or all of these factors may have played a part in the decline of endings, but if O.E. endings were truly functional could so many of them have been lost in the NP without imperilling communication? Did they collapse because they were already *not* fully functional, were they in fact redundant or over-ridden by other grammatical features? Satisfactory communication could hardly have occurred if both many of the case endings were no longer functional *and* word-order was as variable as it was in O.E. If this is a chicken-and-egg question, the answer may not be clear-cut either. It is very possible that, at least in prose, O.E. word-order was sufficiently often SVO/C to allow the collapse of some endings, and that this collapse became a condition for further restriction of word-order.

By the late M.E. period, too, there was a growing number of prepositions available to express case-relationship which in O.E. had been largely a matter of distinct endings (Strang 1970: pp. 274–5). *To* and *for* are increasingly found with datives and *of* became an alternative to the genitive case endings (as it still is: *the baby's cot* and *the cot of the baby*). *By* becomes a way of expressing agency in the passive construction, possibly influenced by the French use of *par* ('Harold was killed by an arrow in the eye'). The great majority of prepositions are of O.E. origin, but many of them flourished in M.E. and were supplemented by others anglicized from French (e.g. *during*) or Latin (e.g. *except*).

In discussing the NP, we should remember that pronouns may replace nouns. **Pronouns**, however, require a specificity of reference which nouns need not have. After all, if *I* love *her* it need not follow that *she* loves *me*. Many of the O.E. pronouns are easily recognizable as the ancestors of their modern forms (*ich, wē, ūs, hē, his, hire*, for example), but in O.E. there was no *she*; no *they, them* and *their*; and no *its*. *They, them* and *their* were brought by the Scandinavians, although it took some time for the new forms to spread over the whole country during the M.E. period. *She* is first recorded in the mid twelfth century (in the *Peterborough Chronicle*). There are various explanations of its origin in English. It too may have been a Scandinavian borrowing. Or, more probably, it may have evolved through a complex shift of stress patterns from either its O.E. counterpart *hēo* or the nominative singular feminine form of the O.E. definite article, *sēo*. *Its* first appears in 1600, but the Authorized Version of the Bible (1611) does not use it and the First Folio, the collected edition of Shakespeare's plays, published in 1623, seven years after his death, uses *its* only in the later plays.

In O.E. *þū* ('thou') and *þē* ('thee') were simply singular, with no thought of restricting them to religious contexts. *ȝē* ('ye') and *ēow* ('you') were the corresponding plural forms. During the M.E. period *ye* and *you* continued as plural forms but were also used as polite singular forms to superiors – or at least to equals – and by contrast *thou* was used to inferiors (a much older man speaking to a younger, say, or a master to his apprentice) or else to especially close friends or members of one's own family. This, like much else at that time, happened under the influence of French. In Chaucer's *Canterbury Tales*, the Host, the self-appointed master of ceremonies on the pilgrimage, addresses the aristocratic pilgrims (Knight, Monk, Prioress) as 'you' but those he regards as his social inferiors (Miller, Pardoner, Parson) as 'thou'. This distinction can often be seen in Shakespeare too. Hamlet calls Claudius *you*, not only out of politeness as subject to king but also formally and coldly because there is so little love lost between them. He calls Horatio *thou*, as to a close friend, but Horatio addresses Prince Hamlet respectfully as *you*. Antony uses *thou* about Julius Caesar for the first time in his passionate funeral oration in order to illustrate his affection for him. But in Shakespeare the interest is often in an unexpected *you* replacing an expected *thou* or (rather more often) vice versa. In Eastcheap Falstaff familiarly calls Prince Hal *thou* since he believes they are bosom friends, and in *King Lear* Goneril, the king's daughter, signals her love for Edmund by the change of pronoun: 'Decline *your* head: this kiss, if it durst speak,/Would stretch *thy* spirits up into the air.' (IV. ii. 22–3.) Accepted social relationships are being deliberately upset and deviance becomes more interesting than conformity. From the O.E. 'thou', 'thee', 'ye' and 'you', P.D.E. now has, in practice, only *you* for all four uses. In this is compares poorly with some continental languages. The subtlety of the second person pronoun has now disappeared from English, where *Thou*, as John Heath-Stubbs reminds us, refers only to the Almighty:

> You are a secret *thou*.
> Fumbling amongst the devalued currency
> Of 'dear' and 'darling' and 'my love'
> I do not dare to employ it –
>
> Not even in a poem, not even
> If I were a Quaker, any more.
> Beginning as an honorific, the unaffectionate *you*,
> For English speakers, has put *thou* out of business.
>
> So, in our intimate moments,
> We are dumb, in a castle of reserve.
>
> And He alone
> From whom no secrets are hid, to Whom
> All hearts be open,
> Can be a public *Thou*.[3]

THE VERB PHRASE

CATS PURR. In the same way that we have expanded the Noun Phrase we can build blocs to form a Verb Phrase. In the first place, the action does not necessarily take place in the present. CATS *were purring/had purred/should have been purring*, and so on. These complex past tenses are achieved by using auxiliary verbs (*be* and *have*) plus participles (*purring, purred*). Then we can add **adverbials**, perhaps a better term than *adverb* since it covers phrases as well as the single word. In fact it is inexact to consider adverbials as being regularly part of the VP since, as we shall see later, they are the most mobile part of the sentence. In Figure 3.1 I have compromised by treating them as a separate part of the predicate, although if you look carefully you will see that the optional adverbial *very* is here part of the NP forming the subject. Adverbials add to the verb, and they typically answer questions like

Where?   (*underneath, in the corner*)
When?   (*now, the day after tomorrow, some other time*)
How?   (*superbly, fast, carefully, with a flourish*)

or act as intensifiers of the meaning (*very, rather, quite, altogether*) or suggest evaluation or restriction (*possibly, hardly, only, to some extent*). In the case of our cats, they PURR *quietly* (how), *on the mat* (where), *in front of the fire* (where), *on winter evenings* (when). We can even slip in another adverbial, *often* (when) between the end of the NP and the main verb PURR beginning the predicate.

We must take a closer look at the Verb. Probably the first thing to ask about a verb is when the action takes place, the matter of **tense** or time. Is it *present* (cars purr) or *future* (cats *will purr*) or *past* (cats *purred*)? Notice that the future tense in English, unlike its counterparts in French or Latin, is signalled by the auxiliary *will*, but that the past tense has the suffix *-ed*, an analytic and a synthetic feature respectively. Next, perhaps, we want to know if the action is ongoing, completed, or maybe habitual. This feature of the verb is called **aspect** and it is often closely allied to tense. *Progressive* aspect describes a continuing action:

She *is cooking* a meal and he *is waiting* in his car at the lights.
She *was cooking* a meal while he *was waiting* in his car at the lights.

Perfective aspect, on the other hand, tells us that the action has been completed:

She *has cooked* the meal. He *had waited* almost five minutes before the lights changed.

Habitual aspect indicates a regular but not necessarily continuous action:

She always *cooks* the meal around seven. He regularly *waits* a long time at those lights.

I shall have more to say later about the interaction of tense and aspect.

Modality in the verb is more subtle. It is more subjective, expressing attitudes like hypothesis (probability, possibility, uncertainty), permission, desirability, obligation, volition – in fact, exploring the possible range of replies between a blunt Yes or No. This is achieved by the use of one of a number of auxiliary verbs called *modal verbs*.[4] Possibility, for example, is usually expressed by *may* or *might*:

> We may/might go tomorrow if it's fine.

Until recently I would have said that *may* suggested greater probability and that *might* was more tentative, but several students tell me that they do not recognize this distinction. *May*, however, can also convey permission:

> You may do your revision in the library.

This use of *may* is most common with the second person and sounds rather formal. *Could* seems to be on the increase as a rather stronger version of *might*:

> The pound could fall still lower after the recent economic news.

with the implication 'could well'. *Can* and *could* are favourite modal verbs of advertizers and journalists, committing them to absolutely nothing: 'This investment could increase threefold in just a year or two.' That *could* might just prove to mean *will* – but don't count on it. Obligation is usually expressed by using *must* (he *must* go) or occasionally, in a way which now seems old-fashioned, by *shall* (he *shall* go). *Will*, normally expressing futurity, can still carry something of its earlier meaning of 'want to':

> They will certainly go to the party.

both in the future and because they intend to. Not all modals are single words: *to have to, to be able to, to have got to* are phrasal verbs.

But modal verbs can be difficult, and for two reasons. The first is the result of shifts in meaning over the centuries: in O.E. 'I *shall* kill the dragon' meant 'I *must* kill the dragon', not kill it some time in the future. In this game of semantic musical chairs, here and there one of the earlier meanings remains and can still be used in certain contexts. *Can* in O.E. meant 'know', and even now 'Can you swim?' means 'have you learned how to swim?', 'do you know how to swim?', and not, as *can* usually signifies nowadays, 'are you able to swim?' (because you have no physical disability or there is a convenient pool available) or, again,

Can you hand me down that book?

suggests the book is on a high shelf and the addressee is tall enough (i.e. is physically able) to reach it. The second reason is because of their subjective nature. We often like to appear to be expressing fine distinctions, the outcome of careful consideration, and modals are conveniently to hand. They are often dependent on context and their force may be affected by an adverbial:

She may *well* not like that.
He can *certainly* appear abrasive.

Another feature of the verb might be noted at this point. Does the subject of the sentence carry out the action of the verb? If so, the verb is said to be in the **active voice**:

The teacher *corrected* the exercise.

Or is the subject acted upon? In that case the verb will be in the **passive voice** (from the Latin word *patior*, 'I suffer'). The passive is formed by using an auxiliary, *have* or *be*, together with the past participle:

It *was agreed* that there should be no further meetings.
The matter *has been referred* to head office.

If something is inflicted upon the subject of the sentence, the agent is usually preceded by the preposition *by*:

The exercise *was corrected* by the teacher.
The pedestrian *was killed* by a hit-and-run driver.

Passives are apt to seem more impersonal, more remote, and are consequently often a feature of official documents or textbooks. But voice is fairly obvious in English and probably does not give any great difficulty in practice.

Bearing in mind, then, the more complex ideas of tense, aspect and modality, we can now look at the expression of these in P.D.E. in the light of their development from O.E. onwards.

THE DEVELOPMENT OF THE VERB

If increasing simplicity is the order of the day in the NP, the reverse is the case with the VP. O.E., remember, had only present and past tenses. The present served also for the future, as it still can:

> I *leave* next week.

where a good deal can be achieved by the addition of the appropriate adverbial. A much greater sophistication in both tense and aspect is evident by Elizabethan English. Here the model followed is, as usual, Latin, but whereas Latin marked the different tenses by different endings, so many of the original endings had by that time disappeared from English that the auxiliaries *be, have* and *do* were increasingly pressed into service. These three verbs which Crystal (1988: p. 53) terms *primary verbs*, can function in English either as main (full or lexical) verbs or as auxiliaries. Compare:

> We are pensioners.

and

> We are reading.

or, again

> I have a cat.

and

> I have been gardening.

The uses of *be* and *have* as auxiliaries are easy to understand and some of them (e.g. to indicate aspect or the passive voice) have already been illustrated. *Do*, however, is rather more complicated. As a full lexical verb it means 'carry out', 'perform':

> She *does* the housework but he *does* the shopping.
> They both *did* their best.

Do can also substitute for another verb or verb phrase used earlier in the sentence, usually to avoid a clumsy repetition:

We ought to spend more time in the garden, like the neighbours
do (spend more time in the garden).

As an auxiliary, *do* has several different uses. The normal M.E.
method of asking questions is simple inversion of subject and verb
– SV for statements and VS for questions. This is still common in
Shakespeare and with modal verbs is still the only permissible form
today. We also use it in 'wh' questions (see below):

> *Parted you* in good terms? *Found you* no displeasure in him?
>> (*King Lear*, I. ii. 154)

> *Should I* go to that meeting? *Will he* be there too?
> Where *has he come* from?

But Shakespeare, like us, often introduces questions by *do*:

> *Do you know* this noble gentleman, Edmund?
>> (*King Lear*, I. i. 23)

> *Do you happen to know* where he is just now?

and this interrogative use of *do* can be found from the close of
the fourteenth century. From about the same time occurs the
occasional use of *do* in negative constructions – O.E. *ne* and M.E.
not had been sufficient without the use of *do* – although it becomes
much more common in the seventeenth century:

> I know your lady *does not love* her husband.
>> (*King Lear*, IV. v. 23)

> *Doesn't he come* to see you very often?
> He *did not paint* that door very well.

Our occasional habit of reinforcing the imperative with *do*:

> *Do* drive carefully!

can be found in early M.E., although this does not occur very
often. We can of course use *do* for more general emphasis,
especially if we are contradicting a previous remark:

> No, I *did* meet him last week.

although this emphatic use of *do* does not seem to occur much
before the fifteenth century. A semantically empty use of *do*,
where it appears to have no real meaning but to function only
as a tense marker, can be found occasionally as early as the

thirteenth century but achieved fairly common use only in the later M.E. and Tudor periods; two examples come close together in *King Lear*:

> Methought thy very gait *did prophesy*
> A royal nobleness. I must embrace thee.
> Let sorrow split my heart if ever I
> *Did hate* thee or thy father.

(V. iii. 173–6)

(*did prophesy*, 'prophesied'; *Did hate*, 'hated')

No doubt one of the main reasons for the use of 'dummy' *do* (as it is sometimes called) was the metrical one: *loves* is one syllable and *does love* two. But it is possible that this use of *do* might have suggested a more formal or conservative style. However that may be, the usage becomes less common during the first half of the seventeenth century, just when *do* in negative constructions is gaining ground, as if there were felt to be an upper limit on the number of uses of *do* at any one time.

So what we are left with in P.D.E. is *do* used (especially) as

a. auxiliary verb in questions,
b. auxiliary verb in negative constructions,

and also (but less often) as

c. full lexical verb,
d. substitute verb,
e. for emphasis.

We need fewer endings than O.E., but, strangely enough, some of the more common of these were not universal in O.E., or indeed in M.E. The third person singular present tense ending, -*s*, was a northern form in both O.E. and M.E. The corresponding form in Midland and Southern dialects was -*eth* which can still be found in the Authorized Version of the Bible and sometimes in Shakespeare:

> For every one that ask*eth* receiv*eth*; and he that sek*eth* find*eth*; and to him that knock*eth* it shall be opened.

(*Luke* xi. 10)

> The quality of mercy is not strained,
> It dropp*eth* as the gentle rain from heaven
> Upon the place beneath. It is twice blest,

It bless*eth* him that give*s* and him that take*s*.
(*The Merchant of Venice* IV. i. 181–4)

In Shakespeare, once more metre plays its part: *droppeth* and *blesseth*, but the monosyllables *gives* and *takes*. Gradually *-s* became the preferred form in all kinds of writing and *-eth* suggested formality or conservatism. (*Hath, doth* and *saith* are, however, common until the middle of the seventeenth century.)

Present participle *-ing*, which we use especially in continuous tenses:

> We are studying *Macbeth* this term.
> I was writing my essay all yesterday evening.

is first found with that ending in the Midlands and South during the M.E. period. But another, and different, *-ing* occurs in the verbal noun:

> I like driving/roller-skating/horse-riding, etc.

This should not be confused with the present participle. The *verbal noun* (alternatively called the *gerund*) is really more noun than verb. In the above example it could be replaced by a noun (I like *cricket*) and it can be preceded by a determiner, as nouns can but present participles cannot:

> *My* driving is terrible.

but hardly

> *I was my driving to work.

Some sentences with the *-ing* form are rather more difficult to classify:

> I like driving to work.
> Changing the tyre took up another ten minutes.

Are these participles or verbal nouns? They are not part of continuous tenses with *be* (I was driving to work) nor do they refer directly to the subject as in:

> Driving to work I passed two quite bad accidents.
> (While I was driving . . .)

They could be preceded by the article or a possessive:

> I like [the act of] driving to work.
> I like my driving to work.

thus making the construction one with a verbal noun, but it sounds rather odd. One suggested solution, which has something to commend it, is to call *driving* here 'the *-ing* infinitive', since it can easily be replaced by *to drive*:

I like to drive to work.

Most of our verbs now form their past tense and past participle by using the suffix *-ed*, and we can think of this as the regular form. It derives from the so-called 'weak' verbs of O.E. Already in O.E. these weak verbs were more numerous than the other kind, 'strong' verbs, but when we learn O.E. strong verbs appear to be more numerous than they actually are. This is because they are more difficult grammatically and because included in their number are a lot of frequently-used verbs such as *eat, come, drive* and *see*. Strong verbs change from present to past tense by a change of the stem vowel and often a further change in the vowel of the past participle: *drive, drove, driven; swim; swam, swum; see, saw, seen*. The past participle of these verbs does not end in *-ed* (as it does in weak verbs) but in *-en*. The *-en* often remains in full, as in *driven, spoken*, but has sometimes been reduced, as in *begun, swum*, and occasionally has disappeared altogether, as in *drunk*, O.E. *druncen*. We still therefore have strong verbs, although the proportion of them in English has been getting smaller, partly because some words which disappeared from the language were, naturally enough, verbs, and partly because from M.E. on virtually all verbs entering English have been treated as weak verbs. In addition, some other verbs, strong in O.E., have since become weak, for example *chew, flow, help, laugh, lose, mourn, shave, shoot, sleep, step, wash, weigh, yell, yield*. Far fewer have moved in the opposite direction, from weak to strong. *Strive*, formerly weak, now has a past tense *strove*, perhaps on the analogy of *drive/drove*. *Wear* too was weak in O.E. but is now strong: *wear/wore*; again analogy may have played its part (*tear/tore*). *Dig* has a weak past tense, *digged*, as late as Shakespeare, the Authorized Version and Milton, but it is now *dug*. We still perhaps hesitate over whether the cocks *crew* or *crowed*, whether *wove* or *weaved* is the past tense of *weave*, and while the coalman *heaved* a full sack on his back he probably turned the corner and *hove* in sight. Still other verbs seem to be hovering between strong and weak. *Mow* has a past tense *mowed*, but the strong past participle *mown* is

quite common – similarly with *swell, swelled, swollen*. *Teach/taught,*
sell/sold, keep/kept and a few others both change the stem vowel
in the past (the sign of a strong verb) but the past tense and
past participle end in *-d* or *-t* (as happens in weak verbs). Yet
other verbs, but not too many, remain stubbornly the same
throughout the sequence present, past tense, past participle:
cut, let, broadcast, for instance. A few originally strong past
participles survive as adjectives: *molten* metal, *ill-gotten* gains, a
sodden raincoat.

With a single present tense and a single past tense as the norm,
O.E. was poor in the expression of aspect. The single past tense,
for instance, refers to past time without saying anything about its
connection with the present: the cat *purred* (but when?). The past
tense with *have* (sometimes called the 'perfect' tense, as it is in
Latin) connects past time with present, either because the past
action is continued up to the present or because the past action
has results bearing on the present. Compare:

> Yesterday we *walked* into town.

with

> I *have walked* a long way today.

(with perhaps some way still to go) and

> Fleming *discovered* penicillin,

(an act, in the past) with

> Fleming *has explained* how penicillin can heal.

(in a way still considered to be valid).

We can also push the event further back into the past, using a
tense (with *had*) which Latin termed the pluperfect and is now
sometimes called *past perfect*. The perfect and past perfect tenses
enable us to relate events which are out of temporal sequence:

> I *came* [past] into the room and *went up* [past] to the man I *had met*
> [past perfect] earlier.

> She's already *left* [perfect].
> (said by someone speaking now)

This can even extend to the 'future perfect':

> By the time he *stops* work [present with future significance], she
> *will* already *have made* [future perfect] the sandwiches.

The new sequence of tenses is sometimes assisted by a friendly
adverb, like *earlier* or *already* in the examples given. Sometimes
the adverb will help even with the straightforward past tense:

> I *read* that book (once? recently?).

O.E. did not have an inflected future tense either, although, as
I suggested, the O.E. context often makes a future significance
clear. Only gradually in M.E. did the modal verbs *shall* and *will*,
followed by the infinitive of the verb, come to be used for the
future tense, and even now there is still often an underlying idea
of the older meanings, compulsion for *shall* and *volition* for will. 'I
shall be 21 next year' suggests not only futurity but also the nature
of things (I'm 20 now); 'We *shall* get wet through before we get
there' (in the future, but also because it is raining heavily). 'He'*ll* go
to the match next Saturday' implies not only an action in the future
but very probably that he wants to go. The trouble seems to be
that English has three ideas to express – compulsion, volition and
futurity – and only two auxiliary verbs, *shall* and *will*, to do this.

ADVERBIALS

We have not yet looked in enough detail at **adverbials** which are
the most mobile part of the sentence. The category of adverbial is
in fact something of a catch-all one, containing several words or
phrases which somehow do not fit conveniently anywhere else.
Most single-word adverbs end in -*ly* (which comes from O.E.
-*līce*) but not all: We travelled *fast*; *Soon* we'll be there; She'll *never*
make it; He works *nights*; They *always* say that. These are adverbs
too. And what about *not, also* or *perhaps*? They may as well be
included, although you could call *not* a negative particle if you
wanted a separate category. Some adverbials (called *conjuncts*) relate
clauses, sentences or even paragraphs, most obviously, perhaps,
those used to form a list: *first, secondly, next, finally*, but also
*however, meanwhile, consequently, therefore, instead, in other words,
by the way*:

> The contemporary reader entering the field of critical theory *for
> the first time* must often feel a little like Alice passing through the

looking-glass. *Up until this point* he or she has, with few questions, accepted that words have fixed meanings and that language is a simple and accurate reflection of reality. But Humpty's total disregard for commonly accepted practices and his anarchic and subjective use of words presents us with a text so bizarre that we cannot relate it to our own experience. The first thing we must learn, like Alice, is that language cannot mirror reality. *As the story continues*, Humpty goes on to teach Alice that, *contrary to her expectations*, language itself can construct meaning. He does this by trying to make sense of the poem 'Jabberwocky' and, *at first*, his efforts are founded on logical criteria: '"Brillig" means four o'clock in the afternoon – the time when you begin broiling things for dinner.' It's not long, *however*, before the words appear almost to provoke their own interpretations.[5]

These conjuncts not only help us to put matters in the right order, they also assist the smooth flow of the argument. Still other adverbials, *disjuncts*, comment, not on the single word or phrase but on the whole clause or sentence:

Unfortunately, we couldn't come to the wedding.
To our surprise, almost the whole family attended.
Honestly, I couldn't care less.

To return to our original sentence about the cats, the verb PURR was followed by one adverb (*quietly*) and three adverbials in the *form* of prepositional phrases: *on the mat, in front of the fire, on winter evenings*. However, they *function* here as adverbials. The prepositional phrase, incidentally, can have other functions too, for example:

as iO   She gave a tip *to the waiter*.
as sC   He seems *under the weather*.
as oC   Mary put the letter *in the envelope*.

It was for these reasons that I hesitated, in the tree diagram on p. 52, over where to place the adverbials. To include them as part of the VP, might indicate that that is where they always occur. I have compromised by placing them in the Predicate (but not within the VP) since that is where they will most often appear. But, even in this particular sentence, the optional intensifier *very* crops up within the subject NP.

The stylistic uses of the mobility of adverbs can be finally indicated by consideration of these three sentences:

1. *On Saturdays* we *usually* go out for a meal.
2. *Usually* we go out for a meal *on Saturdays*.
3. We go out for a meal *on Saturdays usually*.

Number one is a statement, no more. Number two emphasizes the two adverbials by foregrounding them, putting them in emphatic positions at beginning and end. Number three is more tentative, as if someone had suggested a different way of spending the time.

CONVERSION

One consequence of the loss of many of the inflections used in O.E. and M.E. is that it is frequently not possible any more to state categorically that a particular word is a noun or a verb, or whatever. It depends on its use in a particular context, and on its function. In earlier English the ending would have indicated what part of speech it was. Nowadays, when most words have no distinctive endings, we cannot be so sure:

> It gets *light* earlier in the morning once the clocks go back. (adjective)
> In the evening, however, we have to switch on the *light* much earlier. (noun)
> We need a torch to *light* our way down the path. (verb)

Or take the word *station*. It is usually a noun:

> The *station* is some way from the town.

but it can be an adjective:

> The taxi deposited me in the *station* forecourt with only a couple of minutes to spare.

or even a verb:

> The batsman was scoring so freely that the captain decided to *station* more fielders just inside the boundary.

The practice of **Conversion**, using one part of speech as if it were another but without any change in its form, is the conscious exploitation of this and seems to be on the increase. Nouns become verbs, verbs nouns, adjectives nouns, and so on. We *service* a car, *process* information, *video* or *tape* a programme, *host* a party and (two recent transformations of nouns into verbs) *privilege* a particular viewpoint or *rubbish* someone or something we do not like. We like to think we are in the *know* or, if not, we can be given a *hand-out*; sometimes we feel like a good *cry* (in all these examples the appearance of the article is a mark of the noun). Two rare cases of auxiliary verb into noun (both still seem colloquial) are:

> That's a *must*.
> They're putting on something of a *do* for George's retirement.

Adjective turns into noun in 'to go to the *bad*' or using the *spare* (tyre) to replace a *flat*; noun into adjective in the *key* man and *factory* made; adverb into verb in to *down* tools (the infinitive marker *to* confirms the verb); adjective into verb in to *better* one's self. There seems to be no end to it. Recently the government has been advised to *tough out* the recession; this is probably a conversion influenced by the metaphor *ride out*. With some conversions there is also a shift of stress: *prótest, óbject, pérfume, réfuse* are nouns, but *protést, objéct, perfúme, refúse* are verbs.

Conversion achieves both the novelty and the economy desired by both journalists and poets. We are not expecting to see the familiar word used in that unfamiliar way and we are pulled up short to concentrate on a striking idea or a fresh metaphor. Such remarkable plasticity of language would not have been easily possible much before Shakespeare's time. With the decay and eventual disappearance of so many endings during the M.E. period, Renaissance writers were free to exploit this new use of words. Not surprisingly, Shakespeare was alert to the impact conversion could make. There are examples in almost every play. Lear calls Goneril and Regan these *pelican* daughters. In time of famine the mother pelican saves its young by allowing them to peck her own breast, but in a striking reversal of the old story Lear complains that his daughters are tearing him to pieces. Edgar says of Gloucester 'He *childed* as I *fathered*', turning two nouns into verbs and achieving a reversal of the expected relationship. Victorious Roman generals led their captives triumphantly in procession, and such pageants could easily be played on stage. Cleopatra will have none of it. She will die rather than see 'Some squeaking Cleopatra *boy* my greatness'. But, on the Elizabethan stage, women's parts were played by boys, incredible as it may seem to us that a boy actor could be capable of playing Cleopatra. Here, then, there is an additional, non-linguistic effect: not only does the noun *boy* become a verb but the words are spoken by a boy player. So in these cases – and many others – Shakespeare uses conversion to draw our attention to a novel idea and often combines it with a striking metaphor.[6]

TYPES OF SENTENCE

Our sentence about the cats was in the form of a **statement**; the analysis of it has simply demonstrated its constituent parts and, in a very general way, how these developed over the centuries. Obviously not all sentences are statements (sometimes called declaratives). Sentences may be in the form of **questions** (interrogatives), or **commands** (imperatives, directives) or even simple **exclamations**.

The last of these raises the question of what constitutes a sentence. Does it have to contain a verb? Most people would regard 'Good heavens!' or 'What a nice day!' as complete utterances and so perhaps sentences, even though the first of these examples seems to demand a preceding remark to which this is the response. Commands, too, seem simple, but there are many ways of giving a command (which is why several linguists prefer the title *directives*). *Go away!*, *Push off!*, and the like, probably have to be accepted, however reluctantly. *Come in!*, *Have a good time!*, *Take care!* appear much less threatening. Conversation is usually a cooperative business. For instance, *Do come in; Come in, please; Let's start, then*, while they remain commands, suggest that the speaker is quite friendly, and in writing we probably omit the exclamation mark.

One of the main reasons we use language is to give the other person information which he or she does not know (or we think they do not know). Such sentences are statements but, if the other person asks for information that is a question. Several questions demand Yes or No as an answer:

> Is it time for coffee?
> Have you seen her recently?

Sometimes we start with a statement but turn it into a question at the end:

> You came back yesterday, didn't you?
> It's a bitterly cold day, isn't it?

Such 'tag' questions also demand an answer, and the speaker almost always knows what answer to expect. While tags are superfluous to the core of meaning, they can be useful indicators of either cooperation or competition. They may act as bonding between A and B, versus C:

> We can manage that, can't we?
> They just don't understand, do they?

Or else the listener may be coerced into agreement with the speaker who assumes temporary dominance in the conversation:

> Well, you'll just have to put up with it, won't you?

Two other ways where the form in which we put the question makes our feelings evident are, first, by keeping the intonation rising:

> You find grammar difficult.

may be a simple statement if our voice drops at the end, but an (incredulous) question instead if we keep the intonation level high (as if there were more to come, in the form of the reply, before the exchange is complete). The second way is to make a statement which, by virtue of its implication, has the function of a question.

> I suppose you're going to do that homework.
> You haven't finished that homework yet.

are probably saying, in effect, 'You haven't finished your home-work, have you?' and, if the answer (as expected) is no, 'for goodness sake get on with it'. In fact we have a whole range of much more polite questions:

> Do you happen to know . . .?
> Are you by any chance . . .?
> Could you by any chance . . .?

Most questions, however, are either '*Wh-* questions', so called from their opening words:

> *Where* are you going?
> *Who* on earth told you that?
> *Why* didn't they come then?
> *How* did she get to know him?

(the inclusion of *How?* in the list perhaps makes the alternative title, 'Information Questions' more descriptive) or else formed by using the auxiliary *do*:

> *Do* you go there often?
> *Did* you see her yesterday?

Wh- questions have their verb preceding the subject, and so do questions with modal verbs:

> *Shall* we start in a few minutes?
> *Can* we come round this evening?

Questions with *do*, on the other hand, simply place the auxiliary in front of what would otherwise be a statement. Asking questions by inverting subject and verb was the only way in O.E. and M.E. Even in Shakespeare it is a perfectly natural way, although he has plenty of questions with *do* as well. In the latter part of Act I, scene ii, Horatio, Marcellus and Bernardo tell Hamlet that they are sure that the apparition they have seen is the ghost of Hamlet's father. Hamlet's first two questions are the natural ones: 'But where was this?' and 'Did you speak to it?', one *Wh-* question and one question with *do*, but as his interest rises he uses tag-questions, questions by inversion, and questions ('And fixed his eyes upon you?') which are simply questions by means of their intonation pattern:

Hamlet:	Hold *you* the watch tonight?
All:	We do, my lord.
Hamlet:	Armed, *say you*?
All:	Armed, my lord.
Hamlet:	*From top to toe*?
All:	My lord, from head to foot.
Hamlet:	Then *saw you* not his face?
Horatio:	O yes, my lord. He wore his beaver up.
Hamlet:	What, *looked he* frowningly?
Horatio:	A countenance more in sorrow than in anger.
Hamlet:	*Pale or red*?
Horatio:	Nay, very pale.
Hamlet:	*And fixed his eyes upon you*?
Horatio:	Most constantly.
Hamlet:	I would I had been there.

Horatio:	It would have much amazed you.
Hamlet:	Very like, very like. *Stayed it* long?
Horatio:	While one with moderate haste might tell a hundred.
Marcellus and Bernardo:	Longer, longer.
Horatio:	Not when I saw't.
Hamlet:	His beard was grizzled, *no*?

(I. ii. 225–42)

Hamlet's growing excitement would have been far less well conveyed by using the more relaxed form with *do*. Elsewhere Shakespeare uses both kinds of question within the same short passage:

What *did* he when thou sawest him? What *said he*? How *looked he*? Wherein *went he*? What *makes he* here? *Did he ask* for me?

(*As You Like It* III. ii. 213–15)

Rosalind, in her eagerness to ask Celia about Orlando, almost runs out of breath.

Longer Sentences

The sentences I have used for illustration (apart from the extended one about the cats) have all been short and not especially elegant. Naturally, however, longer, more complex and more mannered sentences are often used, especially in written English. Sentences are composed of clauses. The traditional clause has a NP + VP structure, although this can be very simple:

The boy loved the girl.

is both a clause and a sentence. When they become part of longer sentences, such clauses are known as **main clauses**:

From the moment he first saw her, *the boy loved the girl*.[7]

Many clauses contain S and V but are not sentences; they appear incomplete and we wait for more information:

From the moment he first saw her . . .
When he came into the room . . .

Although she doesn't get on with her husband . . .
If it were to rain tomorrow . . .

These are **subordinate clauses**, the less essential part of the sentence, the something extra which is added to the main clause:

When he came into the room, *I got up.*
Although she doesn't get on with her husband, *they're still together.*
If it were to rain tomorrow, *I shouldn't go.*

In all these examples the subordinate clause precedes the main clause. But this order is not obligatory:

We cleared away the dishes once the dinner was finished.
The boy loved the girl from the moment he first saw her.
I got up when he came into the room.

Now if we had said:

He came into the room *and* I got up.

we should have conveyed two pieces of information, two main clauses of equal weight, simply joined together by the conjunction *and*. Similarly:

I rang him earlier *but* he couldn't come today.
We could pick you up *or* you could call for us.

Such sentences are called **coordinate structures**; each clause is of equal weight. We can go on adding more information, although the result will seem uninspiring and rather like a list:

You asked Bob *and* he said he would come *but* he wants to come on Saturday *and* Michael can't come then.

The order of clauses in the coordinate sentence cannot change:

*And he said he would come, you asked Bob.

as opposed to many subordinate sentences where the order is not important (except, perhaps, stylistically):

After you've packed away your toys, *you can all have your tea.*

More than one subordinate clause in a single sentence is also possible, but with several subordinate clauses the sentence becomes more complex and also more 'literary':

> When it got dark, and after the procession was over, *we went home,*
> so that we could be back by ten o'clock, as we had promised.

Sometimes two parts of the argument of a sentence are linked by **correlatives**. Towards the end of the Preface to his edition of Shakespeare (1765), Dr Johnson argues that we should be cautious about emending what the early texts say since their readers were closer to Shakespeare's own language:

> For *though* much credit is not due to the fidelity, nor any to the
> judgement of the first publishers, *yet* they who had the copy
> before their eyes were more likely to read it right, than we who
> read it only by imagination.

Correlatives are fixed pairs of words on which a sentence can pivot; having heard one, we wait for the other. At their simplest they repeat the same word: *the* more *the* merrier, *the* sooner *the* better. Other examples are *neither . . . nor, not only . . . but also* (a translation of the Latin construction *non solum . . . sed etiam . . .*), *although . . . nevertheless.* Often (as in Johnson's sentence) the negative half of the statement comes first and the more positive aspect (or at least an important qualification) follows.

Subordinate clauses can be of several kinds. We have already considered ones stating a condition (*If . . .*), making a concession (*Although . . .*), giving a cause or a result (*because . . ., so that . . .*), simply noting time (*when . . .*) or introduced by a participle (*Having* finally settled down *. . .*). To this list we should add **relative clauses** which are introduced by *who, whom, which, that,* and occasionally *where.* These pronouns usually follow the noun and post-modify it. They often split the main clause:

> The woman *who came in* wasn't my wife.
> The woman *whom I took out* wasn't my wife.
> The school *which I attended* is now a comprehensive.
> The house *that I bought* was built in 1960.
> The room *where we were* is the study.

The relative pronoun can often be omitted, especially in a less formal style:

> The house I bought was built in 1960.

In the above examples the relative pronoun is *restrictive*: it limits the noun to which it refers to one particular woman, school, house or room. *Non-restrictive* relative clauses do not do this. They are to some extent separable from the rest of the sentence, providing extra information which could be dispensed with:

> The meeting, *which had been planned for some time*, eventually took place last week.
> I sold the car to my brother, *who later sold it to a friend of his.*

Notice that there are no commas with restrictive relative clauses, but commas are used to mark off non-restrictive relative clauses. *Who* was first used as a relative pronoun in 1297 and *whom* and *which* in 1175. It was not until Early Modern English that *which* became the most common relative pronoun, supplanting *that*. In both M.E. and E. Mod Eng., *which* and *that* can be used to refer to people as well as to things ('Our father *which* art in heaven'). It was during the eighteenth century that *who* was gradually restricted to people only, a distinction we still keep.[8]

Another type of clause is the **noun clause** (so called because it can function in place of a noun). Noun clauses can act as S, O or C of a full sentence:

> *What this country needs* is a wages policy.   (S)
> I didn't see *what he had done*.   (O)
> He was sorry *that she hadn't come*.   (C)

As with relative clauses, the subordinator (e.g. *that*) in a noun clause can be omitted:

> I heard (that) he's given up his job.

Infinitive clauses are rather similar:

> *To stop now* would be throwing everything away.   (S)
> The headmaster began *to address the assembly*.   (O)
> She was far too young *to get married*.   (C)

GRAMMATICAL ACCEPTABILITY

We should now be in a stronger position to reconsider the disputed sentences at the beginning of this chapter. Questions of simplicity and ambiguity should emerge as rather more important than old-style 'grammaticality'.

1. *Hopefully the economic situation will get better. Hopefully* seems no different from the other disjuncts mentioned above (*unfortunately, to our surprise, honestly*). Why then all the fuss about

this particular adverbial? Alternatives such as 'It is hoped
that . . .' seem both longer and much more formal.

2. *Everybody is entitled to their opinion.* Once we might have said
'to *his* opinion', where the masculine form *his* was intended to
be a common form including (or, as it was sometimes quaintly
put, 'embracing') *her.* Feminists will have none of this, but 'his
or her opinion' or 'her and his opinion' sounds clumsy. So
although *everyone* is strictly singular (*every one*), the plural *their*
seems an acceptable way out, especially as we may assume a
variety of opinions.

3. *There's an article in the paper about how men leave their wives when
they get fat.* In this third sentence *they* could refer either to *men*
or to *wives*, but it is placed closer to *wives* and perhaps the idea
of fat husbands deserting svelte wives is less easily imagined
than slim, elegant husbands leaving enormous wives.

4. *I only want some peace.* We have seen that adverbials are more
mobile than other parts of speech. Ideally *only* should be placed
as close as possible to the word it emphasizes, but 'I want only
some peace' sounds distinctly odd, like a foreigner learning
English. The idea of a single wish is surely uppermost here.

5. *He only saw Bill yesterday.* This is more ambiguous. Does *only*
limit *He* (nobody else saw Bill) or *Bill* (he didn't see Tom) or
yesterday (i.e. very recently)? All these are possible but the last
one, with *yesterday* foregrounded at the end of the sentence, is
surely the most likely. In writing we would have to rephrase
the sentence if we intended one of the other interpretations. In
speech, stress and intonation would remove any ambiguity.

6. *I intend to really get down to my revision next week.* The emphatic
placing of a particular word is behind the reason for splitting
many infinitives. 'I really intend to get down to my revision
next week' is grammatically correct but it may not mean quite
the same. It might suggest that the revision was going to start
next week, whereas our sentence more probably implies that
the revision had already started but that next week is to see
a more concentrated effort. In practice we nowadays split
infinitives more often than we used to, unless the resulting
sentence sounds ugly: 'She worked much more overtime *to
considerably increase* her salary' or 'I decided *to positively and
without question tell* him tomorrow'. In any case, there is no
good historical reason for regarding *to* as part of the infinitive.

O.E. infinitives did not use *to* but ended in *-an* for strong verbs and *-an* or *-ian* for weak verbs. Very occasionally we find an O.E. infinitive preceded by *to* (mostly to express purpose, 'in order to') and even in M.E. there is often nothing to choose in meaning between infinitives without *to* but ending in *-(i)en* and those preceded by *to* or even *for to*. So we cannot logically claim that *to* is part of the infinitive any more than that *the* is part of the noun.

7. *There was a large amount of people at the match but less than at last week's.* I have to admit that I make a distinction between 'count' and 'mass' and would write *number of people* and *fewer than* (whereas I would write *a large amount of money* and *less money than before*). Yet this too may be a distinction that is breaking down. Grammar is not immutable. If no distinction is needed to prevent ambiguity, and if an economical form of expression is available, the earlier distinction may gradually disappear.

8. *Driving away from the town the street is the third on the left.* In practice there would be little difficulty in understanding this sentence and even less if the main and subordinate clauses were reversed: 'The street is the third on the left driving away from the town'. But *Driving* at the beginning of the sentence does not have a subject of its own (this is often called a 'dangling' participle) and the street can hardly be doing the driving. Ideally the sentence should be recast to provide a subject: 'If you drive away from the town, the street is the third on the left'.

9. *If he was to come tomorrow, I shouldn't be here.* Perhaps only someone older or someone writing formally would replace *was* by *were*. The use of the inflected subjunctive to express an hypothesis (as opposed to the indicative which was considered the mood of fact) was a feature of O.E. and to some extent of M.E. too. Even as late as Shakespeare, Hamlet is determined to approach the Ghost 'I'll cross it though it *blast* me' (not the indicative *blasts*). We now have other ways of expressing supposition or uncertainty and the separate subjunctive endings survive mostly in fossilized phrases, especially with the verb 'to be': *Be* that as it may; Praise *be* to God; I propose Mr Smith *be* elected chairman; Long *live* the Queen! – these are simply formulae.

I am not (I hope) arguing that in grammar anything goes. Nor that the above examples are the only possible ones, although I believe they include those usages which people most often object to. I am suggesting that *prescriptive* views of grammar, while they have the clarity of rules which are not to be broken, are far too inflexible. They are, as we shall see in a later chapter, the twentieth-century expression of certain eighteenth- and nineteenth-century viewpoints which were part of the search for authority in language. Today's grammarians are much more *descriptive* in their approach, looking for what we actually *say* as well as what we *write*, often beginning their work with a corpus of material recorded without the speakers' knowledge, or, if it is written, of as great a variety of subject-matter as possible. This involves much more flexibility. Yet it is not without its own standards. They are appropriateness to subject and reader (or listener); economy and unambiguity of expression and, to some extent, euphony too. Don't reach for the red pencil over every split infinitive, but 'to remorselessly and without exception criticize infelicities of expression' – well, maybe.

NOTES

1. A good brief treatment of grammar and syntax is the chapter 'Patterns and Constructions' in Quirk and Stein 1990. Rather longer, but still admirably straightforward, are Greenbaum 1991, Crystal 1988 and Thomas 1993.

2. Nigel Fabb, *Sentence Structure* (London and New York: Routledge, 1994), pp. 21, 94, does not use the term *determiner*, but divides the words which can be found at the beginning of a NP into
    articles (*the, a/an*)
    demonstratives (*this, that, these, those*)
    numerals (e.g. *one, fifty, three hundred and twenty-seven*)
    quantifiers (e.g. *some, many, every, no*)
    genitive noun phrase (e.g. *John's* book).

3. J. Heath-Stubbs, 'Use of Personal Pronouns: a Lesson in English Grammar', *Collected Poems* 1943–1987 (Manchester: Carcenet, 1988), p. 374.

4. *The Oxford Dictionary of English Grammar*, Eds. S. Chalker and E. Weiner, 1994, conveniently lists (p. 244) the distinct characteristics of modal verbs:

a.   they have no -*s* forms, infinitives, or participles;
b.   they do not have the set of tenses formed with *be* or *have* which most verbs have;
c.   they form questions by inversion and negatives by adding *not* or *n't*;
d.   they must be used as auxiliaries to lexical verbs.

5.   *The Bloomsbury Guide to English Literature*, Ed. M. Wynne-Davies, London: Bloomsbury, 1989, p. 33.

6.   Later writers practise conversion too, if not so often or so dramatically. As Joe Gargery does to Pip in Dickens's *Great Expectations* Chapter 27: 'you have that growed', said Joe, 'and that swelled and that *gentle-folked*', Joe considered a little before he discovered this word; 'as, to be sure, you are a honour to your king and country'. (Notice the parenthesis which emphasizes the conversion of noun into verb.)

7.   I have italicized the main clauses, except in the section on relatives.

8.   M. Montgomery, (1989) 'The Standardization of English Relative Clauses' in *Standardizing English: Essays in the History of Language Change in Honor of J. H. Fisher* (Tennessee Studies in Literature 31): pp. 113–38.

EXERCISES

1.   Take these sentences to pieces and describe the parts in the same way as I did with the sentence about the cats:

> Wherever you looked, small, fresh-faced, newly-scrubbed children were running up and down, round and about, all over the place, quite out of control.

> In answer to your enquiry, the fully-completed form was posted to the local office last week in a separate envelope.

> The management issued formal notices of redundancy to half of the workforce at the end of the week.

> We regularly hire a video to watch at home over the weekend.

2.   In this chapter I have taken a strong line against prescriptive grammars, full of rules which must never be broken. Yet English must surely have *some* rules? It does, of course, such as the one which says that the subject and the verb must agree in form: the cat *purrs* but cats *purr*. How many more can you think of?

3. These two extracts come from a leaflet on National Savings
    Children's Bonus Bonds. The first is from the main part of the
    leaflet, the second from 'Terms and Conditions', in smaller print
    at the end. How do they differ in their grammar and syntax (and
    also in the choice of vocabulary)?

    A. How easy is it to cash bonds in?
        Very. A few weeks before the holder's 21st birthday, we send
        a repayment form to the last address we have on file. (So
        it's important to let us know if the holder has moved in the
        meantime.) As no further interest is received after the 21st
        birthday, it's worth sending it back to us in good time.

        And to cash in a bond before the 21st birthday, simply ask
        at your post office for a Children's Bonus Bond Repayment
        Form and a pre-addressed envelope. Send the completed form
        to National Savings, Glasgow.

    B. Introduction and eligibility.
        National Savings Children's Bonus Bonds Issue F are a
        Government security issued under the National Loans Act
        1968. They may be bought by a person aged 16 or over for
        a child or young person aged under 16 on the purchase date,
        who will be the bondholder. Bonds may only be held in the
        name of, and for the beneficial ownership of, the bondholder.
        A bond may not be held by two or more bondholders jointly.
        For each bond purchased a person with parental responsibility
        must be nominated to receive correspondence and control the
        bond until the bondholder is 16.

4. These three extracts were actually printed in newspapers. Rewrite
    them so that they are not ambiguous, even if they are no longer
    funny.

    A. For sale. Desirable semi-detached gentleman's residence.
    B. Bargain. Old Converted Fisherman's 3 Bed Cottage. Close to
        Morecambe central.
    C. 20 million copies of the Parent's Charter to be delivered to
        every home in the country.

Chapter 4

How Words Mean

We like to believe that we mean what we say and that we say what we mean. We have already seen that collocation, the company words keep, may play an important part in our choice of words, so that some words which appear to be synonyms would, in fact, be used in quite different contexts. This is one difficulty in learning a foreign language. Most of us have suffered the mortification of having a translation – of which we were secretly quite proud – returned with a word or two underlined as incorrect. 'But', we reply indignantly, 'that's what it gave in the dictionary'. The response to *that* is that no Frenchman, or German, or Italian, or whoever, would use the word in that particular context. The title of this chapter, read just like that, is pretentious: words are notoriously slippery and there are very many ways of stating or hinting at meaning. T. S. Eliot put it memorably, if unduly pessimistically:

> Trying to learn to use words, and every attempt
> Is a wholly new start, and a different kind of failure
> Because one has only learnt to get the better of words
> For the thing one no longer has to say, or the way in which
> One is no longer disposed to say it. And so each venture
> Is a new beginning, a raid on the inarticulate
> With shabby equipment always deteriorating
> In the general mess of imprecision of feeling,
> Undisciplined squads of emotion.
>
> (*Four Quartets* (East Coker))

I want, more modestly, to consider three aspects of meaning: semantics, pragmatics and cohesion.

SEMANTICS

Semantics, from the Greek *sema*, a sign, is the aspect of language which deals with meaning. It goes without saying that signs are conventional. There is no inherent reason why a *candle*, a *kitten* or an *umbrella* should be called by these particular names, but that is what they happen to be called in English. Words have the potential for developing in different ways and carrying different associations at different times and in different places. The sheer number of loan words borrowed into English over the centuries has allowed us to discriminate carefully, to use them, together with native words, to produce quite fine semantic shading.[1] Earlier I gave a few examples of apparent synonyms in English which turned out not to be exact synonyms at all. Look back at these (p. 26) and then add some rather longer lists such as:

   aged, older, obsolete, obsolescent;
   push, propel, shove;
   scent, aroma, odour, stench;
   wellbeing, felicity, happiness, wealth, enjoyment;
   female, feminine, feminist, womanly, womanish, effeminate;
   poor, needy, impecunious, deprived, destitute, disadvantaged,
   underprivileged.

What are the differences within the groups? What sort of contexts do they have?

   The problem may become more acute when we read the literature of earlier periods, and historical change of meaning, semantic change, is what will concern me most here. I shall not, therefore, discuss semantics in the sense of meaningfulness, fascinating as this is: the apparent absurdity of 'She's 20, going on 40' or of some metaphors ('He's an old woman'; 'the whole road came to see me in hospital') or the ambiguity of 'I don't like worrying neighbours' and 'people like me'. What I am concerned with instead is why, in the Church of England Communion service, we pray that the Queen's advisers 'may truly and *indifferently* minister justice to the punishment of wickedness and vice' (admittedly the 1928 Prayer Book reads *impartially*). Why should James II have allegedly described St Paul's Cathedral as 'amusing, awful, artificial', or Dr Johnson certainly said of Milton's *Lycidas* that it was 'easy, popular, and therefore disgusting'?

James *understood* the words as meaning 'attractive, awe-inspiring and skilfully constructed' and Dr Johnson meant something like 'pleasant, popular (in the better sense) and therefore without true refinement' (obviously not his favourite poem, but less damning criticism than we might have thought). Or again, Lady Macbeth, immediately after the murder of Duncan, tells her distracted husband to 'Get on your nightgown, lest occasion call us/ And show us to be watchers'. It *is* night, and the Macbeths have to pretend to have been asleep and to have been disturbed by the knocking at the gate, but we are not to imagine him wandering around in the nude. *Nightgown* is equivalent to our dressing-gown. Near the beginning of *The Rape of the Lock*, Belinda, the society lady, has risen from her bed fashionably late: 'And now, unveiled, the Toilet stands displayed'. By *Toilet* Pope understood 'dressing table', and the poem goes on to describe Belinda's numerous aids to beauty. In all of these cases the modern meaning clearly would not make sense, although the appearance of the word has not changed.

At this point a few warnings may be in order. Some people, although perhaps fewer than was once the case, believe that semantic change is in some way a corruption of the language. Words should mean what their etymology says they ought to mean, what they once *did* mean. For such diehards, *aggravate* means 'to make worse' and not 'to annoy' and *dilemma* means a choice between two undesirable alternatives and not simply 'problem'. Taken to its extreme, this approach would result in *calculation* meaning 'counting pebbles' (Latin *calx*, 'stone'); *manufacture*, 'make by hand' (*manu*); *prestige*, 'illusion' (*prestigiae*, 'conjuring tricks'); and *expedient* freeing someone caught by the foot (*ex pede*). Although the etymological meaning may be relevant for understanding earlier writers, especially in the case of loan words (the Ghost in *Hamlet* is 'th'extravagant and erring spirit', i.e. 'out of bounds and wandering about'), the word must normally mean what it conveys in good Modern English. Nor is change of meaning confined to lexical words. The modal verbs (see p. 60) have been especially susceptible to differences of sense. In O.E. *Ic sceal gan* meant 'I must go', 'I have to go'; today, unless emphasized (in which case it means 'I'm really going to go', denying the contrary, stated or implied), it simply signifies the future. The large *Oxford English Dictionary* (*OED*), with its dated contexts, is particularly useful for charting changes of meaning. But our old friend context may well alert us to the fact that there is a possible difficulty. When, in his Miller's Tale, Chaucer says students are *ful subtil and ful queynte*, we surely expect *queynte* to be a synonym of *subtil* ('crafty', 'artful'). In M.E. *queynt* could mean 'intricate', 'elaborate', because more than the usual amount of time and trouble had been expended. In this Chaucerian context it carries the sense of 'clever', 'knowing', perhaps (as this particular story illustrates) too clever for their own good, and not today's idea of being attractively old-fashioned: a *quaint* country cottage with roses round the door, for example. But in the underlying sense of something in some way unusual we may be able to trace the direction of semantic change.

That words may change their meanings is self-evident. *When* they changed their meaning the *OED* can usually tell us. *In what ways* they changed their meanings is somewhat more difficult to classify, and we ought to speak of broad categories of change rather than of fixed laws in the way we speak of sound laws. There are several possible ways of classifying semantic change. The one I adopt here is traditional and has the merit of being quite simple. I give in brackets alternative titles for the different categories.

1. **Narrowing** (Restriction or Specialization) of meaning. As a society becomes more advanced it will need more sophisticated terms for distinguishing shades of meaning. This is sometimes achieved by borrowing words. O.E. *dēor* (P.D.E. *deer*) referred to any kind of animal, as the cognate word in German, *Tier*, still does. But once the general terms *beast* (from French) and *animal* (from Latin) had been borrowed into M.E., *deer* was free to signify only the particular species, with antlers, that it does now. *Old* (O.E.) still means 'from the past', but we now have *ancient* (fourteenth century French), 'very old' and *antique* (sixteenth century French or Latin), 'old-fashioned', for greater discrimination. In *Beowulf* the Dragon is sometimes referred to by the Latin loan *draca*, but at other times by the native word *wyrm*. Presumably a *worm* was anything that wriggled, no matter what its size. Similarly a *fowl* (O.E. *fugol*, and in the title of Chaucer's *Parliament of Fowls*) was simply a bird. *Bridd* in O.E. meant 'young bird', 'chick', but eventually

signified any kind of bird, and so *fowl* became banished to the farmyard. When Chaucer says of his Prioress 'And al was *conscience* and tendre herte', the word comes close to our idea of sensitivity (as *tendre herte* suggests). Yet eight lines earlier ('But for to speken of hire *conscience*') there had been no reason to suppose that *conscience* meant other than the moral faculty which enables us to distinguish right from wrong – the only meaning left to us nowadays. Chaucer may be subtly suggesting that a rather sentimental feeling for small animals is, for her, almost as important. Her moral judgement shows itself only within a limited range, whether she realizes it or not.

2. **Widening** (Extension or Generalization) of meaning. This is the opposite of 1. and seems less common. *Bridd*, mentioned in the preceding paragraph as part of the semantic development of *fowl*, is one example. A *journey* was originally a day's walk (French *jour*, 'day') and a *journal* appeared daily. The limits have now been removed: the travel may be of any duration and by any method and the periodical must simply appear regularly. Something of the same kind appears to have taken place during the early years of Christianity in England when O.E. *dryhten*, 'lord', 'ruler', also acquired the sense of 'Lord (God)' and *gāst*, 'spirit', was used additionally of the Holy Ghost. In a similar way, *clæne*, 'clean', could also mean 'pure', 'innocent'. Some few words indeed have recently almost widened themselves out of useful existence. Is an *operation* medical (its primary sense today), military, financial, or merely something that is carried out, its etymological meaning: 'The *operation* of the hedge-trimmer should be undertaken with proper care'? Is *capital* a city, a letter, or accumulated wealth? *Business* and *condition* have gone the same way. Some adverbs, such as *extremely*, *awfully*, and maybe *literally*, seem to be joining them. The intensifying adverbs *exceeding* and *wondrous*, common in E. Mod. E., were probably eventually drained of much real meaning through overuse.

3. **Transfer** (Lateralization) of meaning. Here no noticeable narrowing or widening takes place and the word appears to move sideways. Until the nineteenth century *car* was a wheeled vehicle, not one driven by an internal combustion

engine. *Tūn* in O.E. meant 'enclosure'; by M.E. it is better translated 'village' and in Modern English *town* is much bigger still. Society has simply marched on and things have become more complicated.

4. **Elevation** (Amelioration) of meaning. Categories 1, 2 and 3 are concerned with the range of meaning; 4 and 5 show words moving up or down on a scale of acceptability. Here a word acquires a meaning which meets with more approval than formerly. In the sixteenth and seventeenth centuries (and so in Shakespeare) *politician* often suggests intrigue and scheming; now the word has (always?) returned to its earlier sense of someone concerned with government, a statesman. The Anglo-Saxons might not always have felt too sorry for a *wrecca*, an exile, miserable but occasionally despicable; we might be more sympathetic to a (poor) *wretch*. For an O.E. writer, *cniht* was simply a boy or even a servant. Chaucer's *knyght* on horseback has clearly risen several steps on the social ladder. From a M.E. meaning of 'foolish', 'wanton', *nice* proceeded, via the meaning 'precise', 'subtle' (still present in the phrase *a nice point*) to the current sense of 'agreeable', 'pleasant'. Pride was the first of the seven deadly sins and *luxury* signified 'lasciviousness' or a shameful indulgence in costly things. *Coax* once meant to fool somebody, to 'take them in'. Although the meaning had changed by the sixteenth century to 'fondle' and by the seventeenth to 'wheedle', the phrase *make a cokes of* evidently remained in its original meaning. In Ben Jonson's *Bartholomew Fair* (1614) Cokes is the booby, the foolish character tricked by every rogue he meets in the Fair.

5. **Degredation** (Pejoration) of meaning. Human nature being what it is, this is a category for which it is easy to find examples. *Accident*, originally signifying simply something that happened, is today almost always unpleasant. So is *disease*, formerly simply 'discomfort' (*dis-ease*), not necessarily medical. *Lewd* meant 'unlearned', often 'lay, not clerical' at a time when the Church had a virtual monopoly of education, and a meaning of 'ignorant' was evidently not too far removed from the present 'lascivious'. *Lust* was 'pleasure', more often good than bad and certainly not 'sexual appetite' (which was *luxury*).

But these categories, as I have said, are not especially firm, nor are they mutually exclusive. Could not *accident* and *disease* have been put under Narrowing as well as under Degredation? The change in *harlot* from 'rascal' in M.E. to 'prostitute' later on includes both Narrowing (applied to women only) and Degredation. And odd loose ends persist, usually in fossilized phrases, despite the 'new' meaning. *Quick* is often cited as an example of Transfer, from 'living' (O.E. *cwic*) to 'speedy', but how about 'the *quick* and the dead', 'the *quick* of your nail', even (metaphorically) *quicksands* and *quicklime*? We still say that something happened 'by *accident* or design'. Further categories of change, beyond the five mentioned, are also possible. Some words move from abstract to concrete signification: *wealth* once indicated happiness or abundance, now it suggests a considerable sum of money. Others move in the reverse direction, from concrete to abstract: *gentle*, 'noble of rank', later took on the more abstract sense of the kind of behaviour expected of the well-born. Fortunately 'noble' will serve as a translation for either sense and both are still present in *gentleman*. Later still, *gentle* moved on again to mean 'mild'. A possible, and rather curious, further category of semantic change is that often called *Popular* (or *Folk*) *Etymology* where a word is wrongly interpreted, in the popular mind, as conforming to a known pattern. The second element of O.E. *brydguma* was *guma*, 'man', but when this became obsolete *groom* was wrongly put in its place. A *miniature* in a manuscript is an illumination, often in red (Latin *minium*, 'red lead'), but miniatures were often small (Latin *minimus*) and so the confusion took place. *To eat humble pie*, 'submit to humiliation', is most probably a nineteenth-century confusion or misremembering of the medieval *umble pie*; the *umbles* (or *numbles*) were the animal's entrails and so a source of cheap food. *Buxom*, originally 'obedient', 'compliant', as medieval wives were expected to be, may have acquired the sense 'plump' partly through a suitable-seeming physiognomy but also through the word's resemblance to *bust* and *bosom*. *Enormity* was originally extreme wickedness and *enormousness* extreme size. Fairly recently *enormity* has been used in the latter sense, perhaps conforming to a felt pattern *capacious/capacity*, *sagacious/sagacity*. After all, Falstaff qualifies on both counts. It is possible that *sententious*, once suggesting 'full of meaning', 'complex' but now usually 'pompous', 'verbose', has likewise been influenced by *pretentious*. This type of shift, while seemingly well established, is however particularly prone to the fault of some lengthy discussions of semantic change: they become merely anecdotal.

In the study of semantics one can indeed wander down some fascinating bypaths, such as the examination of *polysemy*, multiple meaning. How many meanings can a word carry at one and the same time before confusion starts to set in? Why should *fair*, which once meant 'beautiful', 'favourable', have come to indicate 'just' (*fair play*, *a fair day's work*) but only 'average' when we ask about someone's health or read a barely satisfactory school report, and do the two uses produce confusion? If I try to inculcate some *team spirit* or tell you to *keep up your spirits*, why am I not advising you to lay in more stocks of whisky and gin? Rather similar to polysemy is the use of some technical words in a more general sense, words such as *allergy*, *chronic*, *dynamo*, *fallout*, *parameter* and *syndrome*. The metaphorical sense which must have been present in their early extension of meaning (e.g. a *human* dynamo) seems now to have largely disappeared, although these words can still be used in their technical sense in scientific contexts. How do metaphors work, in any case? A *lamp post* goes on being a lamp post as well as indicating unusual human tallness and thinness; a *wallflower* is not simply a girl left sitting out at a dance but still a species of flower. How should we explain *warm* feelings or a *sharp* taste? Collocation, the association of words, which I have touched on once or twice, is another interesting matter for exploration. Why do we refer to *rancid* butter, *sour* milk and *mouldy* bread? They are all rotten, yet we would not place *rotten* in front of any of these nouns. Those who complain of gender stereotyping might point out that a man is allowed to be *dynamic* and *masterful* while his female counterpart is called *bossy*, *pushy* or just possibly *feisty*. All this leads our discussion towards the psychology of semantic change and away from semantic change within history. Which still goes on. The obvious example is the contemporary use of *gay* as 'homosexual', whereas Chaucer's Knight who *was not gay* was simply not overdressed. *Disinterested*, 'impartial', has almost taken over the sense of *uninterested*, 'simply not concerned with', probably because *dis-* and *un-* are both negative prefixes. *Imply* and *infer* are nowadays often confused, as are *consist* (of) and *comprise*: the marvellous houses advertised by estate agents often *comprise of* four bedrooms, two living rooms, etc. A juicy law case may carry the report of a *suggestive* remark, although the pejorative sense is absent from the noun used alone (it would have to be an *improper* or *indecent* suggestion). Constant change is here to stay.

PRAGMATICS

The texts which I have used for illustration up to now have been from written English, mostly literary English, although some few used in earlier chapters (advertisements, for instance) are hardly literary, even though they may be carefully organized. A *text* can be described in terms of structure and the rules used to organize it. But most of our daily use of English consists of far less formal exchanges, often in conversation which is a much more interactive business and, of course, a mostly social one too. This is usually called *discourse*.[2] In analysing text we regularly use grammar and semantics. In the analysis of discourse the relatively recent discipline of **pragmatics** is useful too.

What is pragmatics? It is perhaps best defined as the study of how meaning is conveyed. Naturally this will involve a knowledge of the context in which the conversation is carried on, the ways in which the exchange itself is maintained, and how meaning may be *implied* by the utterance or *inferred* from what has been said already. It involves a further examination of our linguistic competence (which I mentioned briefly at the very beginning of the chapter on grammar). If I say

It's hot in here.

the semantics (what the sentence *means*) would signify that the temperature in the room is unduly high. But what I may well *mean by* this remark is 'For goodness sake, open a window'. Or the opposite situation:

The door's open.

semantically states a fact (you can see it's open), but pragmatically means 'Please close it'. Again:

My glass is empty.

semantically means that there's nothing in it, but more than likely indicates 'I'd like some more wine, please'. An utterance, therefore, has both a *sense* (the semantic aspect) and often a *force* (the pragmatic one). The dictionary definition of *pragmatic*, in its non-technical use, is 'practical', 'judging by results', and this is what pragmatics aims to show us. If we were to write out a conversation in full, perhaps directly from a tape-recording of it, we should have to include such things as the hesitations and false starts and also the signals we use to continue the exchange ('I mean', 'You know', 'Right?'). These are features of language which are usually tidied up or eliminated altogether when we produce an edited version of a conversation and which are certainly hardly ever mentioned in grammars of English. In addition, a lot of conversation proceeds by unstated connections between utterances. More often than not we know the person we are speaking to. We may have talked to them about this subject before. We may share (or think we share) the same values. Consequently there may well be a good deal of common ground between us, shared knowledge and attitudes, much of which does not need to be made explicit.

Conversation is normally a cooperative business. If we are asked a question, we usually answer; if we are given information, we usually acknowledge it. We may comment on or elaborate a reply so that the other person temporarily loses his or her 'turn' in the conversation, but generally, unless one of the participants is unduly aggressive or unless the conversation is one where most of the information comes from one side, we try hard to maintain a flow. Conversations must be kept going, for silence is an embarrassment. Some of the ways in which this happens, such as the choice of certain stress and intonation patterns, or of 'tag' questions demanding an answer, or of polite requests which are really commands, we have looked at earlier. There are other, non-verbal, signals, such as nods, shrugs and smiles, where gesture is synchronized with speech.

The principles on which conversation should be (and normally is) conducted have been the concern of some linguistic philosophers. The clearest statement is perhaps that of the American H. P. Grice in 1975 and his arguments have become known as the four **Gricean maxims:**

1. *Quantity*. Make your contribution as informative as is required. Say only what you need to say, neither too little nor too much. Hence remarks like 'To cut a long story short . . .' or 'I won't bore you with the details'.

2. *Quality*. Be truthful. Do not say something you believe to be false or something for which you lack adequate supporting evidence. Hence 'So far as I know . . .' or 'Correct me if I'm wrong, but . . .'
3. *Relation*. Be relevant (to the subject in hand and to remarks already made).
4. *Manner*. Be clear, unambiguous, brief and well-ordered. Obscurity and too great length are to be avoided.[3]

Expressed as bluntly as this, these maxims seem obvious, but surprisingly often we disregard one or more of them for our own purposes. Questions normally demand answers and requests usually elicit information, but these replies do not always materialize (or sometimes not immediately). And we do not always need the full replies: we are quite able to fill in what is 'missing'.

In literature these conversational gambits are most evident in drama. There, time is at a premium, and the dramatist cannot spell everything out lest his audience should fall asleep. Nor is normal conversation very dramatic in itself. The dramatist is interested in misunderstandings (deliberate or not), ambiguity and irony, since these provoke tension and perhaps conflict, as well as furthering the plot. Extreme examples can be seen in writers like Pinter or Beckett, but we can go back a good deal further. Dialogue in Renaissance drama was much more developed than in earlier drama where too many characters talk *at* rather than *to* each other. Shakespeare's early plays are not altogether free of the set speech masquerading as conversation, but he rapidly got better at showing the cut-and-thrust, the here-and-now of the dialogue. In his plays deviance from the norm is sometimes more important than conformity. To illustrate how the audience is meant to make deductions from what is actually said, we can now examine three short passages. The first is the opening of Act IV. scene v., of *Hamlet*:

> Queen: I will not speak with her.
> Gentleman: She is importunate, indeed distract.
>   Her mood will needs be pitied.
> Queen: What would she have?[4]

The Queen enters, answering a question which we have not heard put but whose point becomes obvious. The Gentleman partly agrees with her. Poor Ophelia is in no fit state for the Queen to see her: it would simply be embarrassing. And yet – the strong impression he gives is that Ophelia needs help and support. So his somewhat indirect comment provokes a response although it does not absolutely require one: 'What would she have?' Is this because Gertrude likes to see herself as someone upon whom people can rely for help (as she earlier tried – and lamentably failed – to be a mother to Hamlet)? Is it simply support for the only other woman in the play? Or is she genuinely fond of Ophelia whom she had seen as a future daughter-in-law (V. i. 240)? What we deduce from this short passage may influence our response to the characters. In a production the interpretation would be suggested by the actors, how they speak the lines and what gestures they use. As the Gentleman says a little later:

> Her speech is nothing.
> Yet the unshaped use of it doth move
> The hearers to collection.

> (7–9)

i.e. to grasp something of the meaning.

The second and third examples come from *Macbeth*. In the important scene which closes the long first act (I. vii.), Lady Macbeth taunts her husband with wanting the crown of Scotland but being afraid to kill for it. Macbeth, remember, is a soldier, which is how we first hear of him. Lady Macbeth manages, by seizing on one word in her husband's statement (meant to conclude the conversation – only it does not) to equate killing the king with 'being a man' (the italics are mine):

Macbeth:	Prithee peace.
	I dare do all that may become a *man*:
	Who dares do more is none.
Lady:	What *beast* was't then
	That made you break this enterprise to me?
	When you durst do it, then you were a *man*;
	And to be more than what you were, you would
	Be so much more the *man*.

> (I. vii. 45–51)

As Macbeth gradually realizes that the murder of Duncan is the beginning, not the end, of his troubles, he has to suborn two murderers to kill Banquo and Fleance:

Macbeth:	Was it not yesterday we spoke together?

Murderers: It was, so please your highness.
Macbeth: Well then now,
Have you considered of my speeches? Know
That it was he in the times past which held you
So under fortune, which you thought had been
Our innocent self. This I made good to you
In our last conference; passed in probation with you
How you were borne in hand, how crossed, the instruments,
Who wrought with them, and all things else that might
To half a soul and to a notion crazed
Say, 'Thus did Banquo'.
First Murderer: You made it known to us.
Macbeth: I did so; and went further, which is now
Our point of second meeting. Do you find
Your patience so predominant in your nature
That you can let this go? Are you so gospelled,
To pray for this good man and for his issue,
Whose heavy hand hath bowed you to the grave,
And beggared yours for ever?
First Murderer: We are men, my liege.

                                              (III. i. 73–91)

We have not heard about the earlier meeting before this. The two murderers at first answer deferentially but briefly. The First Murderer is perhaps undecided, perhaps sullen, as his laconic reply, 'You made it known to us', indicates. As the scene continues, Macbeth more and more usurps the conversation, bludgeoning the murderers into agreeing that, having suffered what they have (allegedly) suffered, any sensible man would recognize that all their misfortunes are due to Banquo and would know what to do about it. Ironically, this is another version of 'being a man'. Some linguists refer to conversation as 'problem-solving'. In drama, sometimes more than the single answer is demanded.

COHESION

If we now try to extend our examination of meaning across the sentence into meaning across the paragraph in prose, or within a short poem or section of a longer poem, we shall find that some of the devices already illustrated will stand us in good stead. And

there are further techniques, some of which we probably accept
subconsciously and others which we can recognize as part of the
deliberate strategy of the passage. We may begin with one of
Shakespeare's best-known sonnets (at least in its first line!).

Shall I compare thee to a summer's day?
Thou art more lovely and more temperate.
Rough winds do shake the darling buds of May,
And summer's lease hath all too short a date.   4
Sometime too hot the eye of heaven shines,
And often is his gold complexion dimmed;
And every fair from fair sometime declines,
By chance or nature's changing course untrimmed.   8
But thy eternal summer shall not fade,
Nor lose possession of that fair thou ow'st,
Nor shall Death brag thou wand'rest in his shade,
When in eternal lines to time thou grow'st.   12
　So long as men can breathe or eyes can see,
　So long lives this, and this gives life to thee.

(Sonnet 18)

The normal arrangement of a Shakespeare sonnet is into four
quatrains and a concluding couplet. Each four-line section rhymes
a b a b and the couplet rhymes c c. This of itself produces cohesion
by repetition of the same sounds. The concluding couplet usually
provides a summary of what has been said in the preceding twelve
lines or, alternatively, a contrast to it (sometimes in the form of a
paradox) or, occasionally, an epigram. Sometimes there is a further
break in the argument following line 8. The first word of line 9
here is emphatic and introduces a contrast: 'nature' fades, *But* 'thy
eternal summer' will be seen to last for ever. The arrangement of
the metre and the syntax is directing the developing sense.

Obvious devices of cohesion are the repetition of the same word
or another word formed from the same stem. The *Thou* of the
second line is obviously the same person as the *thee* of the first, the
young man to whom the sonnet is addressed (*thou* also indicates
close friendship, see earlier, p. 57). *So long* at the beginning of the
penultimate line is repeated in the same emphatic position in the
final line and the two are correlatives. *A summer's day* (line 1) is
reflected in *summer's lease* (line 4) and, more importantly, in *thy
eternal summer* (line 9). *Eternal* is repeated in the *eternal lines* of
line 12 and the *Sometime* of line 5 recurs in line 7. Synonyms,

such as *decline(s)* and *fade* aid cohesion, but antonyms (words with opposed sense) can make a stronger impact; there are no good examples here but antonyms are common in Shakespeare's sonnets. *Anaphora*, the way in which the writer refers back to an earlier word or phrase in the text, is another cohesive device. At its simplest, a pronoun refers back to a noun, as the *his* of line 6 avoids repeating the *eye of heaven* (i.e. the sun) of the previous line. *This* (twice) in the final line is more subtle. It does not seem to have a direct antecedent unless it proves to be the *eternal lines* of line 12, the poem itself.

Lexical sets are groups of words which recur in similar contexts. If I say to you *father*, you think at once of *mother* and perhaps *son* and *daughter* or *brother* and *sister*; *uncle, aunt, nephew, niece, cousin* might all be seen as members of a slightly different set reflecting rather more distant relationships. A single word can be a member of more than one lexical set: *horse* might provoke the responses *saddle, bridle, bit* or, if we are thinking of animals in a field, *cow, sheep, donkey*. In Sonnet 18 there are two clear lexical sets. The first is of nature: *summer, temperate, Rough winds, darling buds, summer* (again), *eye of heaven* (sun), *nature* itself, *summer* (yet once more), *shade*. The second set is of time: *summer's day, temperate* (from Latin *tempus*, 'time'), *May, lease* (which lasts for a certain time), *date, sometime* (twice), *often, declines, changing course, eternal* and *time* itself. There are hints of a third set: *lease* (4) which is temporary and *possession* (10), more permanent (since *ow'st* means 'owns') are legal terms and are clearly contrasted.

We are now in a position to see how Shakespeare has cunningly made the vocabulary and syntax mould the argument of his poem. The opening line challenges us with a question. The second line – also a complete sentence – negates the first under the guise of expressing a compliment. The two main lexical sets soon overlap and contrast. Everything in nature is ultimately *untrimmed* and *declines*. Time likewise passes and man's life ends in death. (Death is referred to biblically – his *shade* seems to echo 'the valley of the shadow of death' of the twenty-third Psalm – but also as something which can be vanquished and is perhaps rather vulgar, since *brag* is a colloquial term at odds with the diction of the rest of the poem.) The two lexical sets are linked by the repeated *summer* which is both part of the course of nature and, as a season of the year, also of time. Line 9 signals the change:

But thy eternal summer shall not fade.

introducing the paradox of an *eternal* summer, and this summer *shall not fade* because of the *eternal lines* of line 12. This latter phrase is certainly a pun, perhaps a threefold one. The Sonnets, especially the earlier ones, often appeal to the young man to marry and produce children: *lines* of succession, therefore. Conceivably too, these are *lines* produced by time, wrinkles, the evidence of advancing age. Most important, however, are these written lines, the *lines* of the poem, the (immortal) lines which, by perpetuating the young man's beauty, will overcome Death. The *this* of the last line must, then, be the whole sonnet which *gives life to thee*.

Sonnet 18 illustrated particularly lexical and *syntagmatic* cohesion. The latter is a matter of syntax, connections made across phrases occurring in neighbouring lines rather than through individual words. *Paradigmatic* cohesion is simpler; it consists in the repetition of the same or similar affixes (in grammar a paradigm is a set of inflections, e.g. *amo*, *amas*, *amat*, etc. in Latin or *cyning*, *cyning*, *cyninges*, *cyninge* for the four cases of the singular of one declension of O.E. nouns). Since this type of cohesion did not figure prominently in Sonnet 18, we could take a brief look at the opening of T. S. Eliot's *The Waste Land*:

> April is the cruellest month, breeding
> Lilacs out of the dead land, mixing
> Memory and desire, stirring
> Dull roots with spring rain.
> Winter kept us warm, covering
> Earth in forgetful snow, feeding
> A little life with dried tubers.
> Summer surprised us, coming over the Starnbergersee
> With a shower of rain; we stopped in the colonnade,
> And went on in sunlight, into the Hofgarten,
> And drank coffee, and talked for an hour.

Much of the effect is achieved by the parallelism of the present participles, each ending in *-ing*, each on the end of its line (which runs into the next) but separated from what had come before in that line by the metre and the punctuation. April is indeed the cruellest month, disturbing too: *breeding*, . . . *mixing*, . . . *stirring*. Winter, on the contrary, is comforting: *covering*, . . . *feeding* (together with *kept us warm* forming part of a lexical set of child-rearing). Initially summer is *coming*, but we almost immediately change to dynamic verbs: *stopped*, . . . *went on*, . . . *drank*, . . . *talked*. The lethargy of winter gives place to the activity of summer.

What if a writer deliberately avoids cohesion? It is sometimes said that Milton's vocabulary is difficult and a bar to our comprehension of his poetry. Indeed he often uses words with their etymological (normally Latin) meanings. But his syntax too can seem to us 'un-English', as in the marvellous diminuendo ending to *Paradise Regained*:

> Thus they the Son of God, our Saviour meek,
> Sung victor, and, from heavenly feast refreshed,
> Brought on his way with joy. He, unobserved,
> Home to his mother's house private returned.

The angels have celebrated Christ's victory over Satan in the wilderness. But Christ returns to his parents. The 'normal' order of words would be something like 'They sung [celebrated] the Son of God, our meek Saviour, [as] victor, and brought [him] on his way with joy, refreshed from [his] heavenly feast'. In the last sentence the adverbial *Home to his mother's house* precedes the verb *returned*, and the adjectives *unobserved* and *private*, both qualify *He* (and in Latin their endings would have agreed with *He*). But Milton's order is deliberate and to rewrite the lines a travesty. *Home to his mother's house* is emphasized, foregrounded, by placing it in the emphatic position at the beginning of the line. There is some cohesion here: *from heavenly feast refreshed* is parallel to and contrasts with *Home to his mother's house* and the two phrases are of the same length. Surely, however, the important achievement is that we cannot read these lines quickly. Milton has deliberately slowed the tempo to allow us to follow Christ's footsteps, the unobtrusive return to normality.

The business of binding together phrases, clauses and sentences can, of course, be seen in prose as well as in verse. In verse, however, while the metre may impose some constraints, such as rhyme, it may also tighten up the expression of cohesive figures such as antithesis and antonyms or (as we saw in the Eliot passage) foreground significant words by placing them in emphatic positions within the line. Prose can achieve some of this too, although its nature is to be more expansive. This moving seventeenth-century passage is not especially complex. Its weight comes largely from placing a series of noun phrases in apposition to the subject or object of the sentence:[5]

> It is a thing that everyone suffers, even persons of the lowest
> resolution, of the meanest vertue, of no breeding, of no discourse.
> Take away but the pomps of death, the disguises and solemn
> bug-bears, the tinsell, and the actings by candle-light, and proper
> and phantastic ceremonies, the minstrels and the noise-makers,
> the women and the weepers, the swoonings and the shrikings,
> the Nurses and the Physicians, the dark room and the Ministers,
> the Kinred and the Watchers, and then to die is easie, ready
> and quitted from its troublesom circumstances. It is the same
> harmelesse thing, that a poor shepherd suffered yesterday, or a
> maid servant today; and at the time in which you die, in that very
> night, a thousand creatures die with you, some wise men, and
> many fools; and the wisdom of the first will not quit him, and the
> folly of the latter does not make him unable to die.
> (Jeremy Taylor, *The Rule and Exercises of Holy Dying* (1651),
> Chapter 7.)

In the first sentence *everyone* is expanded to include 'even persons . . . of no discourse' to produce an elaborate subject, most of which follows the verb. But it is in the second sentence that *the pomps of death* are made to seem so unnecessarily pompous and tedious by their extended description: 'the disguises . . . and the Watchers'. Since Taylor's real point is the naturalness and the inevitability of death, he contrasts all this ceremony with the simple 'and then to die is easie' (although this too is extended to 'ready and quitted from its troublesom circumstances'). Thereafter the vocabulary remains simple and the brief expansions become parentheses: 'or a maid servant today', 'in that very night', 'some wise men and many fools'. Yet the style is far from artless. Within the expansions some of the phrases have their own cohesion. 'Of the lowest resolution, of the meanest vertue' repeats the construction of *of* + *the* + adjective + noun and the balance is intensified by the paradigmatic *-est* suffixes. In 'of no breeding, of no discourse' the repetition of *of no* brings the two nouns together. In the lengthy second sentence most of the phrases from 'the minstrels . . . Watchers', are approximately the same length as well as containing two nouns each preceded by the definite article. In the final sentence antithesis is the favoured device: *yesterday . . . today, wise men . . . fools, wisdom of the first . . . folly of the latter*, where the last of these takes up the *wise* and *fools*, turning them into abstract nouns *wisdom* and *folly*.

As befits a novel, Jane Austen's account of how Mr Elton persuades himself that a defeat is in reality a famous victory apparently comes closer to artless narrative where the author chats to the reader with a good deal of empathy between them:

> Mr Elton returned, a very happy man. He had gone away
> rejected and mortified, disappointed in a very sanguine hope,
> after a series of what had appeared to him strong encouragement;
> and not only losing the right lady, but finding himself debased
> to the level of a very wrong one. He had gone away deeply   5
> offended; he came back engaged to another, and to another as
> superior, of course, to the first, as under such circumstances
> what is gained always is to what is lost. He came back gay
> and self-satisfied, eager and busy, caring nothing for Miss
> Woodhouse, and defying Miss Smith.   10
>   The charming Augusta Hawkins, in addition to all the usual
> advantages of perfect beauty and merit, was in possession of an
> independent fortune, of so many thousands as would always be
> called ten, – a point of some dignity, as well as some convenience.
> The story told well; he had not thrown himself away – he had   15
> gained a woman of £10,000 or thereabouts, and he had gained her
> with such delightful rapidity; the first hour of introduction
> had been so very soon followed by distinguishing notice; the
> history which he had to give Mrs Cole of the rise and progress
> of the affair was so glorious; the steps so quick, from the   20
> accidental rencontre to the dinner at Mr Green's, and the
> party at Mrs Brown's – smiles and blushes rising in importance, –
> with consciousness and agitation richly scattered; the lady
> had been so easily impressed, – so sweetly disposed; – had,
> in short, to use a most intelligible phrase, been so very ready   25
> to have him, that vanity and prudence were equally contented.
>
> (*Emma*, (1816))

Half-way through comes the shift to *The story told well* (15) and we can almost hear Mr Elton's own account of the courtship. This is in what is sometimes called Free Indirect Speech (which is quite common in Jane Austen). It is not actually direct speech, which would use the first person and the present tense instead of *he* followed by the past perfect (*he had gained*), but it is the next best thing. Other phrases in this passage give the illusion of actual conversation. *Of course*; *not thrown himself away*; *or thereabouts*; *in short, the dinner at Mr Green's and the party at Mrs Brown's* are what we might well *say*. The apparently casual syntax signalled by the dashes in lines 14, 15, 22 and 24 and the repetition of *he had gained* with the qualification of *with such delightful rapidity* – these too are characteristic of conversation. But there are two other levels on which the passage operates. The Latinate vocabulary of the opening (*rejected, mortified, sanguine*), followed by a number of abstract nouns of Romance origin elsewhere (*encouragement, dignity, consciousness and agitation, vanity and prudence*) suggest Mr Elton's own perception of the importance of the affair. It is within this kind of diction that the cohesion is uppermost: *rejected and mortified, disappointed, debased, offended* and *engaged* (with their repeated *-ed* suffix); *caring* and *defying* (each ending in *-ing* and placed at the head of its clause); the antithesis of *the right lady . . . a very wrong one*; the repetition which emphasizes the antithesis in *He had gone away . . . He came back* and *what is gained . . . what is lost*; the balance of *gay and self-satisfied, eager and busy* and *some dignity as well as some convenience*. But here we begin to perceive the irony, the third level of response. *Convenience* is not really an appropriate word to link with *dignity* – unless, that is, you are really primarily concerned with 'so many thousands as would always be called ten'. The pretentiousness of *accidental rencontre* (instead of 'chance meeting') and *richly scattered* culminate in the balanced 'so easily impressed – so sweetly disposed . . . so very ready to have him'. The last of these (preceded by 'to use a most intelligible phrase') shows that Mr Elton is not only looking for a wife of independent means but is utterly oblivious to the true motivation of the charming Augusta Hawkins. The irony in Jane Austen often works through the deliberate balance and cohesion of questionable qualities.

Drama is different again. For the most part it has to appear more casual, as if it is really spoken and not written, the unpremeditated thought of the characters:

> So, oft it chances in particular men
> That for some vicious mole of nature in them,
> As in their birth, wherein they are not guilty
> (Since nature cannot choose his origin),
> By their o'ergrowth of some complexion,
> Oft breaking down the pales and forts of reason,
> Or by some habit, that too much o'erleavens

> The form of plausive manners – that these men,
> Carrying, I say, the stamp of one defect,
> Being Nature's livery or Fortune's star,
> His virtues else, be they as pure as grace,
> As infinite as man may undergo,
> Shall in the general censure take corruption
> From that particular fault.
>
> (*Hamlet* I. iv. 23–36)

As often, Hamlet is trying to consider all possible reasons for someone's behaviour, to be sure he has weighed up all the evidence before acting – or, more usually, not acting. He is arguing that *particular men . . . shall . . . take corruption/From that particular fault*. That is the main clause. But he suggests various explanations for this: the accident of birth, the exaggeration of a particular disposition (*complexion*), some habit which goes beyond the pattern of approved behaviour (*The form of plausive manners*), the result either of the human condition (*Nature's livery*) or mere Fortune. Each of these is subject to qualification or parenthesis, usually by a subordinate clause, e.g. 'their birth *wherein they are not guilty/(Since Nature cannot choose his origin)*'. Half-way through he has to repeat his subject: *these men/Carrying, I say*, lest we should have forgotten it. In speech we constantly make qualifications, break off and return to our original subject. And the whole argument here is generalized: *particular men . . . these men . . . His virtues*, but there can be no doubt that it is a covert attack on Claudius. We do not need to be Hamlet to conceal what we mean.

NOTES

1. A useful introduction to semantic change is R. Waldron, (1967) *Sense and Sense Development* (London: Andre Deutsch).

2. The distinction is common and is well put by Graddol *et al.* 1987: p. 178.

3. After Yule 1985: p. 110 and Blake 1990: p. 88. For pragmatics in general, see Leech, 1983.

4. I owe this example to Dr A. J. Gilbert.

5. As Blake says (Blake 1990: 37), the NP carries more weight the more it is extended but the VP appears more diffuse the more it is extended. Single verbs seem more dynamic.

EXERCISES

1. What distinction do you make between *wit* and *humour*? What did the words originally mean? What did Shakespeare mean when he spoke of the *humorous* night (*Romeo and Juliet* II. i. 31) and the *humorous* Duke – the wicked one (*As You Like It* I. ii. 255)? What kind of part did Hamlet expect the *humorous* man among the troupe of players to take (II. ii. 322)? Why should Ben Jonson call one of his plays *Every Man in His Humour*? What would a late sixteenth- or early seventeenth-century critic have understood by *wit* and why might he have illustrated it by quoting a *conceit* (from a metaphysical poem, for example)?

2. News At Ten was worse. Cliché-ridden, film obsessed. Implications were 'dramatic', there were 'margins of error', 'cushions of support', mills had 'grist', offers were 'on the table', heads perpetually 'rolled', MPs 'rallied' and agendas were 'tough'. This is writing that the junior sub on the Argus and Gleaner would bin in disgust. Bits of press releases strung together with hackneyed phrases. Try watching the main evening news with your eyes shut.

    (A. A. Gill, writing as television critic, *The Sunday Times*,
    19 June 1994.)

    Find ten or twelve tired collocations of your own and resolve to avoid them when you want to appear interesting or creative.

3. Lear believes that, having divided his kingdom between his two elder daughters, he can stay with them in turn, together with his hundred attendant knights. Gonerill has just rejected this.
    What features of pragmatic theory help to explain the changing relationship between father and daughters?

    Lear: I prithee, daughter do not make me mad.
    I will not trouble thee, my child. Farewell.
    We'll no more meet, no more see one another.
    But yet thou art my flesh, my blood, my daughter –
    Or rather a disease that's in my flesh,
    Which I must needs call mine. Thou art a boil,
    A plague-sore, or embossed carbuncle
    In my corrupted blood. But I'll not chide thee;
    Let shame come when it will, I do not call it;
    I do not bid the Thunder-bearer shoot,
    Nor tell tales of thee to high-judging Jove.
    Mend when thou canst; be better at thy leisure;
    I can be patient; I can stay with Regan,
    I and my hundred knights.

Regan: Not altogether so.
I look'd not for you yet, nor am provided
For your fit welcome. Give ear, sir, to my sister;
For those that mingle reason with your passion
Must be content to think you old, and so –
But she knows what she does.

Lear: Is this well spoken?

Regan: I dare avouch it, sir. What, fifty followers?
Is it not well? What should you need of more?
Yea, or so many, sith that both charge and danger
Speak 'gainst so great a number? How in one house
Should many people under two commands
Hold amity? 'Tis hard; almost impossible.

Gonerill: Why might not you, my Lord, receive attendance
From those that she calls servants, or from mine?

Regan: Why not, my lord? If then they chanc'd to slack ye,
We could control them. If you will come to me,
For now I spy a danger, I entreat you
To bring but five and twenty. To no more
Will I give place or notice.

Lear: I gave you all –

Regan: And in good time you gave it.

(*King Lear* II. iv. 213–45)

4.   What devices help to achieve cohesion in this essay by Bacon:

What is Truth? said jesting Pilate; and would not stay for an answer.
Certainly there be that delight in giddiness, and count it a bondage
to fix a belief; affecting free-will in thinking, as well as in acting.
And though the sects of philosophers of that kind be gone, yet
there remain certain discoursing wits which are of the same veins,
though there be not so much blood in them as was in those of
the ancients. But it is not only the difficulty and labour which
men take in finding out of truth; nor again that when it is found
it imposeth upon men's thoughts, that doth bring lies in favour; but
a natural though corrupt love of the lie itself. One of the later school
of the Grecians examineth the matter, and is at a stand to think what
should be in it, that men should love lies, where neither they make
for pleasure, as with poets, nor for advantage, as with the merchant;
but for the lie's sake. But I cannot tell: this same truth is a naked and
open day-light, that doth not show the masks and mummeries and
triumphs of the world, half so stately and daintily as candle-lights.
Truth may perhaps come to the price of a pearl, that showeth best
by day; but it will not rise to the price of a diamond or carbuncle,

that sheweth best in varied lights. A mixture of a lie doth ever add pleasure. Doth any man doubt, that if there were taken out of men's minds vain opinions, flattering hopes, false valuations, imaginations as one would, and the like, but it would leave the minds of a number of men poor shrunken things, full of melancholy and indisposition, and unpleasing to themselves?

(Of Truth, (1597))

giddiness: frivolity
veins: 1) opinions 2) blood-vessels
mummeries: mimes
triumph: victorious procession (as played on stage)
carbuncle: precious jewel such as a ruby

Chapter 5

Receiving Words

SOUNDS AND SPELLINGS

We can transmit or receive information either in speech or in writing, but we possibly have to do more decoding with speech. Writing is partly decoded for us to an extent we may hardly realize. It is set out into sentences, with capital letters, commas, full stops, question marks and other punctuation, and beyond the sentence into paragraphs, in a way we take for granted. This is even true of the spaces between words. We do not necessarily hear all words in conversation separately, although we may think we do. But, if we try to convey in writing an accurate representation of what we have heard – the stress, the rise and fall of the voice, the dialectally-coloured pronunciation, even the hesitations which are part and parcel of normal speech – we soon become aware of how complex a task that is. This chapter can do little more than state the problems, indicate some of the solutions, and consider how far the difficulties may be due to historical factors.[1]

It is a commonplace that English spelling is quite seriously unrelated to pronunciation. We have surely all heard the joke about the *-ough* group of words – *rough, cough, bough, dough* – and the impossibility of rhyming them. Yet even a single letter can have various pronunciations, for example the *s* in *ease, lease* and *sugar*. The same sound can be interpreted by a variety of letters, most obviously the 'neutral' vowel [ə] by *a* in *banana, America* and *breakfast*; by *o* in *colour* and *opinion*; by *u* in *upon*. A single sound may be spelled by two letters: *scent, loch, quay*, or a letter can be 'silent': the *s* of *island* or *aisle*; the *b* of *doubt* or *debt*; the *p* of *receipt*. We are so trained to spelling in our early years that we ignore the actual value of sounds in speech. We come a little closer to the truth when we speak (as I did earlier) of a 'hard' g or a 'soft' c, but we really require something more exact and complete than that. What is needed is a scientific alphabet where one symbol represents one sound only and each sound is represented by only one symbol, so that a Japanese (for example) who knows this alphabet can pronounce a sound in English which is not present in his own language.

The **International Phonetic Alphabet** (IPA) serves this function. The science of speech sounds is called **phonetics,** from the Greek *phone*. Clearly, in order to cover the full range of sounds, IPA will need more symbols than those in our alphabet. It uses some of the letters of the written alphabet, especially for the consonants, but includes others which have to be learned, such as [ʌ] for the sound in *but, love*; [ɜ:] for the sound in *bird, hurt*; [ɔ:] as in *more*; [ʃ] for the initial sound in *sugar* or the final one in *fish*; and the 'neutral' (or 'reduced') vowel [ə] I used a moment ago. Phonetic symbols are placed between square brackets to avoid confusion with the letters of the written alphabet. Written symbols, called **graphemes,** are placed between angle brackets to indicate that they are a matter of writing only, e.g. <i> before <e>, except after <c>. The 'standard' form of English speech, known as **Received Pronunciation** (RP) has perhaps some forty-six different sounds: vowels, diphthongs and consonants. (Diphthongs are 'gliding vowels' where the voice passes from one vowel towards another; they are consequently transcribed with two symbols which represent the extremes of movement between two positions, as with [ɔɪ] in *boy*, [aʊ] in *out*, [eɪ] in *make*, [ɛə] in *fair*.) Yet our alphabet contains only twenty-six letters and four of these (c,j,q,x) are superfluous because they can be replaced by various other letters. So we need IPA to cover many more sounds than our twenty-two effective letters could manage.

In practice, however, we need to think of cases where two words differ in a single sound only and where changing the one sound into the other will change the meaning of that word. These significant sounds are called **phonemes** and are written between oblique lines. For example, *bat* becomes *pat* by changing the initial consonant and *bad* by changing the final consonant, while changing the vowel turns *bat* into *bit* or *bet*. /b/, /p/, /t/, /d/, /æ/, /ɪ/ and /e/ are therefore all phonemes in English. But phonemes are not international like IPA. What is a phoneme in

English may not be one in another language or even at an earlier stage of English. For us, *sin* and *sing*, *kin* and *king*, *tan* and *tang* differ only in their final sounds, so /n/ and /ŋ/ are phonemes in Present-Day English; /ŋ/ is represented by two letters in spelling, <ng>, but we hear one sound only. In O.E., however, this was not a phonemic distinction. We can reconstruct phonemic systems for O.E. or M.E., and while they would have certain phonemes in common with P.D.E. others would differ.

Other symbols not in the English alphabet are needed to make the distinction between *dilution* and *delusion* and *glacier* and *glazier*: /ʃ/ and /ʒ/. Spelling is no guide at all in *tot* and *yacht* where /t/ contrasts with /j/, but sometimes spelling suggests a difference where there is none: *Thomas*, *Tom* and *Thames* all begin with the phoneme /t/. Always think of what you hear, not what you see written. At the end of this chapter I include a list of phonemes used in RP, the standard pronunciation of P.D.E. understood throughout the British Isles and used as a model for foreign learners of English. In some quarters it is now thought of as élitist, since it is based on an accent associated with the public schools and the professional classes.[2] But so long as we remember that regional dialects need be in no way inferior, the general intelligibility of RP outweighs its suggested social prestige. When I was discussing grammar I spoke of the morpheme as being the smallest significant form. Some morphemes (free morphemes) may be words, like *walk* or *boy*, but a morpheme is not necessarily a word, as in the bound morphemes -*s*, -*ed* and -*ing* of *walks*, *walked* and *walking*. Every morpheme will contain at least one sound and may well contain more than one: -*ing*, for instance, comprises [ɪ] and [ŋ]. So the hierarchy runs: sounds, (phonemes), morphemes, words; phonemes might be excluded as referring to a particular language only.

Sound Change

Sounds change, from one generation to another, although very slightly, almost imperceptibly sometimes. If we notice these changes when we are young, we might say it's how grandpa talks. If, though, we compare O.E. with M.E., or M.E. with Early Modern English, or Early Modern English with P.D.E., the changes begin to show up. There does not appear to be a clear answer to the question 'why do sound changes happen?' Things are not obviously better or more efficient afterwards. The chronology of sound changes is also difficult: it is much easier to say when a sound change is complete than to say when it began, because alternative pronunciations may exist for some time without either being obviously preferred. But it is above all important to distinguish between 'real' sound changes and those changes which are merely graphic, a matter of how the same sound is written differently, as for example O.E. <scip> and P.D.E. <ship>. The study of the system of sounds within a language (or stage of a language such as M.E. or a dialect), their patterns and distribution, is known as **phonology**. The most I can do in this chapter is to consider some of the anomalies in our present spelling and to ask how they arose.

O.E. AND M.E.

Spelling in earlier O.E. is reasonably phonetic, but in late O.E. it begins to fall some way behind actual pronunciation because of the dominance of the Late West Saxon dialect and its elevation into a near-written standard. After the Norman Conquest French scribes were responsible for two kinds of change. Both were spelling changes: the same sounds continued much as before.

a.   The introduction of new letters because the O.E. alphabet was either inadequate or misunderstood by them.
     æ, ð and þ gradually disappeared from the alphabet. <þ>, already more common than <ð> in O.E., became used for both 'th' sounds and from c. 1400 is more and more written <th>.
     ƿ is written <w>, although <uu> (literally 'double u') can be found in early M.E.
     O.E. <cw> is replaced by M.E. <qu>: *cwēne/quene, cwic/quick, cwellan/quellen* ('quell', 'kill').

b.   Discrimination between different O.E. sounds spelled in the same way. The distinction between 'hard' and 'soft' g is increasingly resolved by <g> being used for the 'hard' sound (*god*) and <ʒ>, later <y>, for the softer sound (*ʒer/yer*, 'year').

<gu> is a spelling for <g> in some French borrowings such as *guard, guile, guide,* and this was extended to some non-French words like *guest, guild* and *guilt.*

Similarly 'hard' c is spelled <k> (*cyning* appears as *king* and *cniht* as *kniht*) and 'soft' c as <ch> (O.E. *cēosan, cild* and *cyrice* are respelled *choose, child* and *church*).

Many medieval scribes were careless about leaving *u* open at the top and *n* open at the bottom, nor did they regularly dot *i*. Difficulties could therefore arise with O.E. words like *cuman, sunu, munuc, hunig* through the series of heavy down-strokes and light or non-existent cross-strokes. To avoid confusion the sound [ʊ] was written <o> and not <u> in the vicinity of *m, n,* and *u,* resulting in our spellings *come, son, monk* and *honey.*

Some cases which *do* involve pronunciation change, either between O.E. and M.E. or between M.E. and P.D.E. are:

a. The pronunciation in M.E. of consonants which we usually slur or ignore, e.g. *kniht, folk, gnawen.*
b. The loss of aspiration in M.E. in words like O.E. *hlāford, hlǣfdiȝe, hnecca* which (in most dialects outside the North) became M.E. *lord, ladi, necke.*
c. The replacement of earlier O.E. [ɑː] by M.E. [ɔː] (again, not in the North), turning *hām, hālig* and *sār* into our *home, holy* and *sore* (in the first two of these words [ɔː] became [oː] in the Great Vowel Shift and later still [əʊ]).
d. The introduction of the French diphthong [ɔɪ] in such French loan words as *noise, choice, joy, poison, royal, employ, boil, point.*

We must not assume, however, that there was a fixed spelling in M.E. If any standards existed, they were regional and not national, where different copyists (we are still in the time before printing) had perhaps been trained in the same monastic scriptorium or were at least writing in the same geographical area. The O.E. sound [y], pronounced like the *u* in French *lune,* became [ɪ] in most areas and was spelled <i> in later English (*cyning* becomes *king* and *synne* becomes *sin*) but in the South-Eastern M.E. dialect it was spelled <e>, as in P.D.E. *merry, left,* and in the South-West <u>, as in *dusty, cudgel* and *much.* With *bury,* however, we now have the S.W. spelling with a S.E. pronunciation and with *busy* the S.W. spelling but the 'normal' (i.e. N. and E.) pronunciation.

In many M.E. manuscripts the commonest words, such as 'should' or 'not' can be spelled differently, even on the same page. From about 1430, a spelling system based on manuscripts produced in the London area ('Chancery Standard', see p. 135) gradually gained prominence, but it was the introduction of the printing press which (as with grammar) helped to standardize a single form of spelling, since however rudimentary the press, each copy would be the same as every other, whereas individual copyists naturally produced individual variations.

EARLY MODERN ENGLISH

One of the hallowed topics of histories of the language is the impressively-titled **Great Vowel Shift**. Between Chaucer and Shakespeare, English long, stressed vowels changed their quality, that is, their characteristic resonance and timbre. They were pronounced with the tongue higher and the mouth more closed than formerly. The highest vowels became diphthongized and closer (i.e. with the tongue higher in the mouth) and the lower vowels moved up to take their place. This is often represented diagrammatically:

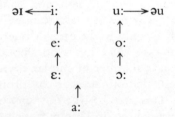

This, however, obscures the fact that the Great Vowel Shift (GVS) was not a series of changes happening one after the other but rather at slightly different speeds during the same period. Broadly speaking, the seven pure long vowels in the diagram are characteristic of fourteenth-century M.E. But by 1500 or so, the two highest vowels, /i:/ front and /u:/ back, had become diphthongs and /e:/ and /o:/ had been raised to take their places. During the sixteenth century, the places thus vacated were filled by the raising of /ɛ:/, /ɔ:/ and /a:/. Chaucer shows the old values and Shakespeare the new ones. But spelling did not change to incorporate the effects of the GVS and the spread of printing in the late fifteenth and sixteenth centuries helped to perpetuate the old spellings. The effect for us is twofold: our present spelling does not always reflect the 'new' pronunciation and there are some odd-looking rhymes and puns in Shakespeare and indeed on into the eighteenth century. In Shakespeare *clean* rhymes with *lane* (both /e:/). After Shakespeare's time, however, his /e:/ was raised further to /i:/, so that in P.D.E. *clean* rhymes with *lean*. However, in a few words (*great*, *break* and *steak* being the most important) the archaic /e:/ has survived into P.D.E. So Shakespeare distinguishes *see* and *sea* or *meet* and *meat* as /i:/ and /e:/ respectively, whereas for us they are both /i:/. Likewise he can pun on *steal* and *stale* and *reason* and *raisin*. Developments, some where a vowel had been shortened before the GVS and so did not participate in that change which affected only long vowels, others the regular outcome of the Shift, and still others occurring afterwards, result in groups of words which are today spelled similarly but pronounced differently: *roof, room, mood* and *food* [u:], contrasted with *blood* and *flood* [ʌ], or *good, stood, foot* [ʊ]. But in the seventeenth century there was a good deal of fluctuation in these three sounds: Dryden rhymes *flood, mood* and *good*. Other early rhymes (not all the result of the GVS) include *rewards* and *cards*, *design* and *coin* (both Pope); *guest* and *feast* (Shakespeare), *feature, nature* and *stature* (Spenser); *earth* and *hearth* (Milton). Rhymes, in fact, can be useful evidence of pronunciation, and not only in the early Modern period. But they have to be used with care. One rhyme does not constitute evidence of sound-change, but a number of similar rhymes, which do not work for us, suggests that our present-day pronunciation will not serve at that point. This may be true not only of an earlier period but also of a modern dialect. In Dublin poor Molly Malone 'died of a *fever*/And no one could *save her*'. 'Treat us *fairly*, travel *early*' pleads a bus advertisement in Liverpool, where *fairly* is often heard as *firly*. *Fair* and *fur* are homophones on Merseyside. The English teacher from the South who heard her pupils speak of the 'furries' in *A Midsummer Night's Dream* momentarily wondered whether the wood near Athens contained a whole layer of characters she hadn't previously noticed.

We have seen, in earlier chapters, the considerable prestige attached to Latin and Greek by English Renaissance writers. Recognizing that several English words were closely related to the original Latin, they replaced the 'missing' letters in words like *adventure, debt, doubt, describe, language, perfect, receipt*. They forgot that such words had been borrowed into English via French, itself derived from Latin. The M.E. spellings <*aventure, dette, doute, descryve, langage, perfit* (or *parfit*), *receit*> naturally reflect a simplification that had already taken place in French. And occasionally these Renaissance etymologists got it wrong. *Admiral* (M.E. *amyrel*) is not from Latin but from Arabic *amir* (compare later *emir*); *anchor* (M.E. *ancre*) and *author* (M.E. *auctor*) are not Greek; while *island* (M.E. *yland*) is actually O.E. *iegland*, not Latin *insula*.

PRESENT DIFFICULTIES

Largely as a result of historical change, then, and the inadequacy of our alphabet to distinguish clearly between sounds, today's English spelling is often a mess. Some of our present difficulties (but these can be exaggerated) stem from confusion in homographs, homophones and homonyms.

Homographs are words with the same spelling but different pronunciation, e.g. <minute> can be a short period of time or an adjective meaning 'very small'. <lead> as a verb means 'be at the front', but there is of course a noun *lead* which is a metal.

Homophones, on the contrary, sound alike but have different spellings. Most common is *there* and *their*, which adults as well as children confuse surprisingly often, but there are several others, for instance *night* and *knight*; *hole* and *whole*; *seem* and *seam*; *cue* and *queue*; *genes* and *jeans*; *pedal* and *peddle*; *chilly* and *chili*; *review* and *revue*; *sight, site* and *cite*; *vain, vein* and *vane*. Some of these are curiosities rather than occasions of difficulty in practice, especially when the homophones are different parts of speech.

Homonyms are identical in both spelling and pronunciation, e.g. *can* is a (tin) can or the verb 'be able'; *hamper* is either a basket or the verb 'impede'; *rest* (noun or verb) means 'repose' or else (noun only) 'the remainder'. In these cases the context would surely make the meaning clear. In a few words an original semantic link has now disappeared and the two spellings have become different, as with <flower> and <flour>, where <flour> was originally the 'flower' of ground meal; and <metal> and <mettle> where the second was a figurative use of the first. Regan's reply to her father Lear: 'I am made of that self mettle as my sister/And price me at her worth' is probably meant as a pun. M.E. spells <person> and <parson> with either meaning, and the ecclesiastical use with <a> was established only in Early Modern English. Originally *tun* (O.E. *tunne*) and *ton* (OF *tonne*) both meant 'cask', but from the eighteenth century *ton* was restricted to weight. These words have therefore ceased to be homonyms.

Where a difference of stress signals the distinction between noun and verb (e.g. '*extract*, noun, and *ex'tract*, verb, or '*record*, noun, and *re'cord*, verb) there is no real problem. Carney (1994: p. 397) suggests '*contract* (noun, 'agreement') and *con'tract* (verb, 'become smaller'), '*converse* (noun, 'the opposite') and *con'verse* (verb, 'chat'), '*object* (noun, 'thing') and *ob'ject* (verb, 'protest') and some other pairs should be regarded nowadays as different lexemes and that they give rise to even less difficulty.

Two basic devices of English spelling may help to give us confidence. Doubling of a consonant usually marks a previous short vowel, e.g. *comma* (contrast *coma*), *hobby*, *supper*. (Unfortunately there are some exceptions to this, especially with <o> before <ll>: *roll*, *swollen*, *wholly* are all pronounced long.) <e> is usually the marker of a preceding long vowel or diphthong, e.g. *mate* (v. *mat*), *prime* (v. *prim*), *pure* (v. *purr*), *white* (v. *Whit* Sunday).

Sometimes analogy may help. The increasingly common confusion between *its* ('of it') and *it's* ('it is') may be resolved by remembering that there is no apostrophe in *hers*, *ours*, *theirs* either. The apostrophe, on the other hand, shows that something is missing:

> it's lost (it *is* lost).
> it's disappeared (it *has* disappeared).
> I'll go (I *will* go).
> Tom doesn't drink (Tom does *not* drink).
> The boy who's been chosen (The boy who *has* been chosen).

The last example may be contrasted with *The boy whose satchel has disappeared* (. . . *of whom* the satchel . . .). Again, simpler words from the same root may resolve a difficulty. To *compliment* is to praise, but to *complement* is to make complete. A *councillor* is a member of a council, but a *counsellor* gives counsel or advice, as with a marriage guidance counsellor. But some distinctions just have to be learned:

The Welfare State has created a whole new race of *dependants*. (noun)

She is completely *dependent* on her weekly giro cheque. (adjective)

Please enclose a stamped, addressed *envelope*. (noun)

The smoke began to *envelop* the whole street. (verb)

This application will look better if you use good *stationery*. (noun, 'writing paper').

Traffic was *stationary* for two miles ahead. (adjective, 'at rest')

STANDARDS OF PRONUNCIATION

Did no one attempt to reconcile English sounds and English spelling or to establish a standard of pronunciation? Indeed they did. Already in the 1580s, Puttenham, in his *Arte of English Poesie*, recommends writers to use 'the usual speech of the Court, and that of London and the shires lying about London within sixty myles and not much above'. Even earlier John Hart, in his *Orthographie* (1569), gives transcriptions of the contemporary pronunciation of English sounds, with examples, and some recognition of variation between the 'learned' and the 'rude', but his tone is too often prescriptive, laying down laws:

> Hereby you may perceive, that our single sounding and use
> of letters, may in process of time, bring our whole nation to a
> certain, perfect and general speaking. Wherein she must be ruled
> by the learned from time to time.

The eighteenth century, and still more the nineteenth with its spread of education, saw several popular works on the subject. Eighteenth-century dictionaries, facing the perennial problem of how to represent pronunciation by an English alphabet inadequate for the purpose, often resorted to special symbols, such as accents or hooks above or below the line, or else a key to pronunciation at the beginning of the work: a^1, a^2, a^3, etc., each with its illustrative words. Thomas Sheridan (the father of the dramatist) was the first to indicate clearly and unmistakably, in his *General Dictionary of the English Language* (1780), the pronunciation of every word. He gives two entries, the first in the usual spelling and the second more or less phonetically. John Walker, whose *Critical Pronouncing Dictionary and Expositor of the English Language* appeared in 1791, was an ex-actor and a teacher of elocution. He is too ready to ignore usage and revere spelling. This is Walker on *'quay* – sometimes written *key'*:

> for if we cannot bring the pronunciation to the spelling, it is looked upon as some improvement to bring the spelling to the pronunciation: a most pernicious practice in language.

His authoritarian tone, however, appealed to the new middle classes of the nineteenth century and his dictionary reached its thirty-fourth edition in 1847.

Spelling Reform

The first spelling reformer was an Augustinian canon called Orm, in about 1200, whose book is a collection of sermons in verse using an elaborate, and in the main consistent, spelling system based on the length of the vowel. Every once in a while today a new proposal for reform is put forward. We must, though, decide whether spelling reform means the complete revision of our spelling on a more or less phonetic basis or whether it means the gradual elimination of a number of irregularities, such as silent letters, in the interests of a more logical spelling. The latter is rather like the American writing of <check> ('cheque'), <center>, <honor>, <dialog> and <theater>. This second solution would be better but the reformers usually intend the first. American spelling, however, is not without its own ambiguities. The regular <license> and <practise> obscures the grammatical distinction which English maintains with <licence> for the noun and <license> for the verb. American standardization on <-ize>, which was originally a Greek verbal suffix, also takes no account of several Latinate verbs which English spells <-ise>, e.g. <advertise>, <exercise>. And could there ever be a single standard, even within the British Isles with the considerable variation of pronunciation in different regions? RP has been proposed, but it is unlikely that this would now be accepted as a neutral, national standard and a foundation for a revised spelling system. Not all educated people speak alike, and even among newsreaders on radio and television (where one might expect RP to prevail) distinct traces of dialectal pronunciation can often be heard. Indeed, radio and television 'personalities' frequently make the most of their regional accents.

In the light of such difficulties within this reasonably small area of the globe, what price a single standard of spelling for Britain, the United States of America, the former Commonwealth countries and anywhere where English is used as a second language? Even if this were conceivable, by what authority could it be imposed? And the commercial problems are enormous: the complete revision of dictionaries and all reference works and the redesign of typewriters, word-processors and printing machinery. Would the benefits compensate for the huge initial outlay? Reformers argue that a new phonetic system would make it so much easier for children to learn to spell. Would it? <Cats> but <dogz>, <jumps> but <runz>, <landed> but <hopt>, <jumpt> and <turnd>? As Carney (1994: pp. 480–1) very reasonably points out, language contains a quite high measure of redundancy which enables skilled readers to skim through a passage quite quickly. If some of the slack in the system were to be removed, more conscious effort would be required. Furthermore, those reformers who identify redundant letters are themselves highly literate. Not so a learner who may need to recognize separate syllables, clearly marked by the spelling, in a way that a new system, based on simplistic notions of economy, may obscure. A new phonetic spelling system might perhaps make some sort of sense for P.D.E. alone, but it would obscure etymological relationships with other languages whose words we have borrowed, and this would work both ways: for foreigners learning our language and for us learning theirs. Finally, how long would a new system last? We cannot put a stop to (or even a brake on) changing pronunciation. Let Dr Johnson, in his Dictionary of 1755, have the last word:

> In this part of the work [spelling] where caprice has long
> wantoned without controul, and vanity fought praise by petty
> reformation, I have endeavoured to proceed with a scholar's
> reverence for antiquity, and a grammarian's regard for the genius
> of our tongue. I have attempted few alterations, and amongst those
> few, perhaps the greater part is from the modern to the ancient
> practice.

STRESS AND INTONATION

Until now I have been talking as if sounds exist in isolation. Of course they do not. Once words are put together into longer units

– phrases, clauses or sentences – stress and intonation become increasingly important. **Stress** is the prominence given to certain syllables in words, and single words indeed have their own stress pattern. Since English is a Germanic language, the majority of words put their stress on the first syllable, but we occasionally need different stress patterns to distinguish nouns like *protest*, *conduct*, *fragment*, *increase* and *transport* from the same words used as verbs. In the written representation of stress the marker is placed immediately before the stressed syllable: hence '*protest* (noun) and *pro'test* (verb). In connected speech, as the speech organs pass from one position to another they are likely to take short cuts because of the speed of the movement: they may drop vowels or make consonants less distinct. There will then be a different stress pattern for the clause or sentence from that of the individual words within it. Consider the different pronunciation of *she* in 'Does she?' (said slowly and with some surprise) and 'Does she know you've come today?'; the difference arises from the changed stress pattern. Of course we retain the ability to emphasize particular words in a sentence: 'No, I said next *Thursday*, not *Wednesday*'; 'Some 'people 'came 'round for 'dinner' (with regular stress, and so not a remarkable statement) versus ''Some people came' (i.e others did not). In a more careful transcription, secondary as well as primary stress would need to be indicated.

In general, however, lexical words, such as nouns, main verbs, adjectives and adverbs, are more strongly stressed than grammatical words, such as determiners, auxiliary verbs, prepositions and conjunctions. Very young children omit unstressed grammatical words: '*Daddy* '*gone*; '*Mummy* '*come* '*now*. As native speakers of English we may confidently predict ends of words or phrases in normal connected speech. It is possible that when we begin to learn a foreign language, we learn words spoken slowly, clearly and often separately, so that later interpretation of normal speech, with its simplified forms, becomes that much more difficult. In informal speech we use reduced pronunciations where a vowel has been elided: [laɪbriː], [hɪstriː], [sekətriː], [dɪfrɪnt] and [præps] for *library*, *history*, *secretary*, *different* and *perhaps*. Consonants may disappear too, especially /d/ and /t/ at the end of a syllable when the following word begins with a consonant: [ðəfækðət], 'the fact that', [fæsfuːd], 'fast food'. Other frequent reductions are [ə'kɔs], ['ɔrediː], ['sɜtənliː]

and [f'ɪnstənts], instead of *of course*, *already*, *certainly* and *for instance*. Alternatively, intrusive letters may be introduced in the interests of smoothness: *law-r and order*, *draw-r-ring room*, *umb-e-rella*, but such examples are better seen as characteristic of substandard speech.

But positioning the stress of a word in continuous speech is not enough. Closely allied to stress is **intonation,** the rise and fall in pitch. It is intonation which largely distinguishes a native from a non-native speaker of a language, or sometimes a regional accent from RP (e.g. the 'sing-song' character of Welsh English). We hardly ever speak on a single level for long. It is by intonation (often combined with a variation in the stress pattern) that we may indicate our feelings about the content of the sentence, feelings such as astonishment or uncertainty. Falling intonation usually indicates that the matter is finished with. Rising intonation suggests things are incomplete, as when a question is asked or a subordinate clause is to be followed by the main clause. This can be best illustrated by examples:

> It's impossible to finish today. (statement)
> Bring your essay. (command)
> What a marvellous idea! (exclamation)

All these fall from a high pitch, fairly near the beginning, to a low one at the end. Two other sentences are different:

> She might be suitable. (some doubt, but it is left unexpressed)
> Can you come Thursday? (question requiring the answer yes or no)

These end with a rising intonation. Different again is:

> When she comes, bring her in.

Here the subordinate clause is unfinished – *When she comes* makes no sense – and the main clause concludes the meaning: hence a rising-falling intonation pattern. Consider the different intonation patterns in:

> I beg your pardon. (I'm sorry)
> I beg your pardon? (What did you say?)
> Your essay was quite good. (indicating praise)
> Your essay was quite good. (but . . .)

PUNCTUATION

How can some of these attitudes be expressed in writing? Obviously punctuation can help: question marks and exclamation marks direct us on how to respond. Italics may be used to emphasize words stressed particularly strongly. Bold-face type (as used in this book) helps to break up the subject-matter into sections or else to emphasize important concepts. A large range of typographical faces and other devices is now available to the printer, and as a result the page can be laid out more clearly and attractively. Novels have always included their own 'stage directions' for stress and intonation (in addition to the quotation marks):

'You'd better find the money', he said menacingly.
'Leave me alone!', she screamed.

Paragraphing may help too. Long paragraphs, often with involved syntax, slow down the movement, as, for example, in the Donne sermon (page 31). Some paragraphs, as in stream-of-consciousness novels, may have very little punctuation in order not to interrupt the flow of the thought. Single-sentence paragraphs are characteristic of much advertising copy, indicating the force of the utterance and perhaps the limited attention-span of some of its readers.

There was probably no standardized system of punctuation for medieval manuscripts but (as with spelling) several systems, consistent within themselves, reflecting the scribe's training in a particular scriptorium. We shall probably never know Shakespeare's own punctuation, since the punctuation of his own drafts (his 'foul papers') would have been obscured in fair copies made for the theatre and later still by compositors in the printing house. The best texts in the First Folio seem, not surprisingly, to use a rhetorical punctuation to assist the actor in delivering his lines, indicating where significant pauses should come. Here are just two examples:

Ophelia: He hath my Lord of late, made many tenders
Of his affection to me.

(*Hamlet*, I. iii. 99)

Polonius is anxious to know how far the affair between his daughter and Hamlet has gone. But how is Ophelia to put it to her suspicious old father? She pauses (at the comma) then chooses the unfortunate phrase *made many tenders*, unfortunate since it simply leads Polonius to demonstrate his cleverness by a number of puns. In his funeral oration Antony first of all makes a statement of fact:

> The Noble Brutus,
> Hath told you Caesar was Ambitious.

> *(Julius Caesar*, III. ii. 84)

But, later in his speech, as he becomes more confident and more sarcastic, he repeats the phrase three times and it is now punctuated differently to allow for the pause before the all-important idea:

> Yet Brutus sayes, he was Ambitious.

We should realize that the punctuation of the Shakespearean texts we use is that of the modern editor, not of the Renaissance printer. It will therefore be less rhetorical and more grammatical, because we read more often than we act, and in cases of doubtful meaning the punctuation can become a form of interpretation.

Capitalization, especially of nouns, was frequently found until the middle of the eighteenth century. Question marks and exclamation marks became more common in the seventeenth century and inverted commas in the eighteenth. The eighteenth century used much more punctuation than we do, in order to reveal the grammatical structure of the sentence; every subordinate clause is apt to be marked off by commas:

> a. The man, who witnessed the accident, has disappeared.
> b. He declared, that he was innocent.

In a. we would remove the commas and take the whole NP (*The man who witnessed the accident*) as the subject, not *The man* alone. In b. we would not pause until we reached the key word *innocent*.

But P.D.E. punctuation does nevertheless aim to reveal something of the grammar of the sentence. The comma, semicolon and colon are really grammatical in intention. The semicolon indicates a stronger pause than the comma, and the full stop at the end of the sentence a stronger pause still. The colon throws the attention forward to what is to come:

> He began his speech in a forceful manner: 'If the company goes on like this, it isn't going to survive'.

Yet we also want the punctuation to be consistent as far as possible with the demands of speech, such as stress and intonation, and generally speaking our punctuation (lighter than that of the eighteenth century) does reflect the intonation of the sentence too.

Of course speech varies considerably with the occasion. When someone is reading from a prepared text the pauses come at constituent (usually grammatical) breaks in the sentence. If, however, the speaker has to think as he goes, he appears to be far less fluent. There will be more pauses and several hesitation markers (*er*, *I think*, *as I said*, *you know*, and the like). In a still fuller representation of speech, paralinguistic features, over and above what the words themselves mean, would also have to be taken into consideration, since these reveal something of the feelings and attitudes of the speaker. Some of them are related to body language (e.g. nods, shrugs, frowns) but they may instead be a variation from the speaker's normal tempo of speech, such as a more precise articulation. There seems to be a running battle between speech and writing. Speech is extremely varied and flexible; writing sometimes seems to be running hard in order to catch up.

PHONEMES OF PRESENT-DAY ENGLISH (RP)

Vowels and Diphthongs

One way to indicate the length in the vowel is to place a horizontal line above the letter, e.g. O.E. *stān*; the absence of such a line indicates that the vowel is short, e.g. O.E. *scip*. In phonetic transcription, length is indicated by dots following the letter, e.g. [e:]

My classification of vowels and diphthongs is based on Carney (1994): pp. xxi–xxii.

Short Vowels

/ɪ/	as in bit
/e/	as in bed
/æ/	as in bat
/ʊ/	as in foot
/ʌ/	as in but
/ɒ/	as in pot
/ə/	as in about

Long Counterparts of the Short Vowels

/aɪ/	as in bite
/i:/	as in bead
/eɪ/	as in make
/aʊ/	as in out
/əʊ/	as in pole

Long Vowels and Diphthongs wholly or partly associated with /r/

/a://	as in part
/ɔ:/	as in more
/ɜ:/	as in girl
/ɪə/	as in pier
/ɛə/	as in fair
/ʊə/	as in poor
/aɪə/	as in fire
/aʊə/	as in flour

Other Long Vowels and Diphthongs

/u:/	as in room
/ju:/	as in duty
/ɔɪ:/	as in boy

From Earlier English

[e:]	as in French été
[ɛ:]	as in French faire
[o:]	as in French eau

Consonants

The classification reflects the place of articulation in the speech organs. Some consonants may be paired: voiced and voiceless.

Plosives (Stops)

Voiced	/b/	as in bet	Voiceless	/p/	as in pet
Voiced	/d/	as in dot	Voiceless	/t/	as in tot
Voiced	/g/	as in gap	Voiceless	/k/	as in cap

Fricatives

Voiced	/v/	as in vine	Voiceless	/f/	as in fine
Voiced	/ð/	as in bathe	Voiceless	/θ/	as in bath
Voiced	/z/	as in zoo	Voiceless	/s/	as in sue
Voiced	/ʒ/	as in azure	Voiceless	/ʃ/	as in ship

Affricates

Voiced	/dʒ/	as in joke	Voiceless	/tʃ/	as in choke

Nasals

/m/   as in mouse
/n/   as in nine
/ŋ/   as in sing

Others

/h/   as in have
/j/   as in yet
/w/   as in was
/l/   as in lose
/r/   as in run

NOTES

1. I have found especially useful Carney (1994) and Scragg (1974).

2. Carney (1994) uses the term Southern British Standard (SBS) in preference to the socially restrictive Received Pronunciation (RP). The recent term 'Estuary English' may appeal because it is both geographically descriptive (S.E. England) and more widely-based socially.

3. There are many more examples in Brown, 1990: pp. 66–77.

EXERCISES

1. How many different phonemes can you produce by changing the individual sounds in *bed*? (Remember these are sounds, not necessarily single letters.)

2. Try to explain the 'un-English' – looking spellings of *biscuit, chord, guilt, icon, quay, receipt, storey, trolley, yoghurt*.

3. Say aloud the following sentences, first of all slowly and distinctly and then at normal speed. What changes in pronunciation take place?

It's evident that this has particularly upset him.
What an extraordinary political decision for Great Britain!
It would be marvellous if there could be a new motorway to the south of England.

4. How many different ways can you read each of these sentences?

John asked Bill and then he asked Fred.
Couldn't she have done something about a present?

Are these matters of stress, intonation or perhaps grammar?

Chapter 6

Correct Words?

There is much talk these days of Standard English and standards of English. But what do we understand by *standard*? Does it mean 'uniformity' or 'measure of value'? For many older people and most politicians it is the second. The earlier chapters of this book have indicated that, so far as vocabulary is concerned, the choice of words often depends on the field of discourse, that is, the subject-matter – whether it is 'legal', 'literary', 'bureaucratic', etc – and on its medium and attitude: is it spoken or written, formal or informal? In the case of grammar, we have seen that some of the older terminology is better suited to a description of Latin, an inflected language, than of English, a much more analytic language. One trouble is that there is often a confusion between non-standard and substandard. Non-standard should not imply blame, simply variation from the usual dimensions of linguistic acceptability (we might write different *from*, but say different *to* or different *than*). Substandard is meant to be deplored: *I dunno, innit?*, *there ain't none left*, or, in vocabulary, *grotty, lolly, nosh, wally, yob* (although these terms might be deliberately employed, by a journalist or novelist wanting to suggest a particular style of speech or behaviour). They are *slang*, normally not to be found outside colloquial speech. *Jargon*, too, departs from the usual vocabulary, but this is different again. These are the difficult words of the expert. We may understand, or at least guess at, some of them (*floppy disk, invisible exports, voice-over, software*) but others merge into an unintelligible technical vocabulary. Part of the trouble defining Standard English is, as Quirk and Stein (1990: p. 114) say, 'we tend to notice someone's use of English only when it is *not* standard', and again, 'Standard English is that kind of English which draws least attention to itself over the widest area and through the widest range of reference' (p. 123). We might, therefore, find it difficult to define just what Standard English is: we are back to the ambiguity of the word *standard*.

In the sense of 'uniformity', a type of English understood over the whole country, not regional, we soon find ourselves talking about the opposite, dialects. A **dialect** is, in the first place, more than just accent, reflecting the region we come from; dialects have special features of grammar and vocabulary too.[1] And they are not, as sometimes supposed, a corruption of Standard English. **Standard English** is itself a dialect, admittedly one believed to be socially superior, but it is a promoted form, granted preeminence for non-linguistic reasons, not for any special linguistic merit. Such reasons, as we shall see, are usually political or cultural: the standard is most often based on the dialect of the capital. We should remember, too, that non-British Englishes have their own standard usages in many respects. We would hardly condemn Americans for using *truck, fender, hood, windshield, gas, sidewalk, railroad, baggage, purse* and *candy*, as opposed to British *lorry, bumper, bonnet, windscreen, petrol, pavement, railway, luggage, handbag* and *sweets*.

STANDARDS AND DIALECT

Most of us, then, will *write* Standard English to the best of our ability, irrespective of the geographical area we hail from. Our *speech* will almost certainly include some dialectal features (especially accent) but how many features will depend on several things: how much we have moved around, our social position or our education. The result may be the difference between people saying 'You're a northener' or, more precisely, 'You come from Yorkshire'. Such features as the development of communication (through the media), the greater ease of transport, the disappearance of a predominantly rural way of life with its associated vocabulary (of farming, for example), and the multilingual population of cities, have all contributed to the decline of dialects, although a north-south distinction at least is probably apparent to most people. Trudgill (1990: p. 66) cites the northern pronunciation of *path*, with the *a* as in *cat*, with the vowel of *calm* to be heard in most of the south. We would almost certainly associate the voicing of *f* and *s* (*vrom* and *zummer*) with the south-west and it is a favourite theatrical device to indicate the simple-minded rustic.

(Incidentally, *vixen*, the comparable form to the masculine *fox*, has even entered Standard English.) Forms like *hisself, theirselves* (on the analogy of *myself*); *hisn, hern, ourn, yourn, theirn* (on the analogy of *mine*); I *reads*, we *buys*, they *sees* (the extension of the -s in he/she *reads*); the retention, from earlier English, of the second person singular forms *thou* and *thee* – all these we would term dialectal, and perhaps particularly southern and western, although in fact they extend beyond these areas. Trudgill (p. 104) has an interesting list of dialectal intensifiers replacing *very*, as in *very tasty*: *gey* (Northumbrian), *gradely* (Lancs), *right* (Central Northern), *wholly* (East), *main* (Wilts and Hants), *well* (Home Counties). How many of us could localize terms of endearment such as *hinny, love, pet, petal*?

All this may sound interesting but, to many people, somewhat removed from late twentieth-century reality. What we all have is an individual **idiolect**, a kind of linguistic fingerprint. It will include features from our place of origin (a regional or an urban dialect) but also others from occupational and social practice (occupational dialect and class dialect), and favourite personal stylistic mannerisms. Idiolect can also be useful in discussions of style in literature: the individualization of a particular character or a distinctive authorial style.

THE GROWTH OF A STANDARD

For most of the O.E. and M.E. periods, the concept of a Standard English would have seemed almost meaningless. The Angles, Saxons and Jutes (plus, probably some Frisians) who invaded Britain in the mid fifth century were organized by tribe and family. Even when smaller tribes consolidated into larger units and we can speak of dialects like Northumbrian, Mercian (the present Midlands), West Saxon and Kentish, we almost certainly simplify. The East Midlands and East Anglia are hardly represented at all in surviving records of O.E. A loose and shifting confederation of sub-kingdoms hardly constitutes political autonomy in the modern sense. Most of the surviving O.E. manuscripts are written in a form of late West Saxon. Many works (including *Beowulf*) had been composed elsewhere and were 'translated' into late West Saxon because of the political and cultural supremacy of Wessex from the late ninth century onwards. This late O.E. 'standard' probably originated in the monastic school at Winchester, an influential religious and cultural centre in the tenth century. It was a written standard only, intelligible over much of the country at the same time as the spoken dialects continued. Although O.E. manuscripts were still copied after the Conquest at some centres like Worcester, the Norman invaders saw no reason to learn O.E. The M.E. period is therefore the period of dialects *par excellence*, written as well as spoken. It begins with the decline of the 'standard' late West Saxon of O.E. and ends with the gradual rise of a new form of standard written English based on a dialect used in London. That, however, is a fifteenth- rather than a fourteenth-century phenomenon. Even at the end of the fifteenth century, there seems to be no established standard in today's sense; Caxton, in his Preface to the *Eneydos* in 1490 (see below) does not appear to realize the new status of the London dialect. And London in O.E. times would have been in the (East) Mercian dialect area, not in Wessex, so that there is no unbroken thread connecting the late West Saxon and the fifteenth-century London-based written standards.

For the M.E. period, we may, if we wish, speak of five major dialect areas, descended from the four mentioned in the discussion of O.E.

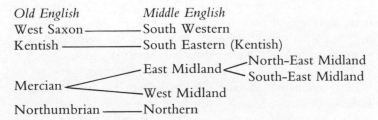

Old English   *Middle English*
West Saxon————— South Western
Kentish ——————— South Eastern (Kentish)
                                   ┌─North-East Midland
                   East Midland─┤South-East Midland
Mercian───────┤
                     West Midland
Northumbrian ———Northern

O.E. Mercian has been split into East Midland and West Midland in M.E., and East Midland can be further divided into North-East Midland and South-East Midland. These divisions are conventional, and useful up to a point, but each of these very large areas consists of a number of dialects, agreeing in the main but with some variations in detail. It is also impossible to give exact dialect boundaries since the regions merge into each other. There are genuine border areas as well: the dialect of one of the greatest M.E. poems, *Sir Gawain and the Green Knight*, probably written in Cheshire or North Staffordshire, is often called 'North-West

Midland' and contains features from both the Northern and the West Midland areas. And people moved. What would happen to the idiolect of someone who was born in one area and moved to another, like the poet William Langland, brought up near the Malvern Hills in Worcester and apparently living in London when he wrote *Piers Plowman*? Time, as well as area, is also important. M.E. conventionally extends from c. 1100 to c. 1500, four centuries. One would expect changes to occur during all that time. The language of the romance *Havelok the Dane*, probably written near Grimsby in the late thirteenth century, is, not surprisingly, more 'modern' than that of the last (mid twelfth century) entries in the *Peterborough Chronicle* from the same dialect area, but these entries are more advanced grammatically than the conservative *Ancrene Wisse* from early thirteenth-century Herefordshire.

Northern appears to have been the progressive dialect in M.E. The decay of endings characteristic of M.E. as a whole had already begun in Northumbrian O.E. Certain features of P.D.E. not found in Chaucer's London (South East Midland) dialect are recorded soonest in the North. Such are the -*s* ending of the third person singular present tense (Chaucer has -*eth*) and *are* as the plural of the present tense of 'to be' (Chaucer has *ben*). Some of these may have been affected by the extensive Scandinavian settlement of the Northern and North-East Midland regions. A true Northern dialect in M.E. will have the complete set of the *th*- forms ('they', 'them', 'their') for the third person plural personal pronoun; Chaucer uses only *they* (S) and has *hem* (O) and *hir* (Genitive).

Post-war work on late M.E. dialects in the universities of Edinburgh and Glasgow culminated in the publication in 1987 of the four volumes of the *Linguistic Atlas of Late Mediaeval English*. This has made possible a much more precise appreciation of the language situation in the period c. 1350 to c. 1450. It is based on a list of some 300 predetermined items (lexical, grammatical, phonological and simply graphic), not all found in any single text, of course. In effect the scribe of a manuscript is made to complete a kind of questionnaire. The *Atlas* contains sample analyses from 2,500 scribes, representing at least one-third of the extant M.E. corpus. The technique used was, first to fit on a map (one map for each main dialect feature) those forms from M.E. manuscripts whose location can be independently fixed by external evidence, like manorial and municipal records or legal instruments such as depositions and conveyances (although until the last quarter of the fourteenth century not very many of these are in English). These are the 'anchor' entries. Then forms corresponding to these, but from other manuscripts whose location is unknown, were added. And so on. Where the maps are densely packed (e.g. in the South-West Midlands) placings of texts of unknown provenance are probably accurate to within 10 miles. At the other extreme (for example Devon or North-West Yorks) we are speaking of 25 miles or more. We are dealing here with the dialect of the *copyist* only and we cannot know how far the manuscript represents the language of the author of the text (unless he signs it) or even how far it is a reflection of the scribe's own spoken language.[2] We must be chary of deducing the spoken from what, after all, is simply the written. Yet each of these dialects does represent an individual form of M.E.: they were read and understood.

As he approaches the end of *Troilus and Criseyde* and visualizes copies of his book being distributed, Chaucer is uneasily conscious of the diversity of English in his own day:

> And for ther is so gret diversite
> In Englissh and in writyng of oure tonge,
> So prey I God that non myswrite the,
> Ne the mysmetre for defaute of tonge.
> And red wherso thow be, or elles songe,
> That thow be understonde, God I biseche.

> V. 1793–8

(*the . . . thow*, the book *mysmetre*, get the metre wrong) but he makes no value judgement here on any one dialect being superior to another. (His *Reeve's Tale*, however, shows a comic exploitation of the Northern dialect.) Nor does Caxton, a century later, in his Preface to *Eneydos*. But John Trevisa (a Cornishman, writing in Gloucestershire) in his translation and adaptation of Ranulph Higden's *Polychronicon* does:

> Also of þe forseyde Saxon tonge, þat is deled a þre, and ys abyde
> scarslych wiþ feaw vplondysch men, and ys gret wondur, for men
> of þe est wiþ men of þe west, as hyt were vnder þe same party
> of heuene, acordeþ more in sounyng of speche þan mcn of þe
> norþ wiþ men of þe souþ. þerfore hyt ys þat Mercii, þat buþ
> men of myddel Engelond, as hyt were parteners of þe endes,

vndurstondeþ betre þe syde longages, Norþeron and Souþeron,
þan Norþeron and Souþeron vndurstondeþ eyþer oþer.

Al þe longage of þe Norþhumbres, and specialych at ʒork, ys
so scharp, slyttyng, and frotyng and vnschape, þat we Souþeron
men may þat longage vnneþe vndurstonde. Y trowe þat þat ys
bycause þat a buþ nyʒ to strange men and aliens, þat spekeþ
strangelych, and also bycause þat þe kynges of Engelond woneþ
alwey fer fram þat contray.

(Similarly with the aforementioned Saxon tongue that is divided
in three and has scarcely remained among a few country men,
and [that] is very strange, for men from the east agree more in
pronunciation with men of the west – as it were under the same
part of heaven – than men of the north do with men of the south.
And so it is that Mercians, who are men of Middle England, as
it were sharers of the extremes, understand better the adjacent
languages, Northern and Southern, than Northern and Southern
understand one another.

All the speech of the Northumbrians, and especially at York,
is so sharp, piercing, grating and formless that we Southern men
may scarcely understand that language. I think that that is because
they are close to strange men and aliens who speak like foreigners,
and also because the kings of England always live far from that
area.)

Trevisa, towards the end of the fourteenth century, has already
grasped that political power is necessary for the growth of a
standard.

London English, which later formed the basis of Standard
English, was not itself a standard in the M.E. period. There is
not very much written in a language that can properly be called
a London dialect in documents before the fourteenth century.
Fourteenth-century London manuscripts are more varied than
earlier manuscripts in subject-matter, technical skill and dialect,
but, paradoxical as it may seem, this is a sign of a developing
national centre. There was migration into London, especially from
East Anglia, in the later thirteenth and early fourteenth centuries,
and also from the central and east Midlands (Leicestershire,
Bedfordshire, Northamptonshire) in the mid fourteenth century.
London was the capital, the seat of the court, the political,
social and administrative centre of the country, the place where
things happened. Here, then, are some of the conditions for
the rise of a standard. Another was the changing status of

French. Throughout the fourteenth century many administrative documents and records, together with private communications between members of the upper classes, both lay and clerical, were still in French, as they had been in the earlier Middle Ages. But this was now a written French, often by professional scribes, a business language to be learned rather than a natural spoken tongue. Hand in hand with this decline of French went the greater use of English, largely reflecting the increasing importance of a professional merchant class and the craft guilds in the towns and, in the country, a rural proletariat (men such as Chaucer's Franklin). Towards the close of the fourteenth century, then, we can see the emergence of a class of 'lettered' laymen, of some standing, who could both read and write English, but were of (at best) limited proficiency in French. Two other factors favouring English were a certain anti-clericalism, not by any means confined to the Lollards, and a patriotism which associated national success with the vernacular: 'our' English and 'their' French. Thomas Usk, a contemporary of Chaucer, is clear about what he sees as the different provinces of the three competing languages:

> Let then clerkes endyten in Latyn, for they have the propertee of science, and the knowing in that facultee; and let Frenchmen in their Frenche also endyten their queynt termes, for it is kyndely to their mouthes; and let us shewe our fantasyes in suche wordes as we lerneden of oure dames tongue.[3]

> (Let scholars write in Latin then, since they have the advantage of learning, and knowledge in that subject; and let Frenchmen also write their elegant terms in their French, for it is natural in their mouths; and let us set out our ideas in such words as we learnt from our mother's tongue.)

After about 1430 English becomes more and more usual in documents such as records, licences, inheritance and transfer of property, and business agreements of most kinds. (Church documents continued to be written in Latin and the law contained a number of French terms.) These new documents were the products of the Chancery, a permanent civil service comprising almost all the national administration except for the Exchequer and by this time located at Westminster. By 1400 there were a hundred or more chancery clerks who lived together in houses and who trained apprentice clerks. The twelve Masters in Chancery were supervisors who were empowered to authenticate new language usages and to sign important letters.[4] Not only were there documents going out from Westminster but, as is the way of bureaucracy everywhere, these frequently demanded replies, and so eventually the replies too began to accommodate their language to the new Chancery Standard. This was a blend of late fourteenth-century London English, as used by Chaucer and Gower, and certain Wycliffite features. For a time, in the mid to late fourteenth century, there was a chance that the Wycliffite language, from the central Midlands, might have become a standard. It is used in most manuscripts of Wyclif's sermons and was spread by his followers, the Lollards, in their preaching and writing from the 1380s onwards. They held that the words of the Bible were all-sufficient for salvation and that a lack of Latinity should be no bar to understanding Christ's teaching – hence their demand for the Bible in English. Lollardy as a sect was not controlled nationwide, but the groups were aware of one another and links were forged by preachers travelling between them:

> They make unlawful conventicles and confederacies, they hold and exercise schools, they make and write books, they do wickedly instruct and inform people.[5]

Much of our knowledge of the movement comes, like this, from its opponents. There is clearly a link between literacy and political awakening: the Peasants Revolt took place in 1381. Why, then, did an incipient Wycliffite standard fail when Chancery Standard succeeded? There are perhaps two main reasons. It was simply 50 years too early, and by the early years of the fifteenth century the establishment had developed an increasing intolerance toward the Lollard movement. In 1407 Archbishop Arundel prohibited the making or the use of English translations of the Bible; there were many prosecutions and it became dangerous to own or read a bible which contained evidence of Wycliffite authorship. What influenced and cemented the spread of Chancery Standard was the introduction of printing into England by Caxton at his Westminster press in 1476, for every copy from a printing press, no matter how rudimentary, is the same as every other. Printing, therefore, is the great stabilizer of language, especially of morphology. Caxton was translator (about one-third of his printed texts were his own translations), editor, printer and publisher. As a businessman he printed what he hoped would sell. His own prologues and epilogues, particularly the Preface to the *Eneydos* (a translation of a French romance based on Virgil's *Aeneid*) in 1490, a year before he died, consider the difficulty in choosing the most acceptable form of English. He had two main concerns. The first was that of dialect differences (still, evidently, a problem); the second, and for him the more serious, was the choice of a suitable style, steering a mean between *playn rude*, 'downright ordinary' and *curyous*, 'elaborate' terms:

> For in these days every man that is in ony reputacyon in his countre wyll utter his commynycacyon and maters in suche maners and termes that fewe men shall understonde theym. And som honest and grete clerkes have ben wyth me and desired me to wryte the moste curyous termes that I coude fynde. And thus bytwene playn rude and curyous I stande abasshed.[6]

(his commynycacyon, what he has to say)

What to do about *curyous* terms will exercise later Renaissance writers, although in their case the words will be Latin rather than French borrowings. Once English had developed a written standard – a spoken standard came some time later – and once its vocabulary had been greatly expanded in the late Middle Ages and the Renaissance, there is a natural demand for a definition of that standard, a yardstick of whether people are using their native language correctly or not. The growth of English dictionaries was a response to this need.

DICTIONARIES

Why do we consult a dictionary? Mostly, I imagine, to discover the meaning or the spelling of a word. Sometimes for reassurance – confirmation or clarification of what we are almost (but not quite) sure is the correct answer – and sometimes to satisfy a wish for authoritative guidance on usage, what is (or is not) allowed in English.[7] Interestingly enough, we speak of 'looking it up in *the* dictionary', as if there were only one, but of course there are very many dictionaries, some general, others reflecting special interests: dictionaries of music, say, or of literary terms. Today, and throughout the centuries, dictionaries have both responded to people's need for information *and* reflected the contemporary feeling of what Standard English should be.

The first dictionary to be printed in England, by Wynkyn
de Worde, Caxton's successor, in 1499, was the *Promptorium
Parvulorum sive Clericum*, designed to help children with their
Latin. It was the first of its kind (there had been earlier lists
of difficult words) to give the English word first and its Latin
equivalent second. There were, too, explanatory glossaries printed
as appendices to some later sixteenth-century books: Speght's 1602
glossary to his edition of Chaucer has some 300 entries. From
Caxton onwards, there was a growing interest in the use of English
in literature (remember his discussion of what style to use) and
also an increasing number of translations of foreign works. As a
result of the Renaissance borrowing of 'inkhorn' terms (pp. 29),
there were obviously more words needing elucidation. All this
produced a climate favourable to dictionary making. Once again,
it was Mulcaster who identified the need:

> It were a thing verie praiseworthie in my opinion, and no lesse
> profitable then praise worthie, if som one well learned and as
> laborious a man, wold gather all the words which we vse in
> our English tung, whether naturall or incorporate, out of all
> professions, as well learned as not, into one dictionarie, and
> besides the right writing, which is incident to the Alphabete,
> wold open vnto vs therin, both their naturall force, and their
> proper vse: that by his honest trauell we might be as able to iudge
> of our own tung, which we haue by rote, as we ar of others,
> which we learn by rule. The want whereof, is the onelie cause
> why, that verie manie men, being excellentlie well learned in foren
> speche, can hardlie discern what theie haue at home, still shooting
> fair, but oft missing far, hard censors ouer other, ill executors
> themselues.
>
> (*The First Part of the Elementarie* (1582).[8])

It is not surprising, then, that the early English dictionaries
concentrated on *hard* words. The title page of what is usually
regarded as the first real English dictionary, *A Table Alphabeticall*,
1604, by Robert Cawdrey (a schoolmaster) advertises its purpose:

> A Table Alphabeticall, conteyning and teaching the true writing,
> and understanding of hard usuall English wordes, borrowed from
> the Hebrew, Greeke, Latine, or French, etc.
> With the interpretation thereof by plaine English words, gathered
> for the benefit and helpe of Ladies, Gentlewomen, or any other
> unskilfull persons.

> Whereby they may the more easilie and better understand many
> hard English wordes, which they shall heare or read in Scriptures,
> Sermons, or elswhere, and also be made able to use the same aptly
> themselves.

His dictionary has some 1,500 entries, several of them with only
a one or two word definition (e.g. *fallacie*, deceit, falshood;
malcontent, discontented; *rigorous*, cruell, and hard). The first surprise on encountering Cawdrey may well be what a slim volume
it is. His may be the first name to occur in most accounts of the
growth of the English dictionary, but he is hardly original. He
drew heavily on Edmund Coote's *English Schoolemaster* (1596),
which included a grammar and prayer book as well as a list of 'hard
words', and Thomas Thomas's *Dictionarium Linguae et Anglicanae*,
a Latin-English dictionary of 1588. John Bullokar's *An English
Expositor* (1616), with almost twice as many words as Cawdrey,
contained 'old words gone out of use' as well as hard words.
We may remember that the reinstatement of these old words
was one of the strategies for increasing the English vocabulary
put forward by those who objected to excessive borrowing from
classical languages. Many more dictionaries appeared in the seventeenth century. Their titles and title pages show that they were still
responding to a demand for definitions of hard words from those
born on the wrong side of the linguistic tracks: Thomas Blount
says that his *Glossographia* (1616) is 'chiefly intended for the more-
knowing Women and the less-knowing Men' and Edward Phillips
calles his dictionary the *New World of Words* (1658). Some, like
Henry Cockeram, *The English Dictionarie* (1623), the first to use
the word 'Dictionary' in its title, extend the appeal of the dictionary
towards that of the encyclopaedia, including some mythology and the
pseudo-science of beasts and birds. Some of the definitions offered are
entertainingly fanciful, e.g. Blount's *Hony-Moon*: 'applyed to those
married persons that love well at first and decline in affection
afterwards: it is hony now, but it will change as the moon'.

Gradually a change came over the concept of a dictionary, to
include more usual words and correspondingly fewer 'hard' ones.
Possibly the first to qualify as a complete dictionary in our terms
was Nathan Bailey's *The Universal Etymological English Dictionary*
of 1721. There were 24 editions by 1782 and its reputation was
high: Mrs Western in Fielding's *Tom Jones* exclaims 'Will you
never learn a proper use of words? Indeed, child, you should

consult Bailey's Dictionary'. *A proper use of words*: the dictionaries of the first half of the eighteenth century were regarded as a way of regulating the language, or, to use a favourite word of theirs, *ascertaining* it (*ascertain* meaning not 'find out about' but 'fix' it, establish it against decay).[9] Dictionaries, it was thought, could settle disputes about spelling and usage, eradicate improprieties, and in general act as a kind of watchdog over the language (Millward, 1988: p. 209). There was a call for an English Academy, on the lines of the Accademia della Crusca (established 1582) and the Académie Française (1635); the latter had actually produced a dictionary in 1694. Such an Academy could pronounce on the virtues – and, more often, the vices – of points of English usage. The idea was supported by Defoe, Swift and Addison among others, and was much discussed in the coffee houses and salons of the time. The title of Swift's letter to the Earl of Oxford is 'A Proposal for Correcting, Improving and Ascertaining the English Tongue' (1712). The court, says Swift, is no use as an arbiter of correctness in English and has not been since the Restoration: 'the Court, which used to be the Standard of Propriety and Correctness of Speech, was then, and, I think, hath ever since continued the worst School in England for that Accomplishment'. Much better to have a committee of 'such Persons, as are generally allowed to be best qualified for such a Work' (it seems to be self-evident to Swift who these persons should be; at any rate he doesn't give names, except for the noble Earl himself) who

> should assemble at some appointed Time and Place, and fix
> on Rules by which they design to proceed . . . . Beside the
> Grammar-part, wherein we are allowed to be very defective, they
> will observe many gross Improprieties, which however authorised
> by Practice, and grown familiar, ought to be discarded. They will
> find many Words that deserve to be utterly thrown out of our
> Language, many more to be corrected; and perhaps not a few,
> long since antiquated, which ought to be restored, on account of
> their Energy and Sound.
>
> But what I have most at heart is, that some Method should
> be thought on for *ascertaining* and *fixing* our Language for ever,
> after such Alterations are made in it as shall be thought requisite.
> For I am of Opinion, that it is better a Language should not be
> wholly perfect, than that it should be perpetually changing; and we
> must give over at one Time, or at length infallibly change for the
> worse.[10]

Latin, of course, is the standard of excellence. Although some (like Swift) recognized that English is unlike Latin in its structure, they do not seem to have accepted the consequences, that you cannot really model English on Latin.

Plans for a large dictionary as part of this scheme were actually drawn up c. 1718, but they – like the Academy itself – failed to materialize. But in 1747 Warburton was still making the same complaint as Swift:

> [The English tongue] is yet destitute of a Test or Standard to apply to, in cases of doubt or difficulty . . . For we have neither Grammar nor Dictionary, neither Chart nor Compass, to guide us through this wide sea of words.[11]

In the same year there appeared Samuel Johnson's *Plan of a Dictionary*:

> . . . a dictionary by which the pronunciation of our language may be fixed, and its attainment facilitated; by which its purity may be preserved, its use ascertained, and its duration lengthened.[12]

Johnson worked on his dictionary from 1747 until its appearance in 1755, from his thirty-seventh to his forty-sixth year. He had very little help, only six amanuenses (five of them Scotsmen!) to whom he was very kind when they fell on bad times. He was regularly chivvied by his publishers, wanting to see some return for the money they had paid to him and which Johnson had of course spent. His dictionary was not the largest in sheer number of words, weighing in at some 40,000 (Bailey had 48,000 in 1730, 60,000 in 1736, and 65,000 in 1755), but in the eyes of his contemporaries Johnson had produced a work to 'fix', 'ascertain', and generally stabilize the language. It also represented genuine English individualism against the impressive, but corporate, productions of the French and Italian academies. Yet, as he worked, Johnson began to see that the idea was impossible. His *Preface*, written last in 1755 and a work well worth reading in itself, shows his change of view:

> Those who have been persuaded to think well of my design, require that it should fix our language and put a stop to those alterations which time and chance have hitherto been suffered to make in it without opposition. With this consequence I will confess that I flattered myself for a while; but now begin to fear that I have indulged expectation which neither reason nor experience can justify.[13]

His fallback position is that he should resist, as far as possible, what he thought to be the imperfections of English (he is actually speaking here about spelling, but he conceived his mission to be wider than this):

> Every language has its anomalies, which, though inconvenient, and in themselves once unnecessary, must be tolerated among the imperfections of human things, and which require only to be registred, that they may not be increased, and ascertained, that they may not be confounded: but every language has likewise its improprieties and absurdities, which it is the duty of the lexicographer to correct or proscribe.

His Dictionary is a terrific one man work, by any standards. The conclusion to the *Preface* shows him as modest about it as he was about anything:

> Thus have I laboured to settle the orthography, display the analogy, regulate the structures, and ascertain the signification of English words, to perform all the parts of a faithful lexicographer: but I have not always executed my own scheme, or satisfied my own expectations. The work, whatever proofs of diligence and attention it may exhibit, is yet capable of many improvements: the orthography which I recommend is still controvertible, the etymology which I adopt is uncertain, and perhaps frequently erroneous; the explanations are sometimes too much contracted, and sometimes too much diffused, the significations are distinguished rather with subtilty than skill, and the attention is harrassed with unnecessary minuteness.

In a letter to Francesco Sastres, written near the end of his life, Johnson ruefully remarks that, 'Dictionaries are like watches, the worst is better than none, and the best cannot be expected to go quite true'.[14] One can have great fun paging through Johnson, as one can with any good dictionary. He includes several unusual words, for example

adscititious,   additional
faddle (verb),   trifle, toy
foody,   eatable, fit for food
maundle (verb),   grumble
nidget,   coward

snudge (verb),   lie close or snug

swaggy,   hanging down because of its weight

but omits most occupational jargon which he regarded as evanescent. Nor does the word *slang* occur in the Dictionary. The eighteenth century, however, had a taste for cant words, especially the language of rogues and vagabonds. Gay's *Beggar's Opera*, 1728, is perhaps the best-known example, and Bailey includes them (as well as some taboo words). Johnson's prejudices emerge most humorously in his definitions:

excise,   a hateful tax levied upon commodities, and adjudged not by the common judges of property, but by wretches hired by those to whom the excise is paid.

oats,   a grain which in England is generally given to horses, but in Scotland supports the people.

opera,   an exotic and irrational entertainment.

lexicographer, a writer of dictionaries, a harmless drudge.

In fact there are fewer such entries than is sometimes implied. Not surprisingly, however, there are some typical eighteenth-century meanings:

enthusiasm   1. a vain confidence of divine favour or communication;
                2. heat of imagination, violence of passion;
                3. elevation of fancy, exaltation of ideas.

gossip   1. One who answers for the child in baptism [i.e. a godparent];
                2. A tippling companion;
                3. One who runs about tattling like women at a lying-in.

penthouse   A shed hanging out aslope from the main wall.

He recognized that the simplest words can be among the most difficult to define and that the definition may end up more complicated than the word itself:

fit,   paroxysm.

network,   any thing reticulated or decussated, at equal distances, with interstices between the intersections.

rust,   the red desqamation of old iron.

Yet many of the questions Johnson raises are those the lexicographer still needs to ask. The core of any dictionary entry is
the *headword* (or *lemma*), with its denotational meaning to follow
(a paraphrase of the headword). But how many compound
words should be included and should they have separate entries?
Johnson includes compounds only if they have different meanings
from their separate components. He therefore lists *woodman* and
highwayman, whose meanings are not transparent (a highwayman
could simply be walking along the highway) but not *coachdriver*
which is self-explanatory. He says he has been careful to list and
define common phrasal verbs (*give over*, *set off*, etc.) since they
can be a special problem for foreigners. What about idioms? The
answer must surely be, as many of those in regular use as the
size of the volume allows. Or slang? Johnson did not like it,
but the most recent (1993) edition of the Shorter Oxford English
Dictionary includes *fab*, *brill* and *naff*; even if these disappear, the
dictionary will stand as a record of past usage. Most difficult of all,
perhaps, is the business of labelling words. Johnson, in his desire
to resist, so far as possible, what he saw as the imperfections of
English, has several labels: *proper* or *improper* 300 times, *low* 217
times, *wrong*, *vulgar* or *inelegant* quite often. Later dictionaries use
ones like *obsolete*, *archaic*, *dialectal*, *literary*, *technical* and *colloquial*,
but the last of these can prove to be difficult: what was colloquial
in 1990 can be quite acceptable in the standard language three or
four years later. A label such as *slang* introduces judgements about
social values, and ones involving matters of sex or race may be
more dangerous still. Even the designation *Americanism* may be
viewed in some quarters as a threat to the English language.

Johnson was the first to make systematic use of illustrative
quotations in an English dictionary. The provision of these to
illustrate historical development of meaning in a word is one of
the greatest advantages of the *OED*. Johnson does not go so far,
and he gives only the author's name, with no specific reference to
an individual work or an act or scene of a Shakespeare play (simply
Pope or *King Lear*). He thought the language of the Elizabethan
period the purest English:

> From the authours which rose in the time of Elizabeth, a speech
> might be formed adequate to all the purposes of use and elegance.
> If the language of theology were extracted from Hooker and the
> translation of the Bible; the terms of natural knowledge from

Bacon; the phrases of policy, war, and navigation from Raleigh; the dialect of poetry and fiction from Spenser and Sidney; and the diction of common life from Shakespeare, few ideas would be lost to mankind, for want of English words, in which they might be expressed.

although Swift, Dryden, Butler (*Hudibras*) and Addison are all well represented. He does not quote from living writers. Shakespeare and the *Authorized Version* have always been among the best-recorded works and so have figured prominently in later dictionaries. The second edition of the *OED* (1989) has indeed been criticized for perpetuating the habit of the first edition and giving too great prominence to literary usage. Johnson is weakest in indicating pronunciation, doing no more than marking the accentuation. Later eighteenth-century dictionaries, such as those of Sheridan and Walker, attempted to remedy this. The problem of pronunciation is still a very real one for the lexicographer. The second edition of *OED* (hereafter *OED 2*) uses the IPA alphabet, whereas *OED 1* had devised its own system. Even so, dictionaries usually indicate only the pronunciation of the word in isolation, not in connected speech with a change of stress pattern and resultant change of pronunciation. Should dictionaries record common alternative pronunciations, such as /ˈaɪðə/ and /ˈiːðə/ for *either* or /əˈgɛn/ and /əˈgeɪn/ for *again*? The better dictionaries do this.

Johnson's *Dictionary* was generally welcomed on its appearance, but the obituaries (he died in 1794) and the early biographies of Johnson show a rather more critical tone, especially from those who were themselves planning new dictionaries. His work on grammar and pronunciation, which were not prime areas of interest for him, was blamed for its incompleteness; he was even castigated for importing 'long-tailed, worm-like words into our language'. But the *Dictionary* was generally accepted as authoritative in the main, even if lacking in some respects. However, a century on, talk about Johnson having fixed the form of the language and settled the proper use of words (both of which he had come to see as impossible) sounded less impressive. By the mid nineteenth century historical linguistics was beginning to be established as a science, largely on the basis of much detailed work by German scholars. The age was one of evolutionary science, the period of Darwin. Two papers given to the Philological Society by

Dean Trench in 1857 show the changing conception of a dictionary, away from prescription towards inclusiveness:

> A dictionary . . . is an inventory of the language . . . It is no task of the maker of it to select the *good* words of a language . . . He is an historian of it, not a critic. Where he counts words to be needless, affected, pedantic, ill put-together, contrary to the genius of the language, there is no objection to his saying so . . . but . . . he is bound to record them. [15]

The original intention, following Trench's criticisms, had been to publish a supplement to the standard dictionaries of the time, but this was soon seen to be inadequate. Hence the title of the *New English Dictionary On Historical Principles* (*NED*) proposed in 1858. An army of voluntary readers was recruited and directions were sent out to them:

> Make a quotation for *every* word that strikes you as rare, obsolete, old-fashioned, new, peculiar, or used in a peculiar way. Take special note of passages which show or imply that a word is either new and tentative, or needing explanation as obsolete or archaic, and which thus help to fix the date of its introduction or disuse. Make *as many* quotations *as you can* for ordinary words, especially when they are used significantly, and tend by the context to explain or suggest their own meaning. [16]

The slips on which the quotations were recorded (there were one and three-quarters *tons* by 1879) were evaluated by assistant editors. The sheer size of the operation made progress much slower than envisaged and the first fascicle (section), *A – Ant*, was not published until 1884. The complete *Dictionary*, covering more than 400,000 words and phrases in about 15,500 pages, was finished in 1928. It had become more reliable during the course of publication (it was published alphabetically) as more sources were examined more carefully. For instance, the Early English Text Society was founded in 1864 and gradually provided reliable texts of early works; it had not been possible for previous dictionaries to be sure how long a word had been in the language nor what had been its original sense. Yet any dictionary is fighting helplessly against the ever-increasing vocabulary of the language, and in 1933 a *Supplement* to the *OED* recorded many additions, especially in scientific vocabulary and colloquialisms. There was also in 1933 a corrected reissue of the whole and the title was changed to the

Oxford English Dictionary. After a gap of 24 years, work began again in 1957 and four more supplements (incorporating the single 1933 supplement) were published between 1972 and 1986. The second edition of the whole, *OED 2*, integrating the supplements, was published in 1989, in 20 volumes containing 290,500 entries.

Its scope is enormous. There is nothing like it in other languages. It aims to give the history and signification of words now in use or known to have been in use since the middle of the twelfth century. Since, as we have seen, there was no standard written English before the fifteenth century, it perforce contains M.E. dialect words. If a word has been used after 1150 (even if it became obsolete) its history is traced back to its earliest recorded form; much of O.E. is therefore included as well. Single words, common compound words and phrases, important affixes, and also variant and obsolete forms of these 'main' words (as *OED 2* calls them) are listed alphabetically. Less frequent derivatives are included under the main word which forms the first element. The treatment of a 'main' word comprises:

I. 1. The usual form in its typical modern spelling (alternative spellings are given if both are in current use, e.g. *inflection* and *inflexion*).
    2. Pronunciation (in IPA for *OED2*)
    3. The part of speech.
    4. Specification or subject label, e.g. *colloquial, figurative, obsolete, technical*.
    5. Principal earlier forms or spellings.
    6. Inflexions (e.g. plurals of nouns and principal parts of verbs).
II. Etymology, including cognate forms from related languages.
III. Meaning. The developing order of senses, illustrated by dated quotations, in chronological sequence and the original spellings (Shakespeare is quoted from the First Folio of 1623).

OED 2 has become less literary in its bias than *OED 1*. The typical early readers for *OED 1* were cultured and educated in the classics; the editors lamented their refusal to include common words on their slips. *OED 2* reflects wide reading in popular as well as in standard sources, 'from Shakespeare to Melody Maker', as its brochure claims. Not only have compounds increased enormously in number during the intervening years, so have phrasal verbs (*measure up to*, *meet up with*) and longer phrases (*put on an act*, *take a dim view of*). What, indeed, constitutes a single unit in the English vocabulary? There are some surprises in datings: *juvenile delinquency* was used by a judge in 1818 and *juvenile delinquent* appears in *Oliver Twist* (1837).[17] Earlier first datings of known words appear regularly and some of the *OED 1* listings have been corrected in *OED 2*.[18]

In contrast to *OED*, we might look briefly at a single-volume modern dictionary which does not claim to be historical in its approach and does not include obsolete, dialectal or highly technical words. This is the *Collins Cobuild English Language Dictionary*, published in 1987. The opening sentence to the Guide to the Use of the Dictionary sets the tone: 'This dictionary is written in ordinary, everyday English'. Definitions are simple and straightforward: for nouns,' A/An X is . . .', for transitive verbs, 'If you X something, you . . .'. Examples are given of typical contexts, collocations or grammatical structures for the particular word. These are mostly taken from the Birmingham University corpus of present-day English, so that they have an air of reality, not of 'made up' sentences: English in use. There are separate entries for common phrasal verbs (*get across*, *get ahead*, *get along*, *get around to*, etc.), for common compounds (such as *immersion-heater*, *package deal*), and for abbreviations and acronyms (*a.m.*, *e.g.*, *i.e.*; *AIDS*, *NATO*). Derived words appear within the main entry: under *touchy* we also find *touchiness*.[19] Pronunciation is RP in IPA symbols. The main entry also cites the plural form of nouns; the comparative and superlative of adjectives; the third person singular present tense, the present participle, the past tense and the past participle of verbs, even of regular verbs. An interesting innovation is a right-hand column which, opposite the entry, provides abbreviated grammar notes and semantic relationships of the word (e.g. synonyms or antonyms – opposite *amateur* also occurs *professional*). This is a dictionary for both native and non-native speakers of English.

Dictionaries today are very conscious of the needs of their users, as, to be fair, some of the seventeenth-century 'hard word' dictionaries also were. New technology is regularly being exploited. There is a greater variety of typefaces, resulting in easier access. Multicolour printing, now becoming cheaper, part in the future. *OED 2* is also available on disk. therefore be easily organized; updatings and even ne can be produced more quickly. *OED 3* is planned for dictionaries move with the times in another way. In a perceptive review of the 1993 *New Shorter Oxford English D* (*Times Literary Supplement*, 22 April 1994), David Noke finds that, in its search for living and dynamic Modern English, its innovations 'present a world of consumerism and designer names'; *dacron, fax, megabyte* and *yuck* are in, but several pre-1700 words are out, unless they were used by a few major authors. Quotations are apt to be from Len Deighton and Jilly Cooper rather than from Chaucer and Milton. How much can you put between one pair of covers (or in this case two stout volumes) at a price the public will pay? Whether we consult it for detailed information about points of language or merely as a help in solving the crossword or the arbiter in a game of Scrabble, the dictionary is trying to become more user-friendly.

LATIN AND A UNIVERSAL LANGUAGE

During the seventeenth century there had been an enormous expansion of trade with the new world: North America, the West Indies and the Far East. One consequence of this was that people became more aware of how many different languages there were. This coincided with the spread of scientific knowledge. The Royal Society was founded in 1660; just over a century later (1768) work began on the *Encyclopaedia Brittanica*. Medieval Europe had had a kind of universal language in the form of medieval Latin. Might there now be a truly universal language for the eighteenth century? Not simply universal *characters*, like mathematical symbols or musical notation, but a completely new language to be based on a new scientific classification of reality. It would not supersede existing languages, but would facilitate international communication. It was believed that from the Creation until the fall of the Tower of Babel 'the whole earth was of one language and of one speech' (*Genesis* xi). As a punishment for man's presumption in seeking to build a tower 'whose top may reach unto heaven', God destroyed the tower and dispersed its builders:

> Therefore is the name of it called Babel [i.e. Confusion]; because
> the Lord did there confound the language of all the earth: and
> from thence did the Lord scatter them abroad upon the face of all
> the earth.
>
> (xi. 9)

Perhaps it was now time to set things right again? The renewed call for a universal language was much discussed in Paris in the 1630s. By the early eighteenth century, in England, the talk was more of a universal *English* and this standard of English was to be achieved by removing the old Germanic roughness to reveal the beauty of its Latin elements:

> The English Language is not capable of a much greater perfection
> than it has already attained. We have trafficked in every country
> for the enriching of it . . . We have laid aside all our harsh antique
> words and retained only those of good sound and energy; the
> most beautiful polish is at length given to our tongue and its
> Teutonic rust quite worn away.[20]

George Campbell, in his *Philosophy of Rhetoric* (1776) uses the same metaphor:

> It is by carefully filing off all roughnesses and inequalities that
> languages, like metals, must be polished.[21]

Furthermore, if the English language could be fixed, the best writers could always be read. Waller lamented in 1693:

> Poets that Lasting Marble seek,
> Must carve in Latin or in Greek:
> We write in Sand . . .
>
> (*Of English Verse*)

Pope, more specifically, looked back to the greatest writer of the previous generation and feared that, all too soon, 'such as Chaucer is shall Dryden be'.

In fact, praise for the virtues of Latin diction was not quite universal. Richard Flecknoe, writing in 1665, saw little international future for English, or for Latin either:

> . . . and lastly for *Latine* and *English* (to tell you true) they
> only served me to stop holes with; the *English* Language
> out of our Dominions being like our *English* money current

with much adoe in neighbouring Countries who traffick
with us, but farther off you must go to *Banquiers* of your
own Nation, or none will take it of your hands. And for
Latin, it being no where a Vulgar Language, but the *Sacred*
and *Erudite* Tongue, take even the Clergy and Schoolmen
themselves (whose proper Language it ought to be) out of
the *Church* or *Schools*, and you cannot doe them a greater
displeasure, than speak Latin to them, so as it rather serves
to *interlard* other Languages, than to make an intire meal
of discourse, and but upon great necessity is never to be
used.[22]

Contrast this with the optimism about the future of English almost
two centuries on, in 1850:

At present the prospects of the English language are the most
splendid that the world has ever seen. It is spreading in each
of the quarters of the globe by fashion, by emigration, and by
conquest. The increase of population alone in the two great states
of Europe and America in which it is spoken, adds to the number
of its speakers in every year that passes, a greater amount than the
whole number of those who speak some of the literary languages
of Europe, either Swedish, or Danish, or Dutch. It is calculated
that before the lapse of the present century, a time that so many
now alive will live to witness, it will be the native and vernacular
language of about one hundred and fifty millions of human
beings.[23]

Perhaps the most interesting – and certainly the most outspoken –
advocate of English at the expense of the classical languages was
the Dorset poet William Barnes (1801–86):

English has become a more mongrel speech by the needless
inbringing of words from Latin, Greek, and French, instead of
words which might have been found in its older form, or in the
speech of landfolk over all England, or might have been formed
from its own roots and stems, as wanting words have been formed
in German and other purer tongues.[24]

Barnes, successively solicitor's clerk, schoolmaster, clergyman,
and both a linguist and philologist, put his theories into practice
in his Dorset poems (which were admired by Hopkins and
Thomas Hardy). He advocated, like the Renaissance opponents of
'inkhorn' terms, the substitution of compounds coined from O.E.

elements for Latin and Greek borrowings: 'When the railway was taken into the hands of more learned men', *terminus* was used instead of '*rail-end*, or *way-end*, or *outending*'. Likewise *speechcraft* should replace 'grammar', *rimecraft* 'arithmetic', *mindsight* 'imagination', *birdlore* 'ornithology' and *workstead* 'laboratory'; in the quotation above he uses *inbringing*, not 'importation' and *landfolk*, not 'people'. But Latin was too firm a part of the English vocabulary to be dislodged, and the eighteenth century had strengthened its position. And if the demand for an English Academy had made no real progress, that for an authoritative dictionary of English fared better. Although, as we have seen, Johnson himself had reservations about what he had achieved, many people believed that his Dictionary had supplied the need.

A STANDARD FOR GRAMMAR

There was a similar search for an authoritative grammar of English. One of the most influential grammars of the second half of the eighteenth century was Robert Lowth's *A Short Introduction to English Grammar* (1762) which went through 22 editions and was still influencing teaching well into the nineteenth century. Lowth begins his Preface with a tribute to the advances English has made during the preceeding two hundred years – but not, unfortunately, in 'Grammatical accuracy'. The trouble, he believes, is the relative simplicity of English grammar in comparison with that of other languages. It is so simple that we scarcely bother about it ('It is not the Language but the practice, that is at fault'.) Authors should be able to express themselves with 'propriety and accuracy', but often they do not. What is needed is a list of Rules:

> The principal design of a Grammar of any Language is to teach us to express ourselves with propriety in that Language, and to enable us to judge of every phrase and form of construction, whether it be right or not. The plain way of doing this is, to lay down rules, and to illustrate them by examples. But beside showing what is right, the matter may be further explained by pointing out what is wrong. (p. 97)[25]

For many eighteenth-century writers, then, grammar is a set of rules existing outside the patterns and usage of English. Rules could be established by the operation of reason and logic. This is in just the same spirit as those who wanted an English Academy. There is little or no room for variation: an expression which is wrong in one case must therefore be wrong in all cases. There is little attempt to distinguish between written and spoken English (written English is the norm) and change in language never seems to be regarded as an improvement. Lowth, however, is occasionally more sensible than we might expect. On verbs: 'it seems better in practice to consider the first [kind] in *-ed* [our weak verbs] as the only Regular form, and the others as deviations from it' (p. 83). He allows that sentences may sometimes end with a preposition, although placing it before the noun or pronoun, (e.g. 'the man to whom . . .') 'is more graceful, as well as more perspicious, and agrees much better with the solemn and elevated Style' (p. 128). His nine parts of speech – Articles, Nouns (Substantives), Pronouns, Adjectives, Verbs, Adverbs, Prepositions, Conjunctions, Interjections – are categories we still use. He sees that connectives are important for the free and logical flow of thought:

> The Connective parts of Sentences are of all others the most important, and require the most care and attention: for it is by these chiefly that the train of thought, the course of reasoning, and the whole progress of the mind in continued discourse of all kinds, is laid open; and on the right use of these the perspicuity, that is, the first and greatest beauty, of style principally depends. (p. 138)

Two things, I think, offend us in Lowth and the other grammarians who think as he does. The first, and more important, is the firm distinctions they make, often on grounds of analogy:

> *He is better than I* (right) v. *He is better than me* (wrong), because the extended form is 'He is better than *I am*'.
> *whether I want to or not* (right) v. *whether I want to or no* (wrong), because the extended form is 'whether I want to *or do not want to*.'
> *thereabout* (right) v. *thereabouts* (wrong). There is no such word as *abouts* in English.
> *It is I* (right) v. *It is me* (wrong), oblivious of the fact that the second might be more emphatic (cf. French *c'est moi*).
> *different from* (right) v. *different to* or *different than* (wrong). One distinguishes *from* and compares *to*.

> In the first person *shall* is the simple future and *will* promises
> or threatens. In the second and third persons *shall* promises or
> threatens and *will* is the simple future.

Likewise the distinction between *lie* (intransitive) and *lay* (transitive) and the condemnation of the double negative (which had been a useful device of emphasis in earlier English). The second annoying feature of Lowth's *Grammar* is the habit of pointing out, in the Notes at the foot of the page, 'errors' in the grammar of major writers, including not only Bacon, Dryden and Pope but also the Authorized Version and even Shakespeare (who, as the American Noah Webster patronisingly said later, 'was a man of little learning, and although, when he wrote the popular language of his day, his use of words was tolerably correct, yet whenever he attempted a style beyond that, he often fell into the grossest improprieties').[26]

There were a few exceptions to all this misapplied vigour. The greatest is Joseph Priestley's *The Rudiments of English Grammar* of 1761, the year before Lowth. Priestley was a chemist and so possibly more disposed to examine the facts and usage of English than to proceed in a dogmatic manner. His is the spirit of Locke, at the close of the seventeenth century, for whom language is an aspect of behaviour, the form and meaning of which are largely determined by convention. Priestley's *Preface* rejects calls for the establishment of an Academy and goes beyond the hallowed appeals to authorities and analogies to invoke custom as the final arbiter:

> . . . the best and the most numerous authorities have been
> carefully followed. Where they have been contradictory, recourse
> hath been had to analogy, as the last resource: For if this should
> decide for neither of two contrary practices, the thing must remain
> undecided, till all-governing custom shall declare in favour of the
> one or the other.[27]

(p. vii)

Priestley's full title is *The Rudiments of English Grammar adapted to the Use of Schools with Observations on Style,* and he proceeds by question and answer: 'What is a NOUN?', 'What are the COMPOUND TENSES of verbs?', 'What is SYNTAX?'. His Notes are not condemnations of the language of great writers but elaborations of the main text, to be used at the discretion of the teacher. He does have rules (or, as he is apt to say, uses) but he is never as censorious as Lowth. Whereas, for Lowth, *You* (singular) *was* is 'an enormous solecism', Priestley says mildly 'ought not the verb . . . to be plural too?' His list of the parts of speech is the same as Lowth's, minus the Articles. They are all defined and examples given. He includes a section on Derivation (i.e. affixation) and has a useful appendix of 'Verbs irregularly inflected' (mostly strong verbs). Priestley's *Grammar* is much more of a reference book than Lowth's. But he also provides, towards the end, some Observations on Style, in which he allows for considerable variation, both in subject-matter and the personality of the writer. He contrasts language and science:

> Language partakes much of the nature of *art* and but little of the nature of *science*; both because improvements in language have their *ne plus ultra*, and because it is a thing not exempt from the influence of fashion and caprice: whereas true science is the same in all places, and in all times, and admits of unbounded improvements.

> (p. 58)

He ends with several illustrative extracts as 'Examples of English Composition', ranging from the simplicity of the Authorized Version to Bolingbroke's *Idea of a Patriot King* and in verse from Pope's *Essay on Man* to Wolsey's soliloquy on his fall, 'Farewell, a long farewell to all my greatness', from Shakespeare's *Henry VIII*.

No doubt many eighteenth-century grammars helped some of their readers to achieve a kind of prestige which distinguished them from ordinary folk. With the growth of education in the nineteenth century, the middle class sought to be separated from the lower classes. So the 'rule-based' grammars of the nineteenth century added condemnations of the split infinitive and made the ending of sentences with a preposition into another forbidden practice. We are of course now more sympathetic to Priestley or to George Campbell's definition of usage as 'present, national and reputable use' (*Philosophy of Rhetoric*, 1776) than to Lowth's strictures. But if Lowth and his successors are too prohibitive and dogmatic for our taste, the demand for rules for the teaching of grammar is still strong and later linguistic theory has not yet supplied a simple and agreed model instead.

NOTES

1. Kastovsky has some brief but useful remarks on dialect in *Cambridge History* I, pp. 292–3.

2. '. . . the works of the *Gawain*-poet were copied not far from where, on other grounds (lexis, rhymes, knowledge of local topography) we would expect him to have lived', *Atlas* I pp. 23–24.

3. Quoted (p. 349) in R. Berndt, 'The Period of the Final Decline of French in Medieval England (Fourteenth and Early Fifteenth Centuries)', *Zeitschrift für Anglistik und Amerikanistik* 20 (1972) pp. 341–69.

4. J. H. Fisher, 'Chancery Standard and Modern Written English', *Journal of the Society of Archivists* 6 (1979): pp. 136–44.

5. Quoted by M. Aston, *Lollards and Reformers* (London: The Hambledon Press, 1984), p. 198.

6. N. F. Blake, *Caxton's Own Prose* (London: Andre Deutsch, 1973), p. 80.

7. A good introduction to dictionaries and their uses is R. Ilson (Ed.), *Dictionaries, Lexicography and Language Learning* (Oxford: Pergamon Press, 1985). For early dictionaries, see J. Schafer, *Early Modern English Lexicography*, 2 vols (Oxford: Oxford University Press, 1989).

8. R. Mulcaster, p. 166.

9. Johnson defines *ascertainment* as 'a settled rule, an established standard'.

10. Compare Lord Chesterfield (to whom Johnson's *Plan of a Dictionary* was addressed:

> I had long lamented that we had no lawful standard of our language set up, for those to repair to, who might chuse to speak and write it grammatically and correctly; and I have as long wished that either some one person of distinguished abilities would undertake the work singly, or that a certain number of gentlemen would form themselves, or be formed by the government, into a society for that purpose.
>
> *The World*, 28 November 1754

Swift's *Proposal* and Chesterfield's essay are both printed in W. F. Bolton, *The English Language: Essays by English and American Men of Letters, 1490–1839* (Cambridge: Cambridge University Press, 1966).

Dryden, in the Dedication to his play *The Rival Ladies* (1664) and Defoe, *Essay upon Projects* (1697) make similar remarks.

11. W. Warburton, Preface to the Pope and Warburton edition of *The Works of Shakespeare* (London 1747), quoted D. T. Starnes and G. E. Noyes, *The English Dictionary from Cawdrey to Johnson* (Chapel Hill: University of North Carolina Press, 1946).

12. Samuel Johnson, *The Plan of a Dictionary*, 1747 (Menston: Scolar Press, 1970).

13. Johnson's *Preface* is quoted from *Johnson's Dictionary, A Modern Selection*, by E. L. McAdam Jnr and George Milne (London: Gollancz, 1963).

14. Quoted from A. Reddick, *The Making of Johnson's Dictionary, 1746–1773* (Cambridge: Cambridge University Press, 1990), p. 9.

15. R. C. Trench, 'On Some Deficiencies in our English Dictionaries', *Transactions of the Philological Society* (1856–7)

16. Quoted from the Introduction to *OED 1*: xv, reprinted in *OED 2*.

17. These examples are taken from the interim report by R. W. Burchfield, 'O.E.D.: A New Supplement', *Essays and Studies* 14 (1961) pp. 35–51.

18. But not all. For a view of *OED 2* as a great opportunity missed, see C. Brewer, 'The Second Edition of The *Oxford English Dictionary*', *Review of English Studies* 44 (1993) pp. 313–42.

19. This can be a problem, especially if the derivative is used more often than the headword. S. I. Landau, *The Art and Craft of Lexicography* (New York: The Scribner Press, 1984), pp. 78–9, complains that adverbs ending in -*ly* are often inadequately treated in dictionaries.

20. Leonard Welstead, *The Perfection of the English Language and the State of Poetry* (1724), quoted H. Darbishire, 'Milton's Poetic Language', *Essays and Studies* 10 (1957), p. 41.

21. G. Campbell, *Philosophy of Rhetoric*, 1776. Quoted S. A. Leonard, *The Doctrine of Correctness in English Usage 1700–1800* (New York: Russell and Russell, 1962), p. 156.

22. *A True and Faithful Account of What We Observed in Ten Years Travell into the Principal Places of Europe, Africa and America* (London, 1665), p. 105. Quoted Bailey 1992: p. 105.

23. T. Watts, 'On the Probable Future Position of the English Language', *Proceedings of the Philological Society* 4 (1850), 212. Quoted Bailey 1992: p. 108.

24. W. Barnes, *Early England and the Saxon-English* (1869), p. 101. Quoted Bailey 1992: p. 194.

25. Lowth is quoted from the Scolar Press facsimile (Menston, 1967). Buchanan, five years later than Lowth, likewise demands rules but begins to sound old-fashioned in his adoption of Latin grammar as a model for English:

> Considering the many grammatical Improprieties to be found in our best Writers, such as SWIFT, ADDISON, POPE, etc., A Systematical English Syntax is not beneath the notice of the Learned themselves. Should it be urged, that in the Time of these Writers, English was but a very little subjected to Grammar, that they had scarcely a single Rule to direct them, a question readily occurs. Had they not the Rules of Latin syntax to direct them?
>
> (*A Regular English Syntax*, 1767, Preface.)

26. Noah Webster, Letter to Dr Ramsey, 1807, quoted Leonard, p. 42.

27. Priestley is quoted from the edition of 1761. John Wallis (1653) is a century earlier but in agreement with Priestley:

> I should not wish you to expect that everything in our Language should correspond exactly to Latin. For in this as in nearly all modern tongues, there is a great difference from the syntax of Greek and Latin (arising mainly because we do not recognize differences of cases). The few who do pay attention to them undertake more labour than the subject is worth.
>
> (Quoted in Tucker 1961: p. 39.)

EXERCISES

1. Do you think it is possible to represent dialect convincingly in literature? The first of these two extracts is from Lancashire in the second half of the nineteenth century, the second is about a Nottinghamshire mining community early this century. How much can you understand? Which features of language are easiest to reproduce and which are hardest?

> Mi gronfeyther – bless him – reet doated o' me –
> He'd tell me aw geet a foine lad;

An' mony a toime say, when aw'rn sit on his knee,
"Eh, bless thee; tha favvers thi dad!"
Then he'd tell mi aunt Betty to beigh me some spice;
An' whenever hoo happen'd to bake,
He'd tell her to reach deawn a pot o' presarves,
An' mak me a noice presarve cake.

God bless him, he's gone; an' a kinder owd mon
Never walk'd o' two legs nor he wur;
Th' last time aw wur o'er theer, an' seed him alive,
He coom back wi' me ever so fur.
Aw geet howd ov his hont when we parted that neet,
An aw think aw shall never forget
Heaw he look'd i' mi face when he'rn goin' away:
It wur th' last time 'at ever we met.

> (Samuel Laycock: *Mi Gronfeyther*.
> *Songs of the People*, Ed. B. Hollingworth (Manchester:
> Manchester University Press, 1977).)

At half-past eleven her husband came. His cheeks were very red and
very shiny above his black moustache. His head nodded slightly. He
was pleased with himself.

'Oh! Oh! waitin' for me, lass? I've bin 'elpin Anthony, an what's
think he's gen me? Nowt b'r a lousy hae'f- crown, an that's ivry
penny –'

'He thinks you've made the rest up in beer', she said shortly.

'An' I 'aven't – that I 'avent. You b'lieve me, I've 'ad very
little this day, I have an' all.' His voice went tender. 'Here,
an' I browt thee a bit o' brandysnap, an' a cocoanut for th'
children.' He laid the gingerbread and the cocoanut, a hairy
object, on the table. 'Nay, tha niver said thankyer for nowt i'
thy life, did ter?'

As a compromise she picked up the cocoanut and shook it, to see
if it had any milk.

'It's a good 'un, you may back yer life o' that. I got it fra'
Bill Hodgkisson. 'Bill,' I says, 'tha non wants them three nuts, does
ter? Arena ter for gi'ein me one for my bit of a lad an' wench?' 'I
ham, Walter, my lad,' 'e says; 'ta'e which on 'em ter's a mind.' An'
so I took one, an' thanked 'im. I didn't like ter shake it afore 'is eyes,
but 'e says, 'Tha'd better ma'e sure it's a good un, Walt.' An' so,
yer see, I knowed it was. He's a nice chap is Bill Hodgkisson, 'e's
a nice chap!'

'A man will part with anything so long as he's drunk, and you're
drunk along with him', said Mrs Morel.

'Eh, tha mucky little 'ussy, who's drunk, I sh'd like ter know?' said Morel.

(D. H. Lawrence, *Sons and Lovers* (1913), Chapter 1)

2. You are planning a dictionary of English twice the size of this book. What kind of information would you include if it was meant primarily for a) native speakers b) non-native speakers?

Linguistic Glossary

Accusative case   The grammatical case expressing the direct object.

Acronym   Strictly, a 'word' formed from the initial letters of a sequence of other words, e.g. *AIDS*, acquired immune deficiency syndrome. More loosely, an abbreviation pronounced as a string of letters, e.g. *MP, EEC.*

Active voice   Where the subject carries out the action of the verb, e.g. The householder *telephoned* the police. Intransitive verbs occur only in the active voice, e.g. The workmen *came* this morning.

Adverbial   A word-class including single-word adverbs (*quickly, now*) and phrases (*in a minute, with great difficulty*) which typically modify verbs and answer questions such as how?, when? and why? Adverbials are an optional part of the sentence and also the most mobile element within it.

Affix   A form which is added to the stem of a word, either at the beginning when it is a PREFIX (*sub*-title, *un*easy) or at the end when it is a SUFFIX (dark*ness*, tobacco*nist*). Both can occur in the same word (*un*reli*able*, *dis*orient*ate*). The process of adding affixes is called AFFIXATION. Since affixes are not words, affixation is usually distinguished from COMPOUNDING where two words are joined together (e.g. *bathmat, top-dog*).

Analytic language   One which uses strategies other than inflections to indicate grammatical relationships, e.g. separate words such as prepositions and auxiliary verbs. P.D.E. is a mainly analytic language.

Anaphora   Reference back to an earlier word or phrase in the text. At its simplest this involves the replacement of an earlier word by a pronoun, e.g. Little Tommy Tucker/sang for *his* supper.

Anglo-Norman   The French spoken and written in England during the earlier part of the M.E. period.

Anglo-Saxon   See OLD ENGLISH.

Antonym   A word with a sense directly opposed to another, e.g. *tall* is the antonym of *short* and *well* of *ill*.

Aspect   The way in which the action of the verb is marked. *Progressive* aspect describes a continuing action (She *is doing* her homework. The boy *was reading* a comic). *Perfective* aspect indicates that the action has been completed (She *has finished* her homework. The boy *has read* the comic.) *Habitual* aspect indicates a regular but not necessarily continuous action (She *settles* down to her homework after tea. The comic *comes* on Fridays.) Clearly aspect is related to TENSE, but tense is more concerned with time and aspect with duration.

Auxiliary verb   A verb in a two (or more) member sequence where the central meaning is carried by the main (the 'lexical' or 'full') verb, e.g. I *was* driving the car, The workmen *have* started. The so–called PRIMARY VERBS (*be, do, have*) can however function as either auxiliary or lexical verbs.

Blend   A word formed from parts of two other words (in this it is unlike a compound where all of each word is included), e.g. *chunnel = channel + tunnel, motel = motor + hotel*. Also called *portmanteau* words.

Celtic   A sub-group of the Indo–European family. The language spoken by the 'ancient Britons', the different dialects of which are now represented by Irish, Scots (Gaelic) and Manx on the one hand and Welsh, Cornish and Breton on the other.

Chancery standard   A form of administrative English used by the fifteenth-century civil servants of the Chancery, based in Westminster. Its spread from c. 1430 on is one of the major factors in the establishment of a standard written English.

Clause   A grammatical unit with at least subject and predicate, so it may sometimes be a complete sentence (e.g. *The bus arrived*) or a subject plus verb sequence within a more complex sentence (The bus *we had been waiting for* arrived.). In the latter cases there is a MAIN CLAUSE, *The bus . . . arrived*, and one or more SUBORDINATE clauses *(which) we had been waiting for*. Subordinate clauses are usually introduced by a connecting word, e.g. *When* she entered the room (subordinate clause), he stood up (main clause).

Cognate   Having the same ancestor, directly related, e.g. English and German are cognate languages; *brotherly* and *fraternal* are cognate words since they are different realizations of the same Indo-European root; <sk> is the cognate Scandinavian spelling to O.E. <sh>.

Cohesion   The means, which may be lexical, grammatical or phonological, of linking smaller units such as words or phrases into larger ones such as sentences or paragraphs. Cohesion can be PARADIGMATIC, repeating items from a recognized set of forms, He felt exhaust*ed*, drain*ed*, play*ed* out, or SYNTAGMATIC by repetition of patterns of phrase, clause, etc., e.g. Studies serve *for Delight, for Ornament* and *for Ability* (Bacon).

Collocation   The habitual association of one word with other words, e.g. *sour milk*, not *rotten milk*. On a larger scale, a feature of LEXICAL SETS, q.v.

Complement   This usually 'completes' the sense following the verb *be* or another linking verb (e.g. *seem, feel*). The subject complement refers back to the subject: He's *a marvellous teacher*; I feel *terrible*. The object complement (unsurprisingly) refers back to the object: The board appointed him *secretary*.

Compound   Where two words are combined into a third without any part of either word being lost, e.g. *milkman, study-bedroom*.

Conjunction   A word used to join two words (slow *and* sure; trick *or* treat) or two clauses (let's pack up *and* go home). Coordinating conjunctions (e.g. *and, but, or*) join words or clauses of equal weight. Subordinating conjunctions (e.g. *although, because, if, when*) introduce subordinate clauses.

Conjugation   The set of forms of a verb, e.g. *eat, eats, eating, ate, eaten*.

Conjunct   A type of adverbial relating clauses or sentences, as in a list, e.g. *For the most part . . . nevertheless . . . in conclusion.*

Connotation An additional 'meaning' of a word, depending on its personal or cultural association for the user, e.g. *police* may suggest protection or fear or repression to different people. The opposite of DENOTATION, q.v.

Content words See LEXICAL WORDS.

Conversion Using one part of speech as if it were another, e.g. to be in the *know* (verb as noun); to *down* tools (adverb as verb). Also called *functional shift* or *zero-derivation*.

Coordination Joining together two units of equal weight, usually by means of a conjunction, e.g. *They put on their coats* and *went for a walk*.

Correlatives A pair of words or phrases joining together two parts of a sentence and making explicit the relationship between them; the sentence 'pivots' on the fixed pair, e.g. *The* more *the* merrier; *Both* his father *and* his grandfather were in the garage business; *If* we set out early, *then* we'll be there by lunch-time.

Dative The grammatical case used for INDIRECT OBJECT or recipient, e.g. The foreman gave *the mechanic* his instructions; The foreman gave his instructions *to the mechanic*.

Declarative A term for the commonest type of sentence, one which makes a statement, e.g. *The first lesson is at nine o'clock*. Its normal word-order is S, V, O/C.

Declension A set of the forms of a noun, pronoun or adjective, showing their different cases, e.g. *he, him, his*.

Denotation The relationship between a word and what it refers to, the primary or 'dictionary' meaning (contrary to CONNO-TATION). Also called *cognotive* or *referential* meaning.

Determiner The part of the NP which precedes the noun itself (and also any adjective(s) that precede the noun) and which limits (or determines) the meaning, e.g. *This* cat; *both* grey cats; *many* young male cats.

Diachronic Concerned with the historical development of a language (contrast SYNCHRONIC; q.v.).

Dialect A variety of a language which may be defined regionally (a west-country dialect), chronologically (M.E. dialects), socially (working-class dialect) or occupationally (student dialect). Characterized by distinctive features of accent, vocabulary or grammar (or all three).

Diphthong A vowel which changes its quality within the same syllable, a 'gliding' vowel; in [taɪm], 'time', the /a/ glides towards /ɪ/.

Direct object, dO. See OBJECT

Discourse A connected stretch of (frequently spoken) language longer than a sentence. *Discourse analysis* investigates the structure of such passages (not only grammatical but semantic and pragmatic) to see how communication takes place.

Disjunct A type of adverbial commenting not on a single word but on the whole clause or sentence, e.g. *Certainly* you couldn't accuse her of that.

Early Modern English (E. Mod. Eng.) English from about 1500 to about 1700.

Etymology The study of the origins of words and the development of their meaning.

Foregrounding Highlighting a word or phrase by taking it out of its expected position and putting it in an emphatic position, typically at the beginning or end of the sentence, e.g. *Considerate* – that's something he'll never be.

Free indirect speech Gives the illusion of listening to actual conversation (direct speech). The speech of the character and the words of the narrator are blended and no quotation marks or reporting clause (e.g. *she said*) appear. cf. examples in the Jane Austen extract, p. 102.

Function words See GRAMMATICAL WORDS.

Grammatical words (also called *Function Words* or *Form Words*) So called because their function in the grammar of the language is more important than their meaning. Pronouns, determiners, prepositions and auxiliary verbs are all grammatical words. They belong to a *closed class* into which new words are hardly ever admitted (contrast the *open class* LEXICAL WORDS). Almost all of them have been in the language since O.E.

Genitive   A case describing ideas like 'possession' or 'close association', e.g. *my father's* car; *Prime Minister's* question time. With animate nouns these relationships are indicated by inflections ('s singular and s' plural), with inanimate nouns most commonly by the 'of genitive' (the door *of the house*) or by a noun acting as an adjective (the *University* Library).

Germanic   A family of related Indo-European languages, including English, German, Dutch, Frisian (West Germanic); Danish, Norwegian, Swedish, Icelandic (North Germanic); and the now extinct Gothic (East Germanic).

Gerund   See VERBAL NOUN.

Grapheme   The smallest contrastive unit of meaning within the writing system. Graphemes are written between angle brackets: <i> before <e> except after <c>.

Great Vowel shift (GVS)   A series of phonological changes, roughly between Chaucer's time and Shakespeare's, in which the long, stressed vowels of English were raised or in some cases diphthongized.

Gricean maxims   The four main principles on which conversation should be based, according to the American linguistic philosopher H. P. Grice. They are: quantity, quality, relation and manner.

Grimm's Law   So called from Jacob Grimm (one of the brothers Grimm) who in the 1820s proposed that a complex system of sound-shifts in consonants characterized Germanic and helped to distinguish it from other Indo-European languages (e.g. *f*ather/*p*ater; li*p*/la*b*ial).

Headword   See NOUN PHRASE and VERB PHRASE.

Homographs   Words with the same spelling but different pronunciation, e.g. <minute>, 'a short period of time' or <minute>, 'very small'; <row> as a verb meaning either 'quarrel' or 'propel a boat'.

Homonyms   Pairs of words identical in both spelling and pronunciation but different in meaning, e.g. *hamper* meaning 'basket' (noun) or 'impede' (verb); *bill* meaning 'account, 'statement of charges' or else 'beak'.

Homophones   Words which sound alike but are spelled differently, e.g. <there> and <their>; <sight>, <site> and <cite>.

Ideolect   The speech habits of an individual, conditioned by age, sex, place of residence, social and professional circles, etc.

Imperative   A form or structure expressing a command, e.g. *Come here!*, *Listen!*, *Close the door!*

Indicative   The mood of a verb which denotes fact (contrast SUBJUNCTIVE, q.v.) and so most commonly used in statements. It is the unmarked mood in English.

Indirect object (iO)   See OBJECT

Indo-European (I.E.)   A linguistic construct, designating the family of cognate languages (including English) once spoken over the larger part of Europe and extending into western Asia and India.

Inflection   An ending, used to mark grammatical categories like case, number, gender, tense.

Intensifier   A type of adverbial that stresses another element more or less strongly: It was *very/exceedingly/perishingly* cold; I *hardly* know her *at all*.

Interrogative   A word or syntactical pattern used to ask questions.

Intonation   The rise and fall in pitch in spoken language and the patterns which result (e.g. to distinguish statements and questions).

Intransitive verb   A verb which does not take a direct object, e.g. We *failed*, but at least we *tried*. (Some verbs can be either transitive or intransitive, e.g. We *failed* the exam.)

Kentish   The O.E. dialect of the county of Kent (then a separate kingdom) and its borders, also found in the Isle of Wight.

Lexeme   An individual and distinct item of vocabulary.

Lexical set   A group of words recurring in similar contexts which reflect the same theme, e.g. *corporal, captain, colonel, general* are all military ranks.

Lexical words (also called *Content words*)   Words where the content is the most important feature (contrast GRAMMATICAL WORDS, q.v.); therefore mostly descriptive words such as nouns, full verbs, adjectives, adverbials. Some are native O.E., many more have been (and continue to be) borrowed. Hence these are open class words.

Lexicon   The stock of words in a particular language.

Main clause   See CLAUSE.

Marked   A form or feature of language distinguished from the norm and hence prominent or deviant in some way, e.g. *cauliflower* (versus the more general *vegetable*), *bitch* (versus *dog*), dog*s* (plural, versus *dog*), *Now* he tells me (foregrounding of *now*).

Mercian   The dialect of O.E. spoken between the Thames and the Humber, i.e. the present-day Midlands.

Middle English (M.E.)   English from about 1100 to about 1500.

Modality   The expression of attitudes such as possibility, permission, desirability, obligation, volition, etc. This is achieved by *modal verbs*, a sub-group of auxiliary verbs, the chief of which are *may, must, can, shall, will*.

Morpheme   The smallest meaningful unit of grammar. It may be a word (a free morpheme) such as *talk* or *boy*, or an affix (a *bound* morpheme with no independent existence) such as talk*ing* or boy*s*. Bound morphemes are sometimes distinguished from *lexical morphemes* used to build new lexical items (but still not full words), e.g. prigg*ish*, *anti*-war.

Morphology   That aspect of language concerned with morphemes in word-structure; it covers both inflection and affixation.

Nominative case   The case used for the subject of the verb.

Northumbrian   The dialect of O.E. north of the Humber and extending into present-day southern Scotland.

Noun clause   A clause which functions as a noun, e.g. *What I need* is a strong drink (S); I decided *that we should continue* (O); It's strange *that he hasn't turned up yet* (C).

Noun phrase (NP)   A single word or group of words functioning like a noun (i.e. it may be S, dO, iO, C): *The staff/the salaried staff/the staff in the office/the staff who come in on Saturdays*. The noun (or pronoun) is the HEADWORD of the N.P.

Object   The part of the sentence affected (or realized) by the (transitive) verb, e.g. The boy fed *the kitten*. *Kitten* is here the DIRECT OBJECT (dO). But if we say The boy gave *the kitten its meal*, *its meal* is the direct object (what was given) and *the kitten* the INDIRECT OBJECT(iO), the recipient of the action of the verb.

Old English (O.E.)   English from about 700 to about 1000, or, if you think of spoken English, from the mid fifth century to about 1100.

Paradigm   The set of the forms belonging to a particular word-class and produced by inflection from a single base form, e.g. P.D.E. weak verbs: *love/loves/loving/loved*, or strong verbs: *break/ breaks/breaking/broke/broken*.

Paradigmatic cohesion   See COHESION.

Passive voice   Where the subject experiences ('suffers') the action of the verb, e.g. *He was knocked down*. The agent may be expressed with *by*: He was knocked down *by a car which didn't stop*.

Phrasal verb   A multiword verb consisting of a verb and one or more particles, but operating as a single unit, e.g. I *took off* my coat; We *set to* and finished the washing-up.

Phoneme   The minimal significant speech sound, in that changing it will change the meaning of the word, e.g. the/ɪ/of *hit* changed into the /æ/ of *hat*. Phonemes are written between slant lines. Unlike the symbols of IPA, phonemes are peculiar to an individual language or to a period of that language.

Phonology   The study of the system of sounds within a language (or stage of a language), their pattern and distribution.

Polysemy   Multiple meaning of a single word, e.g. the adjective *fair* can mean 'beautiful', 'blond', 'equitable', 'honourable', 'average'. The context decides which meaning is intended.

Popular etymology (Folk etymology)   A word is wrongly interpreted in the popular mind as conforming to a known pattern and may be modified in form or meaning to show this, e.g. O.E. *brydguma*, 'bride's man' became *bridegroom*; *sententious*, originally 'full of meaning' and now usually 'pompous' has perhaps been influenced by *pretentious*.

Post-modifier   A word, phrase or clause following the headword of the Noun Phrase, subordinate to it and limiting its meaning, e.g. the boy *from Form Two*; the boy *who came late to the history lesson*.

Pragmatics   The study of how meaning is conveyed, the 'force' of the utterance. Often involving implication or allusion and a knowledge of the extralinguistic context. Semantics asks 'What does this word mean?', pragmatics 'What do you mean by this word?'

Predicate   Grammatically that part of the sentence which is not the subject, e.g. The whole family *ate toast and honey in front of the fire*. Semantically what is said about the subject.

Prefix   See AFFIX.

Primary verb   See AUXILIARY VERB.

Pre-modifier   A word or words preceding the headword of the Noun Phrase and modifying (or limiting) its meaning. It is therefore subordinate to the noun, e.g. The *scruffy ten-year-old* boy; all *the King's* men.

Received pronunciation (RP)   The pronunciation of standard Southern British English, formerly often called 'BBC English' or 'Oxford English'. It is a class dialect rather than a local dialect.

Register   A variety of a language used in particular circumstances and marked by significant occupational, social, stylistic or other features appropriate to that context, e.g. a *military* register, a *legal* register, a *formal* register. Register–switching is important in studies of style.

Relative clause   A subordinate clause attached to a preceding word, phrase or clause (its *antecedent*), usually by a relative pronoun (*who, whom, whose, which, that*). Relative clauses can be *restrictive* (or *defining*), e.g. The necklace *which I bought* turned out to be a fake, i.e. describing a particular necklace, or else *non-restrictive* (*non-defining*), e.g. David, *who you met last week*, is coming to dinner tomorrow, where the relative clause is parenthetical, could easily be omitted, and is usually marked off by commas.

Romance A family of related European languages, descended from Latin, including French, Italian, Spanish, Portuguese and Romanian.

Semantics The aspect of language which deals with meaning.

Stress The force or energy used in the articulation of a syllable. A word will have its own stress pattern, but this may be modified when the word occurs as part of a longer unit such as a sentence.

Strong verb A verb which signifies the change from present to past by a change in the stem vowel and often a further change in the vowel of the past participle (which usually ends in *-en*), e.g. *drive/drove/driven, speak/spoke/spoken*. Nowadays often termed an *irregular* verb.

Subject (S) The person or thing which 'acts out' the verb, e.g. *The girl* wore her best dress. Normally it precedes the verb which agrees with it in number and person, e.g. *He drives* to work every morning; *they drive* to work every morning.

Subjunctive The mood of the verb which typically expresses hypothesis, wish or doubt (and so contrasted with the INDICATIVE, q.v.). Sometimes indicated by a distinctive form, especially in earlier or formal English and in the verb 'to be', e.g. I insist that she *leave* [zero ending] at once; I only wish it *were* possible. In P.D.E. hypothesis is increasingly suggested by modal verbs such as *may, might, should*.

Subordinate clause See CLAUSE.

Suffix See AFFIX.

Synchronic Concerned with the language of a single period of time, often (but not invariably) the present. The opposite of DIACHRONIC, q.v.

Syntagmatic cohesion See COHESION.

Syntax The distribution of words, phrases and clauses in sentences and the set of rules which control this. Often considered alongside MORPHOLOGY, the structure of words.

Synthetic language One which indicates relationships by making changes in the form of the word (e.g. *book/books, man/men*). O.E. was a predominantly synthetic language.

Tag question   Begins as a statement but turns into a question by the addition of a short phrase or clause at the end (which also gives an indication of the answer expected), e.g. Not very clever there, *were you?* Let's break for coffee now, *shall we?*

Tense   The form by which the verb indicates the time at which the action takes place: present (she *speaks/is speaking*), past (she *spoke*, they *hesitated*), past continuous (they *were walking*), perfect (I *have eaten*), past perfect (I *had decided*). The future tense is usually indicated by the modal verbs *shall* and *will* (I *shall* go, they *will* come).

Transitive verb   A verb which takes a direct object, e.g. He *kissed* his wife.

Unmarked   A linguistic feature that is usual and neutral (as opposed to the MARKED form), e.g. How *old* is your son? (unmarked) versus How *young* is your son? (marked).

Verb phrase (VP)   Either a single-word verb (They *came*) or a group of verb forms functioning in the same way (We *have been thinking* of buying a house). The main verb is the HEADWORD of the VP.

Verbal noun   The *-ing* form of the verb used as a noun, e.g. *Smoking* is forbidden on the London Underground; I've mislaid my *knitting*. Also called *gerund*.

Voiced   A speech sound made with the vocal cords vibrating. All vowels in English are voiced.

Voiceless   A speech sound made without vibration of the vocal cords so that breath passes through them unimpeded. Also called *unvoiced*.

Weak verb   A verb which forms its past tense and past participle in *-ed* (*stated*, *loved*) or *-t* (*built*, *swept*). Some grammars call these *regular verbs* since the majority of P.D.E. verbs are weak.

West Saxon   The O.E. dialect of Wessex, central southern and south-west England, the kingdom of Alfred. Written Late West-Saxon (tenth and eleventh centuries) was understood over large areas of England.

Names

Naturally enough people are interested in the names of the places they live in or where they were brought up. And we all have personal names, both surnames and one or more given names. But for the study of the history of the language there is an additional reason why we should be interested. We do not go around changing names every other year, except in a few cases where a name is chosen to celebrate a very important person or event or where a new town or district is established. *Camden Town* (1795) and *Fleetwood* (1836) both celebrate local dignitaries while *Morecambe* was named in the eighteenth century from the Celtic *moricambe*, 'sea bay'. *Southport* dates from 1798 and *Devonport* from 1824; these are both self-explanatory. It follows that names often preserve features of earlier English and reflect the changes which have taken place in the language; some of these features may have become less common in P.D.E. or even have disappeared altogether.

PLACE NAMES[1]

The derivation of some place names may seem self-explanatory: *Bath* ('Roman baths'), *Blackpool, Bradford* ('broad ford'), *Foxholes, Oxford* ('ford used by oxen'), *Portsmouth, Sunderland* ('detached estate'), *Swindon* ('hill where pigs are kept'), *Underbarrow* ('place under the hill'), *Gatwick* ('goat farm') and *Heathrow* ('row of houses on the heath') are not difficult to interpret. Yet we need to be careful. Even if we know that O.E. *-TŪN*[2] (P.D.E. *town*) meant 'enclosure', 'village', *Brighton* was not, as we might surmise, a particularly 'bright' settlement. In 1086 the name is spelled *Britelmestune*, so the first element is a personal name and the settlement was 'the farmstead of (O.E. *-es*, genitive singular)

Beorhthelm'. This is an indication of the prime importance of early spellings. An invaluable source is the Domesday Book of 1086, a survey of England by the commissioners of William I ('the Conqueror'). The names there recorded will, in many cases, be much earlier and, in place-name studies, the evidence from O.E. documents – charters, wills, the *Anglo-Saxon Chronicle* – is even better. Yet even these early spellings must be used with care. If the document is in Latin, the spelling may be Latinized. When we reach M.E., the documents may be written in Latin by clerks whose native language was French. The P.D.E. forms may therefore be the result of respellings trying to reflect changed pronunciation or the attempt of a copyist to represent pronunciation of a word in a language which was not his own.

Again, names which now appear to have different origins may have descended from a single word. O.E. CEASTER (itself a borrowing from the Latin *castra*, 'camp') meant 'fortification', 'walled town'. It would have been pronounced [tʃ] in the south (or in records written in the south) giving: *Chester* (*Legacæster*, 'the camp of the legions' in 735 but simply *Cestre* in Domesday Book) and the second element of *Dorchester*, *Manchester* and *Winchester*. But in the north it was [k] giving: *Doncaster* ('fort on the river Don'), *Lancaster* ('fort on the river Lune') and *Tadcaster* ('town of a man called Tada or Tata'). In the Middle Ages French scribes respelled some of the [tʃ] forms, giving *Bicester*, *Gloucester*, *Leicester*, *Worcester*. Another example of different P.D.E. forms of the same word is O.E. BURH, 'stronghold', 'fortified place', eventually applied to towns and even manor-houses. BURH gives: *Brough* and the spellings in *-borough* (*Marlborough*, *Middlesborough*, *Peterborough*, *Scarborough*) and *-burgh* (*Aldeburgh*, *Edinburgh*). The O.E. dative form of BURH (BYRIG) produces *Bury* and the second element of *Salisbury* and *Shrewsbury*.

The etymology of some P.D.E. forms appears distinctly odd. For all its virtues, *Croydon* does not remind us of 'the valley of the wild crocuses' and even the partisan inhabitants of Glasgow might not think of it as a 'green hollow'. *Liverpool*, on the other hand, has improved from the 'sludge pool' that its name suggests.

Nevertheless, place names do reflect much of our history more directly. The time between the departure of the Romans in 410 AD and the coming of the Angles, Saxons and Jutes in the mid fifth century is something of a grey area. The language of the 'ancient Britons' is usually called Celtic, the different dialects of which are now represented in Irish, Scots and Manx on the one hand and Welsh and Cornish on the other. There are very few Celtic borrowings into O.E. proper; *cross* may be one of them, but even that is rare in O.E. where the normal word is *rōd* ('rood'). But several Celtic place-names survive, especially river names: *Avon*, *Frome*, *Tees*, *Thames*, *Trent*, *Wyre*, and possibly *Severn* and *Wye*. *Dover*, too, meant simply 'river'. Other Celtic names are: *Brent*, *Carlisle*, *Crewe*, *Cumbria*, *Eccles*, *Inverness*, *Kent* and *Leeds*, and the first element of *Manchester*, *Mansfield*, *Pendlebury* (but the *Pennines* are apparently not so called until the eighteenth century), *Rotherham* and *Taunton*. -COMBE, as in *Boscombe*, *Compton*, *Ilfracombe* is probably from O.E. CUMB, 'valley', rather than the cognate Celtic word now represented in Welsh *cwm*.

There are very many place names going back to O.E., so many that it will be easiest to pick out some of the common elements and give one or two examples of each. As in O.E. generally, many of these names are compounds where the specific element precedes the general; for example, *Beaconsfield* is 'the open country (FELD) near the beacon' while *Canterbury*, recorded as *Cantwaraburg* c. 900, is 'the stronghold (BURH) of the Kent (CANT) dwellers (-WARE)'. Place-name specialists often divide names into *habitative*, reflecting settlements, and *topographical*, reflecting features of the landscape. Among the habitative names are:

Stratford and *Stretford*, *Stratton* and *Stretton*, reflecting O.E. dialectal pronunciations of STRÆT (from Latin *via strata*).

Others are those from TŪN, perhaps the most common element of all, in *Preston* ('priest's farmstead'), *Bolton*;

-HAM in *Altrincham*, *Birmingham*, *Grantham*, *Oakham*, meaning 'village', 'estate', probably not used for new names after later M.E. and not to be confused with

HAMM, 'land in the bend of a river', as in the *Anglo-Saxon Chronicle* spelling *Buccingahamme*.

-WĪC ('dwelling', 'farm', but evidently with an additional sense of 'trading centre') as in *Ipswich*, *Norwich*, *Sandwich*. In *Chiswick* and *Keswick* the first element reflects the different southern and northern pronunciations of *čiese*, 'cheese', and in Cheshire -WĪC indicates salt-works, as in the cluster *Northwich*, *Middlewich* and *Nantwich*;

-STOW, 'place', as in *Chepstow*, 'marketplace'.

O.E. elements which reflect the topography of a site include:

FELD, 'open country': *Felsted, Huddersfield, Lichfield, Sheffield*;

-ĒG, 'island' or 'land partly surrounded by water' which was common in early O.E. names and now exists in a variety of spellings such as *Rye*, 'at the island', *Hackney, Hinksey, Tebay*; HALH, 'hollow' in *Hale, Halton, Halifax*;

-DŪN, 'hill', common in the south, e.g. *Hambledon, Maldon*;

-BURNA, 'stream', as in *Blackburn*;

HLAW, 'mound', in *Harlow, Lewes, Wilmslow*;

LEĀH, 'glade', in *Leigh, Bromley, Burnley, Dudley, Hinkley*;

BRYCG, 'bridge', which is easy to spot in *Bridgenorth* and *Cambridge* but perhaps not in P.D.E. *Bristol*, the early spelling of which is *Brycgstow*.

CLIF ('cliff'), HWĪT ('white'), MYNSTER ('church') and WUDU ('wood') are self-explanatory.

The Scandinavians settled chiefly in the north and east, apart from some Norwegian pockets in the north-west, and this is reflected in the place names. Common elements are:

-BY, 'village' in *Corby, Derby, Grimsby, Whitby*, and several others;

HOLM, 'island', in the various *Holmes* and *Cheadle Hulme*; and

-BECK, 'stream', in *Troutbeck*.

Some elements are specifically Danish, e.g.

-TOFT, 'farm' (*Lowestoft*),

-THORP, 'outlying farmstead' (*Thorpe, Milnthorpe, Scunthorpe*), and others are Norwegian, like GARTH, 'enclosure', FELL, 'upland' and

-THWAITE, 'clearing' (*Bassenthwaite, Crosthwaite*).

Since O.E. and Scandinavian were both Germanic languages, there are naturally some cognate elements (O.E. first):

STĀN and STAIN: *Stansted, Stamford* and *Stonehenge*, but *Stainforth, Staincross* and *Stainton*;

CHURCH and KIRK: *Christchurch* and *Whitchurch* versus *Ormskirk* and *Kirkby Lonsdale* ('the church in the village in the Lune valley');

ĊEORL and CARL: *Charlton* and *Chorley* versus *Carleton*;

SHIP and SKIP-: *Shipton* and *Skipton*;

-GATE in the south is probably O.E. *geat*, 'gate' (*Ramsgate, Reigate*) but usually Scandinavian *gata*, 'road' in the north (*Galgate, Harrogate*).

Compared with their extensive influence on the English

vocabulary as a whole, the French seem to have contributed little to place names. But the aristocratic Normans were much more interested in administration than in colonizing the countryside through peasant settlers. The names they gave to their estates still look distinctively French: *Beaulieu*, *Belper* (*beau repaire*), *Belvóir*, *Richmond*. Elsewhere they sometimes added another element celebrating the family inheritance. *Stoke* itself is derived from O.E. STOC, 'outlying farmstead or hamlet', but *Stoke D'Abernon*, *Stoke Fleming*, *Stoke Gifford*, *Stoke Mandeville* and *Stoke Poges* all reflect aristocratic French settlement. *Ashby* is O.E. ÆSC plus Scandinavian -BY, but there are also *Ashby-de-la-Zouche*, *Ashby Folville* and *Ashby Mears*. *Chapel-en-le-Frith*, *Chester-le-Street* and *Bolton-le-Sands* are French additions to existing names. *Devizes* ('on the boundaries') from *devise* and *Grange*, 'outlying farm belonging to a religious house' are among the few simpler names.

To end with a few more oddities. The impressive-sounding *Bere Regis*, *Blandford Forum*, *Chew Magna*, *Huish Episcopi* and *Weston-super-Mare* include additions from medieval Latin; for some reason Dorset seems to have been especially prone. The older names for *York* reflect its varied history. The city appears as *Eboracum* and *Eurwic* in Domesday Book of 1086, but as *Eoforwic*, 'boar farm' in 1070 when the O.E. -WĪC replaces the Latin *acum*. In 865, earlier still, it had been captured by the Scandinavians who called it *Iorvik*. The form *York* was in existence by the thirteenth century. *Nottingham* is *Snotingeham* in Domesday Book, 'the home (HĀM) of the family -ING of a man called *Snot*. (O.E. *snot* meant 'wise', so his name was not as unfortunate as we might think.) *Sn-* was evidently a rather difficult sound for Normans, so the *s-* disappeared in the twelfth century. *Baldock* was founded by the Knights Templars in the twelfth century who called it *Baldac* which was the French form for *Baghdad*. The various *Caldecotes* or *Caldecotts* evidently signified cold, inhospitable shelters (cottages) for travellers, while *Morpeth* was a path where a murder took place. What's in a name, indeed?

PERSONAL NAMES

In considering Celtic influence we saw that river names were important. The full study of place names also includes river names, field names and even street names. But it is to personal names that we must now turn.[3] The first element of several O.E. place names was quite often a personal name, with the compound meaning 'the settlement of Ceolmær, Leofing, Peota, or whoever'. The Anglo-Saxons usually had one name only; 'first name' or 'christian name' is therefore meaningless and 'personal name' is better. These were often based upon roots such as *Beorht*, 'shining', *Cȳne*, 'royal', *þrȳð*, 'power' (the latter is found in women's names). In royal families at least the names are alliterative. Alfred was the son of King Æthelwulf. He had four brothers, Æthelstan, Æthelbald, Æthelberht and Æthelred, and a sister, Æthelswith. (This is one trouble with the fictional Beowulf: he doesn't fit into the family tree if he is the son of Ecgþeow.) Sometimes a man's name shared an element with other family names. St Wulfstan (born c. 1008) was the son of Æthel*stan* and *Wulf*gifu.

Surnames came in following the Norman Conquest but became general only very gradually. They were used by the rich rather than the poor and in the south more than in the north. Nor, in the Middle Ages, were they necessarily hereditary. Tyndale, the translator of the Bible, was known as Hychyns when he lived in Gloucestershire and the fact that Langland's father was Stacy de Rockayle does not necessarily mean that the poet was illegitimate. Nor does the occurrence of *alias* in Latin records suggest anything underhand: John Morys *alias* Rede *alias* Sclattere (cited by Reaney (1976: xiii)), was probably respectable enough in Oseney. As with place names, the earlier the material the better. Charters will usually be in Latin but parish registers often show the laudable efforts of the priest to interpret information given him by his largely illiterate parishioners. As with place names, personal names reflect the course of history. To the O.E. *Alfred*, *Edmund* and *Edward* are eventually added the French-derived *Geoffrey*, *Henry*, *John*, *Richard*, *Robert*, *William* and, for women, *Agnes*, *Alice* and *Maud*. The growth of surnames was almost certainly assisted by the growing bureaucracy of the feudal system. *Robert* was enough for the man himself and for his close friends, but some further identifying label was necessary for the authorities. There is still a paucity of material for women and it is uncertain when matrimonial names became common – probably some time in the fourteenth century.

Surnames (as we may now call them) are traditionally divided into four classes reflecting their origin:

1. **Kinship.** Most of these derive from the father's name. -ING (*Browning, Dunning, Wilding*) is the O.E. suffix and -SON (*Johnson, Robinson, Watson*) often, but not invariably, the Scandinavian one. FITZ- (*Fitzwilliam, Fitzgerald*) is the corresponding Anglo-Norman prefix (compare French *fils*) and MAC- (*Macdonald, McCormack*) the Gaelic one. These affixes correspond to the Latin 'X *filius* ('son of') Y' as found in the charters, but this can surely be only a written description – nobody *said* it. The final -*s* of *Andrews, Parsons, Sims, Stevens* derives from the O.E. genitive singular -*es*; this usually means 'son of' but could mean 'servant of'. Some first names were used as surnames: to the O.E.-derived *Ashton* or *Easton* (*Eādstān*), *Dodd* (*Dodda*) and *White* (*Hwīta*) were later added *Cole, Gunn* and *Swain* from Scandinavian and others such as *Owen* from Welsh.

2. **Occupational.** *Baker, Knight, Smith* and *Thatcher* are from O.E., *Butcher, Carpenter, Draper, Marshall, Tailor* and several others from French. Chaucer's name suggests an ancestor who was a shoe-maker.

3. **Local.** The most general names of this type come from the country of origin, as with *Fleming, Norman, Scott*. Most, however, are considerably more local than this: *Brook, Green*. Early examples of these names are sometimes preceded by *at, by* or *de* and occasionally the present name is the result of metanalysis (wrong division): *Edward æt þæm æsce* (O.E.) became *Edward atten ash* in M.E. as endings got less distinct and finally *Edward Nash*, where the *n* has been transferred from the definite article to the name itself.

4. **Nicknames.** Some of these contain diminutive affixes (*Larkin, Wilson*) or are pet names (*Dickson, Hodgson, Nicholls, Robb, Watkin* from *Richard, Roger, Nicholas, Robert, Walter*). Others are presumably meant to suggest physique (*Long* and *Short*), colouring (*Black, Redhead*) or disposition (*Bull, Lamb*). *Metcalf* was perhaps 'the fat man' – the name is literally 'meat calf' – and *Todd* 'the hairy man', literally 'bushy-tailed, like a fox'. Was *Shakespeare* ironic or merely descriptive? I should like to believe that my own surname derives from French *hosed* (Latin *hosatus*), 'booted' rather than from M.E. *huswyf*, 'mistress of a family', obsolete in this sense by the seventeenth century when it meant 'loose woman'.

It is not always possible to fit a name into just one of these classes. The same man may be variously called 'William son of David', 'William Tanner' or 'William with the beard'. *Waller* could be a maker of walls, a dweller by a stream or well, or a coxcomb (French *galier*). At what stage did names, from whatever origin, become hereditary? There are apparently some examples from the twelfth century and the habit seems to have been established by the end of the fifteenth. As with place names, several personal names are self-explanatory – but, once more, be careful. *Batty* was a pet name from *Bartholomew*, *Bragg* was lively and brisk and *Moody* brave (O.E. *mōdiġ*). *Coward* was not afraid but a cow-herd, *Farmer* a tax-collector and *Pennyfather* a miser. If you want some teasers, try *Boffey*, *Cholmondeley*, *Gaukroger*, *Levick*, *Piercy*, *Pythian* or *Stallworthy*.

NOTES

1. This Appendix has benefited greatly from three recent and excellent studies: Mills (1991) and the chapters by Clark in Hogg (1992) and Blake (1992). There is an attractive booklet, *Home Town*, written by John Dodgson and published by the A. A. (Basingstoke, 1984). Of the several general treatments, the best are Cameron, K. (1988) *English Place-Names*. London: Batsford and Gelling, M. (1988) *Signposts to the Past*. Chichester: Phillimore.
2. I have capitalized common elements in both place-names and surnames.
3. Cottle (1978) is short and very readable. Clark (1992 – see Note 1) also includes personal names. Reaney (1976) is the standard work.

Select Bibliography

I have deliberately kept the Bibliography short. Books and articles cited once or twice only and also editions used appear in the Notes to the appropriate chapter.

Bailey R W 1992 *Images of English: A Cultural History of the Language*. Cambridge: Cambridge University Press.

Barber C 1993 *The English Language: A Historical Introduction*. Cambridge: Cambridge University Press.

Baugh A C and T Cable 1993 *A History of the English Language*. 4th edn. London: Routledge.

Blake N 1990 *An Introduction to the Language of Literature*. London: Routledge.

Blake N 1992 *The Cambridge History of the English Language*, Vol II, 1066–1476. Cambridge: Cambridge University Press.

Boucier G and C Clark 1981 *An Introduction to the History of the English Language*. Cheltenham: Stanley Thornes.

Brown G 1990 *Listening to Spoken English*. 2nd. edn. Harlow: Longman.

Burnley D 1992 *The History of the English Language, A Source Book*. Harlow: Longman.

Burrow J and T Turville-Petre 1992 *A Book of Middle English*. Oxford: Blackwell.

Carney E 1994 *A Survey of English Spelling*. London and New York: Routledge.

Cottle B 1978 *The Penguin Dictionary of Surnames*. Harmondsworth: Penguin.

Crystal D 1988 *Rediscover Grammar*. Harlow: Longman.

Görlach M 1991 *Introduction to Early Modern English*. Cambridge: Cambridge University Press.

Graddol D, J Cheshire and J Swann 1987 *Describing Language*.

Milton Keynes and Philadelphia: Open University Press.

Greenbaum S 1991 *An Introduction to English Grammar*. Harlow: Longman.

Hogg R M 1992 *The Cambridge History of the English Language, Vol. I, The Beginnings to 1066*. Cambridge: Cambridge University Press.

Hussey S S 1992 *The Literary Language of Shakespeare*. 2nd edn. Harlow: Longman.

Lass R 1987 *The Shape of English: Structure and History*. London: Dent.

Leech G N 1983 *Principles of Pragmatics*. Harlow: Longman.

McIntosh A, M L Samuels and M Benskin 1986 *A Linguistic Atlas of Late Mediaeval English*. 4 Vols. Aberdeen: Aberdeen University Press.

Mills A D 1991 *English Place-Names*. Oxford: Oxford University Press.

Millward C 1988 *A Biography of the English Language*. New York and London: Holt, Rinehart and Winston.

Mitchell B and F Robinson 1986 *A Guide to Old English*. 4th. edn. Oxford: Blackwell.

Quirk R and G Stein 1990 *English in Use*. Harlow: Longman.

The Oxford Dictionary of English Etymology. 1966 Ed. C T Onions. Oxford: Clarendon Press.

The Oxford Dictionary of English Grammar. 1994 Ed. S Chalker and E Weiner. Oxford: Clarendon Press.

The Oxford English Dictionary. 1933 Ed. J Murray. 2nd edn. 1989 Ed. J A Simpson and E S C Weiner Oxford: Clarendon Press.

The Oxford Dictionary of New Words. 1991 Ed. S Tulloch Oxford: Clarendon Press.

The New Shorter Oxford English Dictionary. 1993 Ed. L Brown Oxford: Clarendon Press.

Reaney P H 1976 *A Dictionary of British Surnames*, 2nd. edn. London: Routledge.

Robinson O W 1992 *Old English and Its Closest Relatives*. London: Routledge.

Scragg D G 1974 *A History of English Spelling*. Manchester: Manchester University Press and New York: Barnes and Noble.

Spevack M 1974 *The Harvard Concordance to Shakespeare*. Harvard: Harvard University Press.

Strang B 1970 *A History of English*. London: Methuen.

Thomas L 1993 *Beginning Syntax*. Oxford: Blackwell.

Trudgill P 1990 *The Dialects of England*. Oxford: Blackwell.

Tucker S 1961 *English Examined*. Cambridge: Cambridge University Press.

Wales K 1987 *A Dictionary of Stylistics*. Harlow: Longman.

Wardaugh R 1987 *How Conversation Works*. Oxford: Blackwell.

Yule G 1985 *The Study of Language*. Cambridge: Cambridge University Press.

Index

Academy
  English, 140–1, 152, 154
  French, 140
  Italian, 140
acronym, 41
active voice, 61
adverbials, 53, 58–9, 68–70
Aelfric, 2
affixation, 37–9, 155
Alfred, 182
American spelling, 118
American vocabulary, 129
analytic, 48
anaphora, 98
Ancrene Wisse, 132
Anglo-French, 23–4
Anglo-Norman, 22
Anglo-Saxon Chronicle, 174, 175
Anglo-Saxon invasions, 18, 130
antonyms, 98, 148
aspect, 59, 62, 67
Austen, J., 102–3

Babel, 149–50
Bacon, F., 33
Bailey, N., 139, 141, 143
Ball, C., 33
Barnes, W., 151–2
Bartholomew Fair, 89
Beckett, S., 94
Beowulf, 35, 36, 130, 182
Bible

Authorized Version, 2, 3, 64, 154
New English Bible, 2, 3, 5
Wycliffite, 2, 3
blends, 41
Bunyan, J., 14–17
Burchfield, R., 38
Burnley, D., 26

Campbell, G., 150, 155
Carney, E., 116, 119
Caxton, W., 131, 133, 136–7
Cawdrey, R., 138–9
Celtic, 9, 175
Central French, 23
Chancery Standard, 113, 135–6
Chaucer, G., 23, 24–6, 57, 87, 88, 91, 113, 132, 133, 135, 136, 149
Cheke, J., 37
clause, 75
closed class, 6
cohesion, 96–104
Collins Cobuild Dictionary, 148
collocation, 14, 91
command, 72
complement, 51
compounds, 15, 17, 34–43
conjuncts, 68–9
content words (see lexical words)
conversation, 93, 94, 108
conversion, 70–2
coordinate structures, 76
copious language, 31
correlatives, 77, 97

Crystal, D., 62
curious terms, 137

Danelaw, 20
dangling participles, 80
degredation of meaning, 89
determiners, 53
dialects, 110, 129–30
  in Middle English, 131, 132
dictionaries, 137–49
  compound words, 144, 148
  hard words, 138–9, 148
  indicating pronunciation, 145
  labels, 144
diphthong, 109
direct object, 50
directive (see command)
discourse, 92, 128
disjuncts, 69
do, 62–4
Domesday Book, 174
Donne, J., 31–3, 122

Early English Text Society, 146
Early Modern English, 7, 88
elevation of meaning, 89
Eliot, T.S., 84, 99–100
Encyclopaedia Brittanica, 149
etymological meaning, 86

First Folio (Shakespeare), 30, 57, 122
Flecknoe, R., 150
folk etymology (see popular etymology)
form, 50
free indirect speech, 102
French, decline of, 135
  in personal names, 178, 179
  in place names, 177
Frisian, 9
function, 50
future perfect, 67–8
future tense, 68

Germanic, 7, 9, 10, 25, 27, 35, 36, 120,
  150

Germanic invasions, 1, 9
gerund (see verbal noun)
Gower, J., 136
grapheme, 109
grammatical acceptability, 49, 78–81
grammatical words, 6, 120
Great Vowel Shift, 113, 114
Gricean maxims, 93–4
Grimm's Law, 10

Hart, J., 117
Harvard Concordance to Shakespeare,
  31
Havelok the Dane, 132
headword, 53
Heath-Stubbs, J., 58
hesitation markers, 124
homograph, 115
homonym, 115, 116
homophone, 115
Hughes, T., 42–3

idiolect, ix, 130
imperative, 63
indirect object, 51
Indo-European, 7–9
infinitive, 79–80, 81
infinitive clause, 78
inkhorn terms, 29, 37, 138, 151
International Phonetic Alphabet, 109
intonation, 73, 79, 121
intransitive verb, 51

jargon, 128
Johnson, S., 85–6, 119, 152
  Dictionary, 141–5

kennings, 36
Kentish, 9, 130
Kingman Report, viii, x

Langland, W., 25, 132, 178
Lass, R., xii
Latin grammar, 6, 48, 54, 62
lexical sets, 98

lexical words, 6, 120
Linguistic Atlas of M.E., 132–3
Linguistics, ix
loan translations, 35
loan words, 18, 33–4, 85
　Arabic, 33
　Dutch, 33
　French, 21–7
　German, 33
　Greek, 15, 29–30
　Indian, 33
　Italian, 33
　Latin, 19, 27–33, 103
　Persian, 33
　Russian, 33
　Scandinavian, 18, 20–1, 57, 176
　Spanish, 33
　Turkish, 33
Locke, J., 154
Lollards, 3, 136
London English, 134
Lord's Prayer, 1
Lowth, R., 152–4, 155

main clause, 75
Mercian, 9, 130
metaphor, 85, 91
Middle English, 7, 20
　dialects, 131–3
　grammar, 54, 56, 64, 65, 66
　spelling, 111–13
Millward, C., 140
Milton, J., 85, 100, 114, 149
modality, 60
modal verbs, 60–1
morpheme, 39, 110
Mulcaster, R., 28–9, 36, 138

narrowing of meaning, 87
Nashe, T., 30, 37
National Curriculum, viii
neutral vowel [ə], 108
New English Dictionary, 146
New Shorter Oxford Dictionary, 144, 149
Nice Work, 13

Nokes, D., 149
Norman Conquest, 13, 21, 56
Norman French, 23
Northumbrian, 9, 130
noun, 50
　declension of, 54
　gender, 54
　irregular plurals, 55
noun clause, 78
noun phrase, 53–9

Old English, 3–7, 131
　grammar, 54, 56, 57, 62, 64, 66, 67, 68, 80
　personal names, 178
　place names, 175–6
　spelling, 3–4, 111–12
　vocabulary, 17–19, 21, 26, 88, 89
　written standard, 130–1
open class, 6
Orm, 118
Oxford Dictionary of English Etymology, 14, 31
Oxford English Dictionary, 14, 31, 86–7
　OED1, 145, 147–8
　OED2, 145, 147–8, 149

paradigmatic cohesion, 99
passive voice, 61
past perfect (pluperfect), 67
past tense, 66, 67
Peasants Revolt, 136
perfect tense, 67
personal names, 177–80
Peterborough Chronicle, 22, 57, 132
phonemes, 109, 124–6
　in O.E., 110
phonetics, 109
phonology, 111
Pinter, H., 94
place-names, 173–77
polysemy, 91
Pope, A., 114, 150
popular etymology, 90

post-modifier, 53
pragmatics, 92–6
predicate, 50, 69
pre-modifier, 53
prepositional phrase, 69
prepositions, 55, 56
Present-Day English, 4, 7
Priestley, J., 154–5
primary verbs, 62
Promptorium Parvulorum, 138
pronouns, 57
punctuation, 122–4
Puttenham, G., 117

questions, 63, 72–5, 94
  tag question, 72–3
  wh- question, 63, 73–4
Quirk, R., 128

Rape of the Lock, 86
Received Pronunciation, 109, 110, 118, 121
register, 14
regular verbs (see weak verbs)
relative clause, 77–8
Richard I, 22
Romance vocabulary, 7, 9, 10, 25, 103
Royal Society, 149

Sastres, F., 142
Scandinavian invasions, 13, 19–20, 56, 132, 176
semantics, 85–92
Shakespeare, W., 86, 89, 154
  cohesion, 97–9, 103–4
  compounds, 40–1
  conversion, 71–2
  do, 64, 74
  -eth/ -s, 64–5
  long vowels, 113–14
  new words, 30
  pragmatics, 94–6
  punctuation, 122–3
  questions, 74–5
  rhymes, 114
  second person pronoun, 57–8

Sheridan, T., 117
Sir Gawain and the Green Knight, 131
Skelton, J., 28
slang, 128, 144
sociolinguistics, ix
sound change, 110, 111, 112
Speght, T., 138
spelling
  in O.E., 3–4, 111–12
  in P.D.E., 108, 112, 115–17
  in M.E., 113–13
  Latinate, 5, 115
spelling reform, 118–19
Spenser, E., 28, 114
Standard English, 128–9
Stein, G., 128
Strang, B., 56
stress, 27, 35, 79, 108, 116, 120–1
strong verb, 66–7
stylistics, ix
subjunctive, 80–81
subordinate clause, 76–8
surnames, 182–4
Swift, J., 140–1
synonyms, 97–8, 148
syntax, 6, 7
syntagmatic cohesion, 99
synthetic, 48

Taylor, J., 101–2
tense, 10, 59, 62
text, 92
Tom Jones, 139
transfer of meaning, 88
transitive verb, 51
Trench, Dean, 146
Trevisa, J., 133–4
Trudgill, P., 129, 130

universal language, 149–50
Usk, T., 135

verbal noun, 65
verb phrase, 54, 58–61

Wace, R., 22
Walker, J., 117–18
Waller, E., 150
Warburton, W., 141
Webster, N., 154
weak verb, 11, 66–7, 153

West-Saxon, 9, 130
widening of meaning, 88
Wyclif, J., 2
Wycliffite Bible, 3
Wycliffite language, 136